Opium

CAESAR [recovering his self-possession] : Pardon him, Theodotus: he is a barbarian, and thinks that the customs of his tribe and island are the laws of nature.

Shaw G. B., 1899, *Caesar and Cleopatra*, Act II

Where there is no common power, there is no law; where no law, no injustice. Force and fraud are in war the two cardinal virtues.

Hobbes T., 1651, *Leviathan*, Chapter XIII

Drug sticks to Man like the skin to its flesh.

Pelt J.-M., 1983, *Drogues et plantes magiques.*

Opium

UNCOVERING THE POLITICS OF THE POPPY

Pierre-Arnaud Chouvy

Harvard University Press
Cambridge, Massachusetts
2010

First published by I. B. Tauris & Co Ltd in the United Kingdom, 2009

First Harvard University Press edition, 2010

Library of Congress Cataloging-in-Publication Data
Chouvy, Pierre-Arnaud.
Opium : uncovering the politics of the poppy / Pierre-Arnaud Chouvy.
    p.   cm.
  Includes bibliographical references and index.
  ISBN 978-0-674-05134-8 (cloth : alk. paper)
  1. Opium trade—Political aspects—Asia.   2. Opium trade—Prevention.
3. Opium trade—Asia—History.   4. Drug control—Asia.   I. Title.
  HV5840.A74C46   2010
  363.45095—dc22   2009044012

Contents

Illustrations and Maps

Illustrations

Maps

Acknowledgements

This book is the outcome of years of research and draws from many inspirational writings and people. It also draws on my PhD dissertation (*Les territoires de l'opium*, 2002) but has been expanded vastly. Although all to whom I owe a debt of gratitude cannot be mentioned here, my thanks goes to those who trusted and supported me since I started working on illicit opium production in Asia, in the mid-1990s.

I would like to acknowledge the crucial role played by my friend and colleague, Alain Labrousse, in supporting me in my study of the geopolitics of illicit drugs, an approach that he helped develop through the creation of the former *Observatoire géopolitique des drogues* (OGD: Geopolitical Drug Watch). I wish to express my special gratitude to Laurent Laniel for his friendship and long and fruitful collaboration: he has contributed to the improvement of my work in many ways, notably through his rigorous and helpful comments on this book. I have also benefited from the incomparable insight and advice from another friend and colleague, David Mansfield, whose unique work is extensively quoted in this book. I am grateful to David Stonestreet, my editor at I.B.Tauris, for taking up this project and for his thorough editing of my text. I would like to thank Xavier Bouan, Alain Labrousse, David Mansfield and Margit Vermès for kindly letting me use some of the photos that illustrate these pages. A special thank you must go to my wife, Jennifer, for her support and for never failing to correct my English over the years.

A final acknowledgement must go to the peasant farmers of Asia and elsewhere – who, forced by acute poverty to resort to illicit agricultural drug production, find they must then endure the violence induced by the War on Drugs.

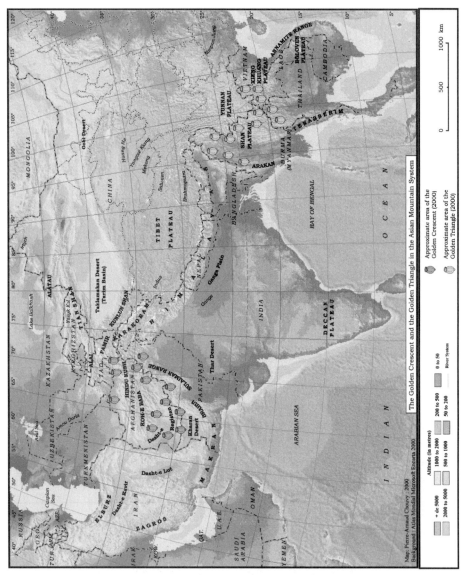

Map I: The Golden Crescent and the Golden Triangle in the Asian Mountain System.

Introduction

Bitter, brownish, and sticky, opium – the sap of the opium poppy, *Papaver somniferum* Linnaeus – is an addictive narcotic drug known since the earliest times. Both a palliative and a poison, the exotic origins of opium and the properties that were frequently, if erroneously, attributed to it, have ensured the West's continuing fascination and the aura of mystery that has long surrounded it.

My concern in this book is the politics and economics of the poppy in Asia, about how, when and why illicit opium production emerged and developed in specific regions of the continent at given periods of history. Its main objective is to explain how and why decades of anti-drug policies have not only failed to achieve their ultimate goal of suppressing illicit opium production but have even failed to reduce it.

The failure of more than a century of prohibition of certain drugs – opium included – is now evident. In fact, one hundred years of global prohibition and about forty years of a US-led War on Drugs have not just failed to suppress illicit opium production: for an increasing number of countries it seems likely to have both stimulated and displaced production.

In 1906, Charles Henry Brent, the first Protestant Episcopal Church Bishop of the Philippines and a staunch opponent of the then booming opium trade, wrote to President Theodore Roosevelt asking that the United States call for an international conference to enforce anti-opium measures in China. The same year, 41,624 tonnes of opium were produced worldwide: 85 per cent in China (35,364 tonnes) and 12 per cent in British India (5,177 tonnes). Opium had long been produced in Asia, most notably by the Mughal rulers of India, and its production, trade and consumption had been banned at different times in various countries, especially in the Chinese Empire (first in 1729). But in the mid-nineteenth century the British imposed their trade in Indian opium upon China through two so-called Opium Wars (1839–42 and 1856–60). This legalisation of the opium trade, imposed upon China by the British with the signing of the Treaty of Tianjin (1858), led eventually to the development of huge Chinese production: China had no choice but to promote an import substitution programme in order to address the deficit in its balance of payments with British India. Yet, in 1906 the Qing government of China launched its first national anti-opium campaign, one year before the British and Chinese governments agreed on a scheduled reduction of the opium trade. In 1909, the United States convened the International Opium Commission in Shanghai and in 1912 the Hague Convention urged its members to limit opiates to medical uses. Thus, less than sixty years after the Treaty of Tianjin legalized the Chinese import of British opium, opium production was on its way to becoming illicit except for medical purposes. This first step toward a global prohibition of *certain* drugs would prove successful, but only initially since the suppression of opium production in China and India eventually stimulated the emergence of illicit production in other areas, notably the so-called Golden Triangle and Golden Crescent areas of Southeast and Southwest Asia.

Following the multilateral efforts of the League of Nations (1919–46), then of the United Nations (founded in 1945), and after the Communist government in Beijing succeeded in eliminating opium production in China during the period 1949–59, global illicit opium output fell dramatically – to as little as 1,066 tonnes in 1970 (US government sources: McCoy, 1991: 495). But as world production was drastically reduced, so the areas where the opium poppy thrived changed. South of the recently opium-free China, a major new opium producing region emerged: Mainland Southeast Asia's so-called Golden Triangle. By 1970, 67 per cent of the world's illicit opium was harvested in the Golden Triangle, with 23 per cent in the other emerging area: the Golden Crescent. Burma,[1] in the Golden Triangle, alone contributed 47 per cent of the total; Afghanistan, in the Golden Crescent, a mere 10 per cent. Ironically, despite the fact that the world's illicit opium production was at its lowest in 1970, the following year saw both the expression 'Golden Triangle' coined by a US official and the launch of a global War on Drugs by Richard Nixon's administration. But this reduction in global production was short-lived and was mainly the result of the rapid suppression of production in China and India rather than an efficient global prohibition regime. In fact, many argue, as does this book, that the highly repressive War on Drugs proved not only inefficient but also counterproductive. Subsequent development-based policies, which were designed in the early 1970s, would also fail to drive illicit opium production down.

What is undeniable is that between the low of 1970 and the year 1989, illicit worldwide production of opium increased by 218 per cent to 3,395 tonnes (UNODCCP, 2001: 60) and that a marked change in the relative importance of producing countries took place. In 1989, Burma, whose many complex internal conflicts had stimulated opium production, was still the world's leading illicit producer of opium. In fact, Burma's output in 1989 exceeded the total world output for 1970, with 1,544 tonnes or 45 per cent of the global illicit output. But a challenger to world supremacy emerged to the west of the Himalayas: Afghanistan. Afghanistan's opium output increased 800 per cent in thirty years (from 130 tonnes in 1970 to 1,200 tonnes in 1989) and represented 35 per cent of the total world output for 1989. Alone, in 1989 Afghanistan was producing more opium than the entire world had done in 1970. At the close of the 1980s, the Golden Triangle and the Golden Crescent together supplied 96 per cent of the world's illicit opium – a percentage that has remained virtually unchanged into the 2000s.

Despite increased international and national anti-drug efforts, and despite a much better understanding of the dynamics of the global illegal drug markets and of the shortcomings of anti-drug policies and programmes, not much has changed since 1989 and global illicit opium production continues to increase. The only thing that has changed, especially since the mid- and late 1990s, is the relative size and breakdown of production figures. While Thailand, Vietnam and Pakistan drastically reduced their opium output, production has boomed in Burma and Afghanistan. Burma remained the world's premier producer of illicit opium until 1991 (1,728 tonnes), when it was (just) overtaken by Afghanistan (1,980 tonnes). Then, in a matter of a few years, Afghanistan's opium output snowballed, breaking record after record (3,416 tonnes in 1994, 4,565 tonnes in 1999 and 6,100 tonnes in 2006) and in 2007 its huge 8,200-tonne opium crop reportedly amounted to 93 per cent of the global output. In 2007, Afghanistan produced more opium than the entire world had done in 2006 (6,610 tonnes).

The steady increase in global opium production since the early 1970s has occurred despite the many efforts by the international community to suppress or reduce illegal opium poppy cultivation worldwide. Countless forced eradication campaigns, and many crop substitution and alternative development programmes, have failed. It can even be argued, as is done in this book, that forced eradication campaigns have been counterproductive, causing – at least to some extent – an increase in illicit opium production. Of course, the reasons for such a global failure are many and complex, rooted in the long history and politics of Asia and of the poppy. Opium production has clearly benefited from the turmoil of Asian history and geopolitics. The nineteenth-century Opium Wars, the twentieth-century Cold War and the many local conflicts waged by proxy in Burma, Laos, and Afghanistan, and even the twenty-first-century War on Terrorism in Afghanistan and Pakistan, have all fuelled the continent's illicit opium production. Illicit drug economies and war economies share a long and common history and have shared many territories in Asia and elsewhere.

Yet, illicit opium production has benefited not only from synergies between war economies and drug economies: it has also thrived on economic underdevelopment and poverty, whether war-induced or not. It is now widely acknowledged that the vast majority of Asian opium farmers grow poppies in order to combat poverty and, above all, food insecurity. Despite this fact (and the vast majority of Asian opium farmers are among the poorest of the poor), many observers and policy makers still doubt that farmers engage in illegal opium production out of need – and not out of greed. In 2007, even the United Nations Office on Drugs and Crime bluntly argued that Afghan opium production was not linked to poverty – 'much to the contrary'. In fact, history and geography show that illicit opium production never thrives better than when war and poverty overlap, as in Afghanistan and Burma. Part of the problem, in both Afghanistan and Burma, is that illicit opium production largely outlasts war. War often transforms political and economic realities and time is needed for war-torn countries to achieve the transition from war economy to peace economy. In predominantly rural countries such as Afghanistan and Burma, where conflict has lasted for decades and hampered economic growth and development, it seems that the suppression of illicit opium production can only proceed from the establishment of peace and the initial reconstruction of the state and of the economy.

But opium suppression policies have also failed because they have been – for the most part – inadequate, ill-funded, and improperly sequenced. In spite of three international 'conventions on narcotic drugs' (1961, 1971, 1988), the launch in 1971 of a global War on Drugs by the United States, and the creation of a specialized anti-drug body within the United Nations (UNFDAC: 1972; UNDCP: 1991; UNODC: 2002), the 'Drug Free World' proclaimed by the motto of the UN anti-drug agency has proved an elusive goal.

The politics favouring poppy cultivation have proven considerably more successful than the policies designed and implemented in order to ban it. Neither the War on Drugs nor development approaches have reduced illicit opium production in Asia – quite the opposite. Why have anti-drug policies failed despite four decades of continuing and increasing effort? What are the shortcomings and limitations of forced eradication, alternative development, 'silver bullets' and other 'quick fixes'? The following pages will attempt to provides answers to these and other questions and in doing so it will be necessary to call upon a rich and extensive literature that includes the disciplines of history, geography, anthropology, politics, agronomy and development. Such is the great diversity and complexity of illicit opium production in Asia.

The first half of the book (chapters 1 to 5), draws on the complex history and geopolitics of the opium poppy in Asia, from Neolithic times to the mid-twentieth-century emergence of the Golden Triangle and the Golden Crescent, to the most recent developments in opium production in Afghanistan and Burma. How, where and when did illicit opium production take place in Asia? Who contributed to the emergence of the Golden Triangle and the Golden Crescent, and why? How and where did opium and heroin trafficking occur? Chapters 1 to 5 give a detailed overview of the roots and dynamics of illicit opium production and of drug trafficking in both the Golden Triangle and the Golden Crescent.

The following chapters first detail and explain how and why illicit opium production thrived in certain regions and countries of Asia and not in others. What relations existed and still exist between war and drugs, between war economies and drug economies? Did illicit opium production finance terrorism or did the strategic imperatives of the War on Terrorism put the War on Drugs on hold?

Alongside such geopolitical and geostrategic considerations, this book also offers a detailed look at the diversity and complexity of the agricultural and economic contexts of opium poppy cultivation in both Southeast and Southwest Asia. How and why is opium production undertaken in Asia, and by whom? Why do some Asian farmers resort to illicit opium production in spite of its labour intensiveness and poor economic yield? Understanding the 'drivers' of opium poppy cultivation and the motivations of opium farmers is a prerequisite to understanding the reasons for the successes and failures of anti-drug policies. How and why did forty years of forced eradication, crop substitution, and alternative development programmes not only fail to suppress illicit opium production but even to hamper its growth? In conclusion the book details and analyses the shortcomings, insufficiencies, and potentialities of anti-drug policies by reviewing the anti-drug history of Asia's opium producing countries.

1. Opium poppy fields in Dir district, NWFP, Pakistan.

1

Opium: a Drug in Motion through Time and Space

Opiates are derivatives of opium[1] and are among the most widely used drugs in the contemporary world, mostly as pain-relievers but also as so-called recreational drugs. Opiates, however, are the only true *narcotic* drugs since they cause stupor, induce sleep and relieve pain – as the etymology tells us. Hence, morphine, the principal alkaloid of opium, is an analgesic and a sedative that has an effect on the central nervous system, whilst cocaine, an alkaloid obtained from coca leaves, is a topical anaesthetic which, used as a stimulant, provokes euphoric effects. Under international legislation on mind and body altering substances,[2] yet regardless of their respective effects or potency, opiates can be divided into licit and illicit drugs. Thus morphine is widely used as a licit substance in modern medicine, whilst heroin is now mostly consumed as an illicit product.[3]

The exact geographic origin of the opium poppy still puzzles botanists, historians, and geographers alike but the plant proved itself able to adapt to most ecological environments and spread across all of Europe and Asia and can now also be found in both North and South America, Australia and even Africa, growing under diverse climates and on extremely different soils (Chouvy, 2001, 2002a). As with other cultivars – such as *Nicotiana tabacum* (tobacco) or *Erythroxylon coca* (coca) – *Papaver somniferum* stands out because no truly wild population or specimens exist. This suggests that the history of the opium poppy is clearly linked to the history of human settlement and to cultivation, prompting questions about the symbiosis that developed between the plant and humans, and indicating a very old selection process of drug plants by humans over many thousands of years.

One cannot understand what has most likely been a long and complex relationship between human societies and the opium poppy if the geographic origin and the history of the plant are not explained at least in some detail. As A.-G. Haudricourt and L. Hédin stressed, 'The narrow dependence of Man and his crop plants ... can be well understood only if one constantly keeps in mind the conditions under which the vegetable varieties and species occur and are distributed geographically' (Haudricourt and Hédin, 1943: 21). As for the nature of this relation, it is particularly well expressed by biologist and pharmacognosist J.-M. Pelt, who wrote that the 'drug sticks to Man like the skin to his flesh' (Pelt, 1983: 14).

THE OPIUM POPPY AND MANKIND

There are differing ideas about the botanical evolution of the opium poppy but all varieties of *Papaver somniferum* appear to have developed in and around human settlements, either in the areas created and maintained by people or on the peripheries, on dumping grounds and around cultivated fields, for example. One idea, put forth by J.M. de Wet and J.R. Harlan, is that selection would have operated according to a double process of artificial selection and natural selection (Wet de, Harlan, 1975: 99–107). Seeds coming from the cultivated wild plant would have escaped and colonized peripheral spaces modified or disturbed by human activity. Some 'escaped' poppies would then have adapted gradually to continuing human disturbance of its habitat.

Human settlement and the beginnings of agriculture probably benefited the opium poppy by enlarging the habitat most favourable to its development, together with other weeds no doubt, some of which also had psychoactive properties and which often entered opium-based preparations. This was the case for *Datura stramonium* L. (often known as Jimson Weed), for example, which was part of the Greek *nepenthe*, the potion used to induce forgetfulness of pain or sorrow.

Given its beauty – its bright and colourful flowers – people must have noticed the poppy at a very early stage. Its many useful properties – food, oil, medicine, fodder, recreation and, or, ritual – not to mention its facilitated growth in and around human settlements, must have ensured the continuing association with people and its spread along transcontinental migration routes.

THE GEOGRAPHIC ORIGIN AND HISTORIC SPREAD OF THE OPIUM POPPY (MAP II)

Archaeological evidence has led specialists to believe that the opium poppy probably originated somewhere between the Western Mediterranean and Asia Minor. It is, however, on the Neolithic lakeshore dwellings of Neuchâtel, Switzerland, that some of the oldest paleobotanical remains of opium poppy seeds and capsules have been found. Fossil evidence has also been found in Cueva de los Murciélagos, in southern Spain, but no similar findings have been made in the Eastern Mediterranean or in Asia Minor (Merlin, 1984: 173–5). In his book, *On the Trail of the Ancient Opium Poppy*, M.D. Merlin concludes: 'Although most of the fossil evidence for the opium poppy comes from west central Europe, we do have a small amount of direct evidence from other Neolithic and Bronze Age locations in southern Spain, the Rhineland, Austria, Czechoslovakia, Poland, and perhaps Turkey'. He then suggests that 'the opium poppy was spread out of central Europe and down into the eastern Mediterranean region during the later part of the prehistoric period (i.e., the late Bronze Age) (Merlin, 1984: 282–3).

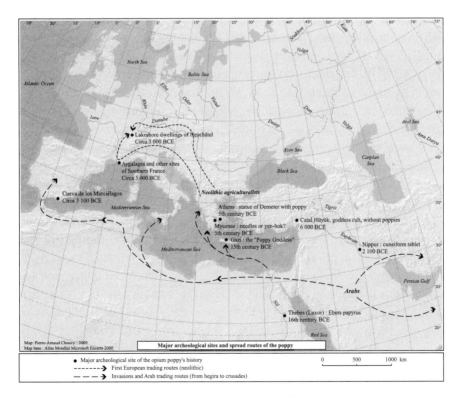

Map II: Major archeological sites and spread routes of the poppy.

It is now commonly accepted that the opium poppy probably originated in Europe and was part of the trading activity of the earliest migrations between the different peoples of Europe and Asia. Indeed, it has been suggested that seeds of *Papaver somniferum*, and even some opium, may have been included in the extensive trading undertaken by the Sumerians, whose commercial network reached all the way to the Mediterranean to the west and the Indian subcontinent to the east. Thus, poppy seeds as well as opium must have been exchanged for thousands of years, by both sea and land, making opium use an ancient practice in various regions.

There is no doubt that the Egyptians traded opium – the so-called *opium thebaicum*, for instance, whose reputation was well established in the thirteenth century BCE (Latimer and Goldberg, 1981: 17). Indeed, it is probable that it was the Egyptians who were responsible for the spread of opium poppy cultivation within Europe, by introducing it to the Greeks. In southernmost Europe, the use of opium clearly declined after the fall of the Roman Empire (fifth century CE), only to reappear much later with the return from the crusades (thirteenth century CE), thus underlining the role of the Arabs in the geographical spread of opium.

It is generally believed that the Arabs played the major role in spreading the opium poppy and opium-related knowledge to the rest of the world. They early understood and exploited the commercial potential of opium and spread its consumption all the more easily as their empire rapidly expanded. Trade, which was accompanied by the spread of Islam, formed an integral part of their traditions. Where the Arabs went opium followed, whether by caravan or aboard dhows, whose most skilful navigators benefited from the monsoon winds which the Phoenicians had sailed before them.

The Arabs supposedly introduced opium to India, after having conquered Spain, Egypt, Asia Minor, Turkistan, Persia and certain parts of India in the seventh century, although some suppose that Alexander the Great (356–323 BCE) had already introduced it ten centuries earlier. In India, however, the first known reference to the opium poppy dates only from 1000 CE, whereas one has to wait until 1200 CE to find opium mentioned from an explicitly medical point of view (Husain and Sharma, 1983: 25).

It is again the Arabs who are reputed to have introduced opium and the knowledge of its uses to China in the eighth century, in spite of the fact that there are Chinese texts referring to its use as early as 987 BCE and again in the third century (Booth, 1998: 104). These texts hardly leave any doubt that opium was known and used in China before the Arabs ever traded in it. However, the leading role that the Arabs took in the spread of the opium poppy is clear if one only looks at the etymological similarities of 'opium' in many languages: *afiun* in Arabic and Persian, *opium* in French and

English, *opos* or *opion* in Greek, *afium* in Turkish, *ahipen* in Sanskrit, *aphin* in Hindi. As for the Chinese *Fu-yung* (*ya-pien*), linguists maintain that it also comes from the Arabic *afiun*.

The Arabs might not have introduced opium into China but they undoubtedly traded in it, at least to make up the shortages in Chinese production. However, with the decline of Arab influence and the unprecedented development of the European maritime trade, the commerce in opium was taken on by the Venetians after the lagoon city became the main centre of European trade (from the thirteenth century on). At that time opium was highly prized in Europe, since all the great navigators were charged, among other things, with bringing back the famous panacea from their voyages. Hence the Portuguese took over the opium trade with Vasco de Gama (1460–1524). They bought opium in India, where poppy cultivation was strongly encouraged by the Mughal emperors for the substantial income it brought them. Then, by settling in Macao in 1557, the Portuguese permanently took over from the Arabs. As for the famous Indian opium from Bengal and Malwa, it quickly became highly coveted by the Dutch and the British, who spread its use in Java and in China, respectively.

It is, however, only when the European maritime powers, as a result of their great expeditions, initiated an era of globalization, that the opium trade took on a brand new dimension: interpenetration and interdependence of the world's markets were to inaugurate new dynamics and to lay down the conditions for the global drugs trade.

Indeed, with hermit Romano Pane allegedly being the first Westerner to witness tobacco inhaling in fifteenth century Hispaniola, a brand new era in the diffusion of opiates began: beyond tobacco it was opium which could now be smoked, like hashish, and later, cocaine or even crack. The introduction by the Portuguese and the Spaniards of the pipe and tobacco in Southeast Asia, whose use was later taken over and spread by the Dutch, spurred opium consumption in a way that the British quickly and skilfully exploited. Opium was efficiently produced and traded by colonial monopolies to ensure the profitability of their colonies and, at least for the British, to balance their trade deficit with China. Fearing that payment for Chinese imported goods (tea consumption was growing fast in Britain when only China produced the leaves) would deplete their silver reserves, the British resorted to opium, a product of their Indian colony, as a means of payment: 'A triangle traffic developed in which opium smuggling yielded the silver later used to buy tea legally, which was then shipped to London' (Meyer and Parssinen, 1998: 9).

The first shipment of Indian opium arrived in Canton in 1773, eventually leading China to mass addiction. Although opposed by the Chinese rulers, the trade continued unabated for decades until two so-called 'Opium Wars'[4]

(1839–42 and 1856–60) between the British, who wished to maintain the trade, and the Chinese who tried to put an end to it. The treaty of Nanjing (1842), which ended the first war, gave Hong Kong to the British. Hong Kong would go on to become the world's main heroin hub in the twentieth century. China, confronted with exploding opium consumption, eventually fostered local poppy production as a way of balancing its own growing trade deficit: China, as the biggest opium-consuming country ever, then became the world's leading producer as well (35,364 metric tonnes in 1906: 85 per cent of world production). The Treaty of Nanjing also included a provision for extra-territoriality: i.e. 'the right for British subjects in China to be judged by their own consuls and tried under their own legal system [. . .]. The privilege, later granted to other foreign powers, created enforcement-free safety zones used by traffickers when drugs once again became illegal in twentieth-century China' (Meyer and Parssinen, 1998: 10–11).

Beyond its strictly financial dimension – the fact that it was deeply integrated into global colonial trading together with tea, sugar, silver, and cotton – the opium trade entered a system in which British capitalism transformed certain substances 'from upper-class luxuries to working-class necessities'. Indeed, opiates, 'like coffee, or chocolate or tea [. . .] provide stimulus to greater effort without providing nutrition [. . .]' (Mintz, 1985: 186). In Asia, where most of today's illicit opium and heroin are produced, 'opium prepared the ground for capitalism by creating mass markets and proletarian consumers while undermining the morale and morality of elites' (Trocki, 1999: 53). In Asia, 'opium, both in the case of capitalist development as well as in the case of colonial finance, served to tighten up those key areas of "slack" in European systems and facilitated the global connections that in effect, were the [British] empire' (Trocki, 1999: 59). Indeed, as Carl Trocki documents, Chinese labour in the colonial economies of Southeast Asia had two advantages: it enabled production by the coolies (opium consumption being used both to dull the worker's pain and as a prophylactic against diarrhoea and fever caused by dysentery, malaria, typhoid and intestinal parasites); and provided revenue (in the form of taxes) available from opium farms (or monopolies), as only Chinese were allowed to smoke opium. As a matter of fact, the coolies' pay was taken back by the colonial system through the opium farm system: 'opium was not peripheral to the system [. . .] but rather it was central [. . .]. If the cost of employing labor were not recaptured by the capitalist and recycled, as it were, there would have been no profit.' (Trocki, 1999: 144–7). As Timothy Brook and Bob Tadashi Wakabayashi put it, opium 'gave foreign powers the financial wherewithal to make colonial empire-building feasible' (Brook, Wakabayashi, 2000: 1). However, it is also true that colonial empire-building clearly made large-scale opium production, trading and consumption feasible.

Having been used to make the European colonies in Asia viable and even profitable, the opium poppy then spread on a global scale: it accompanied Chinese immigrant workers (coolies) to the Americas, rendered Japanese expansionist policies in septentrional China (Manchuria) lucrative and developed on the successes of the modern drug traffickers.

Today, this narcotic plant thrives to a greater or lesser extent across the surface of the entire planet: in Asia of course, where for decades the Golden Triangle (Burma, Laos, Thailand) and the Golden Crescent (Afghanistan, Iran, Pakistan) have been the two most important areas in the world for illicit opiates production; but also in Europe (France, Spain), India, and Tasmania, where one can find licit crops for the pharmaceutical industry; in Africa, where the poppy has asserted its presence along the Gulf of Guinea ; and finally in North, Central and South America, where Mexico is one of the world's most important producers of illicit opium (and heroin), and where certain Andean states, already involved in coca growing, have witnessed an increase in poppy cultivation, a testament to the interest that drug traffickers take in diversification.

THE OPIUM POPPY, FROM EARLY USE TO PROHIBITION AND CRIMINALIZATION

Asia, where most illicit – as well as licit – opium is produced, has a long association with psychoactive substances. Many of them – cannabis, opium, datura, etc. – have been found throughout the continent for centuries and sometimes thousand of years, and have been used, either separately or in combination, for a variety of purposes, as in India's *saddhus* rituals, where spirituality can be accessed by way of hashish consumption. Different societies established traditional uses for such substances (or so-called 'drugs') such that they have become part of social codes (as in Persia), religious rituals (as in India), and local pharmacopoeia (as in China). Centuries ago, before the pipe was introduced into Asia by the Europeans, opiates were consumed by ingestion, by way of opium poppy decoctions or by eating opium, sometimes in sophisticated and even tasteful preparations. Such consumption was traditional, both ritually and medically. With opium smoking, a recreational use emerged both in Asia and Europe in the eighteenth century (later in North America) and gave rise to a fully-blown social and economic phenomenon.

Addiction was facilitated when the intake of alkaloids was made easier, echoing to some extent what happened when tobacco became available in ready-made cigarettes (North Carolina cigarettes had even been marketed in China to help wean the Chinese from opium) (Courtwright, 2001: 112–22). Addiction to narcotics was further facilitated by the discovery of the first alkaloid – morphine (1805–6) – by the invention of the hypodermic syringe (1851), and by the rapid advances in the pharmaceutical industry that led to the production of heroin (by Bayer in 1898). In fact, 'opium made the same transition earlier accomplished by sugar and tobacco, from an exotic chemical to a fully "capitalist" drug commodity' (Trocki, 1999: 58). The advent of injecting drugs by syringe not only potentially led to severe addiction but also to contracting blood-borne diseases such as hepatitis and HIV/AIDS.

Now more than ever, the modern trade in illicit drugs is shaped and stimulated by mercantilism, even more so as it grows on the fertile and complex terrain of both poverty and armed conflict. In fact, a direct relation between illicit drugs production, poverty and war appears to exist (Chouvy, 2002a). Illicit drug production and drug trafficking have always, it would seem, been the outcome of both economic and political events.

However, the trade in narcotics was deeply disrupted when addiction became a social (even religious) issue in Western countries, especially in the United States, where the Chinese had brought opium smoking with them in the earliest days of the gold rush and where anti-Chinese sentiment swept California as early as the mid-1870s: on 15 November 1875, in San Francisco, an ordinance made it a misdemeanour to keep or frequent opium dens, thus calling the first shot in the prohibition of certain drugs in the United States. As would so often be the case in more than a century of global prohibition, the effect of the law proved counterproductive: it did not eliminate the dens but forced them underground and made their commerce more lucrative.

Before prohibition became global many opiate-based substances were legally and easily available, some being produced by pharmaceutical companies that are today major manufacturers and distributors of widely known medicines. Laudanum, a medicinal tincture of opium, has probably been the most widely used opiate-based substance in the Western world for more than two hundred years. Opiate-based medicines were numerous and marketed for a variety of purposes to different parts of society. In the United States, for example, Stickney and Poor's paregoric, or 'Mrs Winslow's Soothing Syrup', were widely used by mothers and child-care workers. Although immoderate opiate consumption had been a real social and health problem in the nineteenth century (especially), the very existence and availability of such substances had clearly contributed to relieving pain and treating disease at a time when mortality from malaria, cholera and dysentery was high. As sanitary conditions in the Western world improved, however, and as other pain-relievers were discovered and made more easily available, the serious side effects of chronic opiate use became a growing issue. The best-known and most widely-used pain-reliever (moderate though) was, and still is, acetylsalicylic acid – or aspirin – a non-narcotic analgesic derived from extracts of the bark of the willow tree (*Spiraea ulmaria* L.), which was rediscovered in 1899 and manufactured, again, by Bayer. In fact, before Germany lost World War I and the Treaty of Versailles was signed in 1919, Aspirin and Heroin were trademarks owned by Bayer.

By the end of the nineteenth century opium prohibition was already on its way: Britain passed the Opium Act in 1878 in an attempt to reduce opium consumption in its colonies by restricting it to registered Chinese smokers and Indian eaters. In Burma, for example, the (ethnic) Burmese (Burmans) and the other non-Chinese or non-Indian Burmese people, were banned from legally purchasing and consuming opium. However, about ten years later, in 1886, the Shan States of northern Burma were annexed by the British into their empire. Tribal refugees and migrants from Southern China began settling in the area, bringing with them the opium poppy, opium production techniques and the beginnings of a new economy. The strict monopoly that the British had tried to enforce on the production and trade of Indian opium had proven counterproductive, increasing prices and helping to foster illicit opium production in the Shan States and making smuggling to both Burma proper and neighbouring Siam (Thailand after 1939) all the more lucrative.

In the United States, Congress imposed a tax on both opium and morphine use in 1890 in an attempt to enforce some kind of federal legislation on narcotics. However, these early moves to reduce opiate consumption coincided with the commercial production of heroin (1898). Heroin was then thought to be non-addictive and the perfect cure for opium and morphine addicts but in fact rapidly increasing rates of heroin addiction were observed in the United States as early as 1903, eleven years before Congress regulated opium use through the 1914 Harrison Act, which made illegal the non-medical use of cocaine and opiate drugs and criminalized some 200,000 users of narcotics in the country (Harrison, Backenheimer and Inciardi, 1995). Five years later, in 1908, Britain and China finally agreed on a treaty restricting the opium trade although opium production and addiction would not disappear from China until Communist rule in the early 1950s.

The Anglo-Oriental Society for the Suppression of the Opium Trade was founded in Britain in 1874. Funded and inspired by the Quakers, they supported a successful 1906 motion that the Indo-Chinese opium trade was 'morally indefensible', a trade that William Gladstone, British prime minister at the time, had once described as 'most infamous and atrocious' (Booth: 1998, 156–7). In return, the Chinese issued an edict prohibiting opium poppy cultivation in China and both parties agreed on respective deadlines for opium suppression. Major agricultural changes were accordingly needed in India, where the poppy acreage was halved between 1905 and 1910. As for China, extensive efforts were also directed at suppressing opium poppy cultivation and at weaning the nation off opium consumption. However, the political upheaval that disrupted China, first after the 1911 Wuchang Uprising and then after the death of Chinese president Yuan Shikai in 1916, considerably limited the scope of the government's suppression agenda. Opium production and consumption resumed as internecine wars were waged by local warlords, who depended on income from opium production.

Many Chinese farmers were in fact coerced to produce opium in lieu of food crops, setting a symbiotic relationship between the illicit drugs economy and the war economy that would later repeat itself in the Golden Triangle and the Golden Crescent, when some of the Cold War proxies and covert operations would be financed by the illicit drugs economy.

With the beginning of the twentieth century, a major change took place in the way narcotics and other drugs were addressed politically, socially and economically. Until then only the Indian-Chinese opium trade had been targeted by prohibitionists. Having annexed the Philippine Islands in 1898 and implemented local opium prohibition in 1908, the United States initiated a global policy aimed at reducing both production and consumption of certain drugs (Davenport-Hines, 2001: 155–60). At the instigation of the United States, the International Opium Commission, was convened in Shanghai in 1909. The first of its kind, it failed, however, either to draft a convention or even to get a single country to abide to a common policy. Two years later, in 1911, the Hague Conference gathered twelve nations together, leading to a 1912 Convention that implemented international control of opium production and an overall prohibition of the non-medical use of opiates. However, as happened in China during the same period, World War I put a halt to the Convention's agenda and drug production and consumption quickly resumed, if only through the war-induced demand for painkillers. At the end of the war, the Treaty of Versailles (1919) adopted control measures on opium as it removed Bayer's monopoly on the Aspirin and Heroin trademarks. In 1921, the League of Nations established the Advisory Committee on the Traffic in Opium and other Dangerous Drugs, thus enabling international cooperation in, and the monitoring of, drug control.

Various international conferences were subsequently convened to deal with drug production, trade and consumption, and world opium production was reduced, from 42,000 tonnes in 1906 to 8,000 tonnes in 1934. After World War II, further international conferences determined which countries could legally grow opium poppies to meet the needs of the pharmaceutical industry (1953), and discussed how to tighten control on certain classified drugs: the Single Convention on Narcotic Drugs, signed by eighty countries, was held in 1961 and led to the foundation in 1968 of the still-extant International Narcotics Control Board (INCB), an 'independent and quasi-judicial control organ for the implementation of the United Nations drug conventions'.[5] The year 1971 saw the birth of the United Nations Fund for Drug Abuse Control (UNFDAC), whose goal was to address economically illicit opium production through the implementation of crop substitution programs and alternative development projects in countries illegally producing opium. The United Nations (UN) then created the International Drug Control Programme (UNDCP, 1991), later to be part of the Office for Drug Control and Crime Prevention (UNODCCP, 1997), renamed in 2002 the Office on Drugs and Crime (UNODC). The 1971 Convention on Psychotropic Substances and the 1988 Convention Against Illicit Traffic in Narcotic Drugs and Psychotropic Substances were the last two conventions aimed at helping legislate and control the illicit drugs industry worldwide. As stated by the INCB, 'From the beginning, the basic aim of the international drug control treaties has been to limit the use of drugs to medical and scientific purposes only'.

In order to assess the achievements of international drug control, a United Nations General Assembly Special Session (UNGASS) on the World Drug Problem was convened in New York in June 1998, ten years after the adoption of the 1988 Convention. While the proposal for an independent evaluation of drug control efforts was dismissed, partly by the United States and Great Britain, Pino Arlacchi, UNDCP director since September 1997, planned for illicit drug production to be eliminated or significantly reduced within ten years. A global strategy to reduce illicit drug supply and demand by 2008 was thereby adopted without any prior evaluation of past and current anti-drug policies. The United Nations reaffirmed its 'unwavering determination and commitment to overcoming the world drug problem through domestic and international strategies to reduce both the illicit supply of and demand for drugs'. Since 'participation of non-governmental organisations at UNGASS was largely limited to critique from outside',[6] 'the need for a comprehensive approach towards the elimination of illicit narcotic crops' (UN General Assembly Political Declaration, 10 June 1998[7]) was easily affirmed. No matter how unrealistic the goal being set, 'A Drug Free World' was called for. Five years later, at the time of the 2003 Mid-Term Review of UNGASS, no significant and sustainable reduction of opium or coca production had taken place: the huge expanse of Moroccan cannabis cultivation had finally been confirmed by the first UNODC survey of the country (UNODC, 2003d; Chouvy, 2005c), production of synthetic drugs was clearly increasing, and opium production was growing in the new Western-backed Afghanistan. Still, Antonio Maria Costa, UNODC director since May 2002, referred to 'encouraging progress towards still distant goals', and the goals and targets of the UNGASS were merely reaffirmed (Blickman and Bewley-Taylor, 2006: 1).

2. Opium poppy field in Dir district, NWFP, Pakistan.

2

Opium and Heroin in Asia: Early History and Geopolitics

While opiates continue to be used worldwide, legally and illegally, as painkillers or even as panaceas, both by allopathic medicine and by non-allopathic medicines, most of the world's opium is still produced illegally and fuels a thriving illicit drugs industry based around morphine and heroin.

Today, at least ten countries produce opium illegally. Nineteen others grow opium poppies legally for the pharmaceutical industry, under strict state control. India is the world's only licit opium *exporter*.[1] All other licit opiates exporters extract the alkaloids directly from 'poppy straw' (Concentrate of Poppy Straw): i.e. from the plant itself, not from opium (Chouvy, 2006a). In 2005, 439 tonnes of opium were legally produced in India whilst at least 4,620 tonnes were produced *illegally* in the rest of the world (GOI, 2006: 113–14; UNODC, 2006c: 57). In 2007, 6,322 hectares of illegally cultivated opium poppies were eradicated in West Bengal alone,[2] i.e. an area not much smaller than the 7,833 hectares harvested under licence for the whole of India in 2004–5 (GOI, 2005: 98).

Interestingly, Afghanistan and Burma – the source of more than 90 per cent of the world's illicit opium for years – were denied the right to be legal producers in the 1950s. Fifty years later, in 2007, after a few years of continually decreasing Burmese production, Afghanistan produced its highest opium crop to date: 8,200 tonnes – or 93 per cent of total illicit world supply (UNODC, 2007b: 1; 2006b).

Since the beginning of commercial opium production – whether licit or illicit – Asian domination has never been challenged, although production has shifted from certain countries and regions to others, showing opium production to be geographically flexible within Asia. The record output levels achieved by the Chinese (35,364 tonnes of opium in 1906: 85 per cent of the global output) are, however, very unlikely to be reached again by any given country, or even globally (at least in absolute values), although Afghanistan, with 93 per cent of the world's opium output in 2007, has achieved an even heavier global domination than China ever did in relative values.[3] Asian opium production has undergone many other deep disruptions in the one hundred years since Charles Henry Brent called for an international conference to enforce anti-opium measures in China. And it is to the two regions that were to become Asia's largest areas of illicit opium production that we now turn: the Golden Triangle and the Golden Crescent.

SOUTHEAST ASIA: FROM THE FALL OF CHINESE OPIUM PRODUCTION TO THE BIRTH OF THE GOLDEN TRIANGLE

Against a background of rapidly increasing opium production in China, increasing opium consumption in the European colonies of Southeast Asia and exorbitant prices imposed by colonial opium monopolies, north-south migrations from China further contributed to the development of large-scale opium production in Mainland Southeast Asia.

Such north-south expansionist movements within China have driven people from southern China to Mainland Southeast Asia since at least the ninth century BCE. Centuries after the Thai and the Shan moved down from Yunnan to settle in Mainland Southeast Asia, others followed along the same routes, bringing their knowledge of opium with them. Historian Ron Renard explains that poppy cultivation was recorded by Chinese historians in western Yunnan, near Burma's Kokang region, in 1736 and that when opium production grew rapidly in and after the 1830s, 'Christian missionaries noted poppy growing in the northern Kachin areas in Burma' (Renard, 1996: 15).

In 1856, the Chinese Empire faced the 'Panthay Rebellion' (1856–73), a separatist uprising by the Hui people. The Hui are Muslims supposedly of Uzbek descent, whom the Burmese call Panthay and the Thai, Chin Haw or Haw. The Panthay Rebellion was a reaction to the southward push of the Han (ethnic Chinese) and to the creation of a Muslim kingdom around Dali (Yunnan) by Du Wenxiu (also known as Sultan Suleiman or as Sultan of Dali). The economic viability of this kingdom was largely due to the development of commercial networks between Yunnan and Southeast Asia. The Panthay had crossed the mountainous tracks of Burma, Siam, Laos, and Vietnam for centuries (on their renowned sturdy mules) before their rebellion was quelled by the Chinese. The Panthay took refuge in the Shan and Wa

States of northeastern Burma, where they founded the city of Panglong, in the Kokang region, in 1875.

The Panthay allied themselves to the Hmong who, in 1853, had also rebelled against the Chinese and fled to Southeast Asia in order to avoid repression. The migrations of the Hmong, Yao, and other slash-and-burn agriculturalist peoples from southern China to Southeast Asia brought with them a knowledge of opium poppy cultivation. Chinese southward expansion and its associated ethnic troubles effectively therefore brought about the influx of well-known caravanning groups (the Hui) and some of the region's most skilled opium producers (the Hmong) into northern Mainland Southeast Asia, where they settled along with the Lahu, Lisu, and Akha: all tribal peoples of the Tibeto-Burman linguistic family. Populating highlands above 800–1,000 metres that were suitable for poppy cultivation, itinerant farmers cleared the land to secure both cash (opium) and staple crops (mountain rice and corn). Thanks to their mules, and to their links with the valleys and plains where regional markets were held, the Hui found outlets for Hmong products and provided them with basic consumer goods by using networks originally established for the tea trade centuries earlier (Forbes, 1986; Forbes and Henley, 1997; Renard, 1996).

In the meantime, and in spite of the large increase in opium production in China, Southeast Asia's colonial opium monopolies abruptly raised their selling prices. As a result, in the early years of the twentieth century, contraband Chinese opium increased considerably, competing with the legal and overtaxed imports of Chinese opium. Siam and French Indochina rapidly suffered from such competition but Southeast Asian opium production would not increase significantly before the Second World War – a century or so after opium producers and caravaners emigrated from southern China to Southeast Asia, in the mid-nineteenth century.

The time-lag between the arrival of opium producers in Southeast Asia and the real development of opium production can be explained, partly, by caution on the part of the colonial monopolies, who drew a large part of their revenue from the sale of opium but not from its production or export. Colonial governments were already faced with a thriving black market in opium from Yunnan, which competed strongly with their sales. To accept and to facilitate local opium production would have further complicated what was already an uncontrollable situation along the northern borders of Siam: colonial domains were poorly controlled and therefore extremely porous.

The 1930s and 1940s, however, witnessed an unprecedented development in opium production in Southeast Asia, from Burma to Tonkin (Siam included). In the early nineteenth century, northeastern Burma was already renowned for high-quality opium produced in its Kokang region, located between the towns of Mong Ko and Panglong, on Yunnan's border with Burma. The region's opium trade benefited from the existing structures and networks of the prolific tea commerce, for Kokang had been a regional hub for the tea trade between Yunnan, Burma and a few Tai kingdoms for hundreds of years. But in the 1930s and 1940s the then fledgling export industry of Shan tea struggled to compete with Indian and Ceylonese teas. The Japanese occupation of Burma seriously disrupted what was a sub-regional to regional tea trade and 'the Shan tea industry reverted to a purely domestic affair after Britain transferred power to an independent Burma in 1948' (Maule, 1991). Lashio, a large town in the north of the Shan States, had long been one the region's main trading centres where tea was traditionally brought by the producers themselves, before they returned with their mules loaded with rice, silver, and jade. When the Second World War made such a trade too dangerous for tea producers, opium – a produce of much greater value – progressively replaced tea in the regional commercial exchanges. Panthay caravaners took advantage of the growing opium trade and extended it to most of the Shan and Kachin States (Maule, 1992; Renard, 1996; Taylor, 1998). As Ron Renard explains: 'Although subject to both the Shan State of Hsenwi and to the Yunnan government at Kunming, Kokang was so remote from the two that it was, in effect, autonomous; an advantageous position for growing such a lucrative crop as opium' (Renard, 1996: 19). After 1900, poppy cultivation, which had already become the 'dominant crop in Kokang and the Wa region', spread 'on hills everywhere higher than 1,200 meters' (Renard, 1996: 29).

The British, who sold Indian opium in Burma, chose to ignore opium production in the Shan and Wa States as well as opium contraband from Yunnan, and they refused to intervene administratively in these frontier regions (Maule, 1992: 26; McCoy, 1991: 109). Siam (which had become Thailand in 1939 under the Phibun government) had also suffered from contraband Chinese and Burmese opium. Acting upon advice from Sir Malcom Delevigne, the British delegate to the League of Nations, reduction measures announced in 1907 by King Chulalongkorn (i.e. the closure of opium dens) were replaced by a policy of encouraging the development of Siamese opium production, which would reduce costs of the imports and would abate contraband (Maule, 1992: 21). At that time, the only means of reducing contraband opium to and within Southeast Asia was to legalize local production and export, as happened in Burma and in Siam.

In French Indochina, the opium monopolies were supplied with Indian, Turkish, and Persian opium until 1899, when Paul Doumer, Governor-General of French Indochina from 1897 to 1902, showed a degree of favour toward cheaper Yunnanese opium. Then, when the Second World War broke out, French monopolies experienced an unprecedented break in supply as Middle Eastern imports were interrupted. In order for the opium monopolies to maintain their profits they needed to develop production within the colonies. From this point on, the Hmong of Laos and of Tonkin were allowed to produce opium legally for the monopolies of French Indochina. These measures provided a strong stimulus to Laotian production during the Second World War, something that, as historian Alfred McCoy explained, had changed the 'hill tribe economy from subsistence agriculture to cash-crop opium farming' (McCoy, 1991: 119). In doing so Indo-Chinese production underwent a 600 per cent increase in four years, from 8.4 tonnes in 1940 to 60.6 tons in 1944 (McCoy, 1991: 115).

However, at the end of the Second World War, despite the disruption in Indian and Chinese supplies, and despite Southeast Asia's recent self-sufficiency in opium, production in the highlands of the Indochinese peninsula was still just beginning. What would soon become the Golden Triangle at this stage produced little more than 80 tonnes of opium a year. The Golden Triangle really only emerged after the radical political change that occurred in China in 1949. The defeat of the Kuomintang (KMT), Chiang Kai-shek's Chinese nationalist troops, by the People's Liberation Army (PLA) of the Chinese Communists, was going to deeply affect opium production in Mainland Southeast Asia.

From 1950 onwards, the PLA imposed the cultivation of substitution crops in southern China, and legal, as well as illegal, opium exports to Southeast Asia quickly stopped. In fact, China really began implementing anti-drug policies in 1952, with its first large Communist and nationalist anti-opium campaign. However, opium poppy eradication in southern China's non-Han areas required more time, effort and diplomacy than in the rest of China's Han-dominated regions. For example, in southwest Yunnan's Baoshan Prefecture, four anti-opium campaigns (1952, 1954, 1964, and 1965) were necessary to clear the region of opium production and consumption (Zhou, 1999: 149–61).

While China was adopting a radical solution to its opium problem, Southeast Asia, within the context of the developing Cold War, began to take the lead in opium production. The sudden prohibition of opium production in Iran in 1955 not only reinforced this situation: it also stimulated Afghan and Turkish production. And the Cold War was soon to give another decisive stimulus to the development of the Golden Triangle. The participation of the United States Central Intelligence Agency (CIA) in the conflict between the KMT and the PLA, and also the French fiscal and anti-independence policies in Indochina, were going to be instrumental in the thriving opium market of Southeast Asia. Communist threats, the French and American Indochina Wars and the existence of a large opium-consuming Chinese diaspora in Southeast Asia, all encouraged the emergence of the Golden Triangle: an area of large-scale commercial production of illicit opium in the heavily forested and rugged hills and mountains of the Indochinese peninsula.

Indeed, Bangkok and Saigon were Southeast Asia's two main centres of opium consumption and were closely linked with the opium producing areas of northeastern Burma and northern French Indochina through the covert operations of the CIA and French special services and military. The Golden Triangle emerged all the more easily because its growing production supplied over one million Southeast Asian opium consumers and offered funding opportunities for French and United States covert operations.

This situation was to have unexpected consequences, increasing the tension and conflict inherent to the region. From 1948 on, the independence of Burma and the ethnic conflict that ensued, coupled with the growing influence of Chinese communism throughout Southeast Asia, considerably increased opium production and trade in the region. With an opium output of about 80 tonnes when the Second World War drew to a close, the three countries of the Golden Triangle managed to produce 700 tonnes of opium in 1970, and Burma alone eventually set a national record with 1, 791 tonnes in 1993 (UNODC, 2006c).

SOUTHWEST ASIA: FROM THE FALL OF PERSIAN OPIUM PRODUCTION TO THE RISE OF THE GOLDEN CRESCENT

In South and Southwest Asia the history of opium production is much older. The spread of opium production in the region that would come to be known as the Golden Crescent, was a by-product of early commerce along the Silk Road, and of Arab maritime trade. Indeed, places such as Kunduz and Kabul in Afghanistan, Peshawar in Pakistan, and the Makran coast of Pakistan served as commercial hubs and relays for merchants who undoubtedly traded in opium as early as the first century CE. Opium was later produced in India under state monopoly by the Mughal emperors (1526–1857), and Babur and Humayun, two famous emperors, were known to be inveterate opium-eaters (opium was not smoked then). 'Bengal opium' was produced north of Calcutta; 'Malwa opium', north of Bombay. Opium had also been produced in Persia and Turkey for centuries and Persian opium production actually far outdates Southeast Asian production. From at least the seventeenth century, the region's main opium-producing state was Persia, until the Shah momentarily banned all production and consumption in 1955. However, large-scale commercial production did not start until much later, after mercantilism and world trade turned opium into a global commodity.

The trade in Turkish opium owes part of its success to the fact that the British East India Company long refused to increase the quotas limiting production and export of Bengal opium to China. Malwa and Turkish opium was then traded to China by Parsee tradesmen and American merchants respectively, as the latter were barred from bidding at the Calcutta opium auctions before 1834 (McCoy, 1991: 82–3). Of higher quality than Indian opium, Turkish opium was also widely consumed in Europe during the nineteenth century: in Britain, 'between 1827 and 1869, 80–90 per cent of all imported opium was Turkish' (Booth, 1996: 51–2). British imports of Turkish opium never dropped below 70 per cent, even with the arrival on the market of Persian opium, which was imported directly or via Constantinople, where it was repackaged to look like Turkish opium (Booth, 1996: 52).

In Persia (Iran after 1935), from the mid-nineteenth century until the mid-twentieth century, the opium economy was far from negligible. To enable the import of large quantities of expensive consumer goods and of certain foodstuffs (sugar, rice), the country had to increase the value of its cash crops (opium, cotton, silk and tobacco). In doing so, it ultimately neglected the national production of staple crops such as wheat and barley. With a large part of the population then suffering from malnutrition, this growing concentration on cash cropping was probably responsible for the great famine of 1870–1. Persian opium production benefited greatly from this concentration on the development of cash crops and, by the middle of the 1930s, the country was drawing 15 per cent of its foreign trade revenues from the opium economy (McCoy, 1991: 443).

A lucrative economy and a population with a growing indulgence in opium consumption drove Persian production to 600 tonnes at the turn of the nineteenth century and encouraged the government to resist foreign diplomatic pressure to reduce its rapidly growing production. In 1936, opium production reached 1,350 tonnes (McCoy, 1991: 443). In 1949, 11 per cent of the Iranian population indulged in the pleasures of opium and Tehran boasted no less than 500 opium dens. By the mid-1950s an estimated two million opium addicts consumed as much as two tons of opium a day (Booth, 1996: 252–3). In 1955 the Shah of Iran abruptly prohibited opium production and consumption, reducing the number of opium addicts to approximately 350,000 within three years and leading to the almost complete disappearance of poppy cultivation in the country (McNicoll, 1983).

This prohibitionist policy drastically reduced the number of opium addicts in Iran, but there were rapid and unexpected consequences in the development of a black market in opium: Turkish, Afghan, and Pakistani opium producers quickly responded to the emergence of the lucrative Iranian illicit market. Payment for large quantities of contraband opium with gold severely depleted the Iranian gold reserves, however, and the Shah decided to reverse his prohibitionist policy. In June 1969 a program of licensed poppy cultivation was launched. In reply to the United States, who denounced the serious deterioration in the anti-drug policies they had devised, the Shah replied that Iran would renew its opium ban as soon as its neighbours did (McCoy, 199: 443). Turkish opium production increased as a direct consequence of the Iranian ban and the United States feared that this would lead to the rise of new consumer markets for Turkish opium. Yielding to sustained and heavy pressure from the United States, Turkey shortly banned opium production (1967–74) until it managed to have itself included, along with India, as a 'traditional' opium poppy cultivator, thereby obtaining the right to grow poppies (for the production of concentrate of poppy straw) for the pharmaceutical industry.

Iran thus renewed its former association with opium, and, by 1972, the country had around 400,000 opium consumers, among whom about a quarter (105,000) were registered smokers. Unable to meet their needs out of Iran's national production (217 tonnes in 1972), Iranian opium consumers resorted to 195 tonnes of illegal opium, imported from Turkey as well as from the then nascent Golden Crescent. The entire Afghan crop (about 100 tonnes) and much of Pakistan's lesser production were exported to Iran (McCoy, 1991: 444). Iran's unregistered opium consumers, unable to meet their needs from the black market, turned to the more discreet consumption of heroin, which was then produced in Tehran's clandestine laboratories, and heroin consumption increased rapidly.

In neighbouring Afghanistan, opium production varied between 100 and 300 tonnes a year in the 1970s and what was not exported to Iran was mostly used as a panacea, notably for opium's analgesic effects. Opium was largely prescribed as a remedy for numerous illnesses, and many of the 100,000 opium addicts in Afghanistan during the 1970s probably became addicted via this route (McNicoll, 1983: 34). Opium prohibition had first been established in 1958 in Afghanistan, but it had gone unheeded: at that time the internal political, economic and social situations did not really play in favour of a firm stance from the government, especially since heroin addiction was unknown outside Iran. It is also very unlikely that the government would have been able to enforce coercive measures in regions of production whose tribal populations were, for the most part, isolated from the power centre both geographically and politically.

In the mid-1970s, Pakistan's annual opium production was estimated at between 150 and 200 tonnes. Opium was, and still is, produced mainly in the North-West Frontier Province, along the famous Durand Line that establishes part of Pakistan's international border with Afghanistan. The region's geographic, socio-ethnic, and political features explain in part the development of the opium economy that would take place in Afghanistan from the 1980s on. Indeed, as had occurred in Southeast Asia, the European colonial powers, in this particular case the British, exercised only a very limited, if not inexistent, control over the tribal populations of Afghanistan and Pakistan.

Although the mountainous peripheries of Burma had been largely neglected by the British rulers, in Afghanistan and in Pakistan the tribal areas had been subject to very specific policies. The cost and the psychological impact of the two Anglo-Afghan Wars (1838–42 and 1878–81), lost by the British, had clearly played against the interventionist British colonial policy known as 'Forward Policy'. Here, as everywhere else in the colonial world, the borders, and among them the Durand Line, were the outcome of conflicting spheres of influence and not the result of local physical, ethnic, and political realities. And so the tribal populations of Afghanistan, and especially the Pashtun, were arbitrarily divided by the Indo-Afghan border, which would later (1947) prevail as the Pakistani-Afghan. Known for being martial, the Pashtun are Sunni Muslims with a strong and distinctive tribal structure (at least sixty tribes, each divided in clans and sub-clans). They abide by strict warrior traditions brought together in an unwritten code of honour, the Pashtunwali – blood feud, right and duty of asylum, defence of the honour of the women of one's tribal subsection (*Encyclopedia of Modern Asia*, 2002: 467–8). There are an estimated 10 million Pashtun in Afghanistan (almost 40 per cent of the Afghan population) and around 16 million in Pakistan (8 per cent of the overall population), where they are concentrated in the NWFP (North-West Frontier Province) and Balochistan. The Pashtun have always resisted intervention in their political and legal affairs, and the British thus tried to use them by winning them over. The Tochi Scouts and the Khyber Rifles, for example, were created to keep watch over caravan roads, such as the one crossing the famous Khyber Pass. The British raised very few taxes, at times none, on the trading activities of these populations and they even tried to limit opium production in the region, if not to suppress it altogether. As a result, in 1901, what was then called the North West Province no longer produced any opium. However, opium consumption had not disappeared completely from the region, and some Afghan opium was regularly imported from Jalalabad (McCoy, 1991). The current status of the NWFP and of the Federally Administered Tribal Areas (FATA, tribal territories under federal administration), where the writ of the Pakistani state is limited, is a direct legacy of these British policies.

Pakistan would eventually become one of the world's leading opium producers, achieving its highest output only in 1979 (800 tonnes), just a few years before Afghan opium production doubled in a year for the first time (1982–3: from 300 to 575 tonnes). The Golden Crescent was then only emerging, and Afghanistan was still very far from the global supremacy it would achieve in the 2000s.

3. Opium harvest, Nangarhar province, Afghanistan.

3

Opium and Heroin in Asia: The Golden Triangle and the Golden Crescent

FROM THE BIRTH OF THE GOLDEN TRIANGLE TO BURMA'S DOMINANCE IN SOUTHEAST ASIA

The Golden Triangle is the name given to the area of Mainland Southeast Asia where, from the early 1950s until 1990, most of the world's illicit opium has originated. Opium poppy cultivation has taken place in these border regions since the mid-nineteenth century. Isolated, mountainous and heavily forested, it is an area populated by a large number of extremely diverse ethnic groups, many of them tribal and semi-nomadic slash-and-burn agriculturalists. It is also a region where a number of complex linguistic zones overlap.

The name 'Golden Triangle' was first coined by the United States Vice-Secretary of State, Marshall Green, during a press conference on 12 July 1971 and refers to a broadly triangular area with vertices in Burma, Laos and Thailand, where opium production was concentrated. Green implicitly acknowledged – and probably rightly so – the absence of large-scale commercial opium production in China, perhaps not entirely surprising given that he was speaking three days prior to the announcement by President Nixon of his February 1972 visit to the People's Republic of China, the first official visit of a United States President to Communist China (Renard, 1996: 4). 'Golden' probably refers to the economic importance of the opium produced and traded in the area, which developed considerably in Mainland Southeast Asia over the course of the second half of the twentieth century.

Yet, according to the Swedish journalist and veteran Burma-watcher, Bertil Lintner, the name may well have derived from the fact that the first traders of this three-border region, especially those of the Thai-Burmese border towns of Mae Sai (Thailand) and Tachileck (Burma), exchanged the precious opium for 99 per cent pure gold ingots (Lintner, 1994).

Opium production in Mainland Southeast Asia has always been concentrated in this region – the mountainous borderlands of Burma, Laos, and Thailand, where rugged hills and mountains, heavy monsoon rains and lack of transport infrastructure have long protected rebel armies and illicit crops from the writ of central government and anti-drug agencies. The geography of the region has been favourable to the Golden Triangle's emergence: 'The contraband trade in narcotics flourished all the more because the region's imposing terrain and rivers remain untamed by roads and bridges. The annual monsoon rains thus render the area even more inaccessible for several months each year' (Renard, 1996: 5). After decades of expanding poppy cultivation in the three countries, opium production has progressively decreased, almost completely disappearing from Thailand in the 1990s and seriously decreasing in Laos during the early 2000s. Poppy cultivation is now concentrated in the Kachin and Shan states of north and northeastern Burma, where it had originated in the mid-nineteenth century. Although Burmese opium production also decreased considerably after 1998, it has proven resilient, most certainly aided by Burma's turbulent political history since its independence in 1948, a key factor in its status as Asia's longest-standing illicit opium producer.

The opium economy and the war economy have clearly nurtured one another in a country that has suffered from internal war for the past sixty years and where the world's longest armed insurgency still continues.[1] Indeed, as an extremely valuable economic resource, opium has frequently enabled warring factions to fund their respective war efforts. It has also been used in strategic negotiations, offering both state and non-state actors opportunities to gain political leverage or create ad hoc strategic alliances. The Burmese government, for example, early and repeatedly made use of opium in its negotiation strategy, something that some anti-government forces have directly or indirectly benefited (and suffered) from. Indeed, 'according to the account of Chao Tzang, Olive Yang [who dominated the opium trade in Kokang from the end of the Second World War until the early 1960s] "had been permitted by the Burmese to engage in opium trade in exchange for keeping out the KMT"', until '1962 when the Burmese army occupied Kokang and arrested her and her brother, Edward Yang, the Kokang Prince (Renard, 1996: 56).

Shan State, one of the world's main opium producing areas today, has always been the main source of Burma's opium, a fact partly explained by its recent history. Under British rule, the Shan States were not part of Burma Proper and were therefore not subject to direct British rule. They belonged to the Frontier Areas, where colonial administration was minimal: indirect rule was conducted by the Shan chieftains, or *sawbwa*. On 12 February 1947, Aung San – national hero and then de facto Prime Minister – signed the Panglong Agreement with the leaders of the Shan, Kachin, and Chin, who expressed solidarity and support for a united Burma after independence. Under the terms of the Panglong Agreement, the Frontier Areas were to be fully autonomous in their internal administration.

In 1959, however, Ne Win (1911–2002), Chief of Staff of the Armed Forces and head of the caretaker government (1958–60), robbed Shan *sawbwa* of their political and administrative powers. By so doing, he rendered their traditional private militias ineffective and cash-strapped. Following the 1962 coup d'Etat by Ne Win, the Communist Party of Burma (CPB) – the first group to launch an armed struggle against Burma's central government (1948) – went underground and joined forces with some of the ethnic minorities along the Chinese border, among which figured mostly Kokang, Shan, and Wa guerrilla groups. In 1963, Ne Win – facing repeated rebellion and discontent (Shan, Kachin, Karen and Communist, notably) – encouraged the organization of private militia, called Ka Kwe Ye (KKY) or self-defence groups, whose mission and role was to provide support to the government and the Armed Forces (Tatmadaw) in their combat against the rebels.

Among these militia was the Wa group of Maha Sang (1945–2007), who had fought the CPB between 1966 and 1973. Maha Sang retreated to the Thai border in 1973, created the Wa National Army (WNA) in 1976, and eventually formed an alliance with the Kuomintang (Smith, 1991: 351). By this stage, the Burmese-led CPB, which had received long-expected Chinese help after Rangoon's 1967 anti-Chinese riots, relied mostly on Kokang and Wa troops. In the late 1970s, however, China decided that the CPB had to be 'self-reliant', which it managed by largely relying on its monopoly in cross-border trading with China (70 per cent of the CPB's budget). Then, in 1980, China launched its open-door trade policy and the CPB was rapidly faced with competition from other groups, such as the Kachin Independence Army, along the Burma-China border. Soon, the CPB had no other choice than to resort to the revenues it could derive from opium trading. The CPB already controlled about 70 per cent of all the poppy fields in Burma but had always followed an anti-opium policy, at least until 1976 when a rat invasion in the Wa region forced it to abandon its crop-substitution scheme. In the mid-1980s the CPB started collecting 20 per cent of the opium produced in the areas it controlled, in addition to a 10 per cent local trade tax and a 5 per cent export tax. Opium from the CPB areas was first transported to the Thai border where KMT remnants and Khun Sa (1934–2007) – the Golden Triangle's most notorious drug lord and warlord – bought it and refined it (or not) into heroin. But the CPB also allowed many heroin refineries on its own territory, on payment of 'protection fees' (Lintner, 1994: 291–4).

Opium production and trade developed all the more readily since Ne Win had tacitly authorized the KKY militia to engage in all types of business and trade, including the most profitable activity to be found in the mountainous peripheral regions where the KKY were to restore law and order: opium and heroin trafficking. Among the sixty or so KKY, the two most important were both headed by half-Chinese half-Shan chiefs: Lo Hsing-han and Chan Shi-fu, alias Khun Sa (Lintner, 1994; McCoy, 2003; Smith, 1991). Chan Shi-fu, 'stepson of the ruler of Loimaw (one of the northernmost Shan principalities)' (Renard, 1996: 60), took advantage of the opportunity offered to him with the creation of the KKY and recycled his own militia. Investing himself in the opium business, he was quickly betrayed by the Shan nationalists with whom he had negotiated passage rights for his opium caravans and only began effectively fighting them in 1966: three years after he should have done so as a KKY leader supposedly in Ne Win's service. In the context of ceaseless internecine feuds, largely sparked by the very competitive opium business, Rangoon abolished the KKY in 1973. However, during the ten years that the KKY existed, Chan Shi-fu, self-dubbed 'opium king', and Lo Hsing-han, became the Golden Triangle's two most powerful opium traffickers.

In 1969 Chan Shi-fu was arrested by Rangoon, and his men joined first the Shan State Army (SSA) and then set up the Shan United Army (SUA), in 1972. Lo Hsing-han (who had formed an alliance with factions of the Shan State Army) largely benefited from Chan Shi-fu's imprisonment and dominated the Shan States, but in 1973, one year before Chan Shi-fu's liberation, Lo himself was arrested by Thai police near Mae Hong Son and extradited to Rangoon, where he was jailed until 1980. Chan Shi-fu, free and with his main rival in jail, was now able to secure an immense portion of the regional opium market as the leader of diverse Shan nationalist groups and private armies. In 1976 he rejoined his men and, choosing Khun Sa (a Shan name) as his *nom de guerre*, he proclaimed himself spokesman for the Shan cause. He based himself in Ban Hin Taek, in the hills of northwest Thailand, until 1982. In 1987 Khun Sa's 20,000-strong Mong Tai Army (MTA) was created, after the SUA allied itself to the Tai Revolutionary Council (TRC).

On 18 September 1988, Burma's armed forces seized power under the leadership and command of General Saw Maung: the State Law and Order Council (SLORC) became the official name of the ruling junta and the 1974 constitution was abolished. Saw Maung ruled the country until his retirement for health reasons in 1992, when he gave up his position to General Than Shwe. In 1989, Brigadier General and chief of intelligence (DDSI) Khin Nyunt (number three in the regime), started a politics of conciliation with some of the country's rebel groups, holding talks and agreeing on ceasefires. The first ceasefire agreements between Shan groups and the government were signed in 1989, the same year that the CPB was disbanded and driven out of Burma's northern Shan State by mutinous Kokang and Wa troops. In a matter of a few days, Lo Hsing-han was welcomed back in Kokang, where he set up his new army and established a reputed seventeen heroin refineries. As Alfred McCoy explains, during the 1990s:

> Rangoon's military regime allied openly with leading drug lords, offering protection for those who repatriated illicit assets and used their armies to fight ethnic rebels. By attacking rebels while protecting favored drug lords, Rangoon's military created an effective synergy between borderland security and heroin trafficking (McCoy, 2003: 435).

This strategy probably achieved two things: Burma's record opium crop in 1993, and Khun Sa's demise only three years later.

Khun Sa laid down his arms in 1996 at his headquarters in Homong (in Shan State), and negotiated with the Burmese junta his retirement as a neighbour of Ne Win on the shores of Rangoon's Inya Lake, where he died in October 2007. After Khun Sa's surrender, his Mong Tai Army gave way to a new Shan State Army South (SSA-S), commanded by a former lieutenant of Khun Sa, Colonel Yawd Serk, with headquarters in Doi Tai Leng, across the border from Chiang Mai's Vieng Haeng district, Thailand.

On 15 November 1997, the junta underwent a discreet facelift, changing its official name from State Law and Order Restoration Council (SLORC) to State Peace and Development Council (SPDC). In the following years, Burma's opium production progressively decreased, dropping from a record of 1,791 tonnes in 1993 to a mere 315 tonnes in 2006, before 'unexpectedly' increasing again to 460 tonnes in 2007 (UNODC, 2007c: 1). However, the 1990s also saw the rapid development of methamphetamine production in Shan State: between 500 and 800 million methamphetamine pills (known as *yaa baa*) are thought to have been produced on a yearly basis in Burma in the early 2000s (Chouvy and Meissonnier, 2004).

Opium production abated following bans issued by the leaders of the country's largest opium-producing areas – Shan State's Special Region n° 4 (Mong La) in 1997, Special Region n° 1 (Kokang) in 2003, and Special Region n° 2 (Wa) in 2005. Control of Special Region n° 4 was obtained from the Burmese junta by Sai Lin (also known as Lin Ming Xian), a former Chinese Red Guard who had fought for the CPB and established the National Democratic Alliance Army (NDAA), also known as the Eastern Shan State Army (ESSA), in 1989. The region was declared opium free in 1997 and its capital, Mong La, was turned into a casino resort for Chinese tourists. That same year, Pheung Kya-shin, father-in-law of Sai Lin, leader of the Myanmar National Democratic Alliance Army (MNDAA) and owner of the first heroin refinery ever set up in the CPB-controlled region in the mid-1970s (Lintner, 1994: 293), declared that Kokang was to become opium free by 2001. The Kokang region, or Shan State's Special Region n° 1, was eventually declared opium free in 2003. And Shan State's Special Region n° 2 was to be opium free by 2005 under a pledge (issued in 1995) by Bao You-xiang, chairman of the United Wa State Party (UWSP) and supreme commander of the United Wa State Army (UWSA), who controlled the region. Such pledges proved all the more important as UNODC estimated that Burma's Shan State was producing as much as 90 per cent of the country's opium in the early 2000s: in 2003, 92 per cent of the 810 tonnes of opium produced in Burma originated in Shan State, 34 per cent in the UWSA-held Special Region n° 2. In a matter of only a few years, the Kokang region (2003) and the Wa region (2006) were declared opium free. In the mid-2000s, opium suppression was clearly on its way in northern Shan State, but also in Kachin State, where the Kachin Independence Organization (KIO) pledged to ban opium production after its 1994 ceasefire agreement with the junta. (In the mid-2000s it administrated close to 30 per cent of all Kachin State.) However, opium is still produced in Burma: mostly in southern Shan State, where poppy acreage has increased in 2005, 2006 and 2007 (for 2007, 65 per cent of Burma's poppies were cultivated in South Shan State, 25 per cent in East Shan State), and in parts of Kachin State and Kayah State. In 2007, after years of decline, opium poppy cultivation increased by 29 per cent and opium production rose by 46 per cent (due to higher yields than in 2006) (UNODC, 2007c: 51). Opium prices increased after successive opium bans imposed in North Shan State (Special Regions n° 1, 2, and 4) and it is very likely that as a consequence opium production increased in East Shan State and South Shan State as well.

FROM THE RISE OF THE 'GOLDEN CRESCENT' TO AFGHANISTAN'S GLOBAL SUPREMACY

The name 'Golden Crescent' – of unknown authorship – echoes, of course, that of 'Golden Triangle', its Southeast Asian alter ego. But its 'Crescent' refers to the Muslim dimension of this opium-producing region comprising the countries of Afghanistan, Iran, and Pakistan. In 1979 – around the time when the Golden Crescent really emerged – a CIA report described the outbreak of opium and heroin production in Southwest Asia in these terms: '[Iran's opium boom had] created a new 'golden triangle', comprised of Iran, Pakistan and Afghanistan' (McCoy, 1991: 446). The area of modern opium production known as the Golden Crescent emerged only later, in the late 1970s, twenty years or so after the Golden Triangle's first stirrings in Southeast Asia. Strictly speaking, the Golden Crescent only existed for a few years, between the mid- or late 1970s and the mid-1980s, when Afghanistan's opium production was slowly rising, when Iranian opium was mainly produced for the country's internal consumption and when Pakistan's production was at its highest.

Afghan and Pakistani opium was first marketed for Persian and Indian consumers. The Shah's 1955 opium ban in Iran had stimulated production in Afghanistan and Pakistan and had encouraged the rapid growth of local low-grade *heroin* production and consumption. Until the mid-1970s, the limited amounts of Afghan and Pakistani opium were almost entirely exported to Iran, whose hundreds of thousands of users acted, in the words of former CIA director Richard Helms, 'as a sponge for opiates produced elsewhere in the Middle East, thereby diverting supplies that might otherwise find their way as heroin to the United States' (McCoy, 2003: 469). In 1974 a seizure of 'fairly high-grade heroin' was undertaken for the first time in Tehran, but increasing heroin production in Southwest Asia was still destined for the regional market: i.e. the Iranian market. In the words of Alfred McCoy: 'While Iran absorbed all the opium the region could produce, drug use in both Pakistan and Afghanistan was still uncommon' (McCoy, 2003: 470).

The production and use of heroin in the region, however, was to be drastically altered in a matter of a few years. Pakistan's opium production increased from 90 tonnes in 1971 to 500 tonnes in 1978, then to a record 800 tonnes in 1979. That same year the Iranian Revolution closed the largest, and almost only, outlet for Afghan and Pakistani opium. However, though the new Iranian regime suppressed opium production during the early years of the 1980s it never succeeded in putting a stop to the imported opium from Afghanistan and Pakistan that kept Iranian users supplied. In 1978 – two years after he staged a military coup d'Etat against the government of Prime Minister Zulfikar Ali Bhutto – General Muhammad Zia-ul-Haq of Pakistan announced that the production, commerce and consumption of all intoxicants, opium included, was to be prohibited in Pakistan within one year (Prohibition Order or Enforcement of Hadd). Ironically, this announcement saw the last legal Pakistani opium crop achieve a record figure (Chouvy, 2002a: 96). In order to reduce growing opium stockpiles in Pakistan (the record crop was achieved the same year that Khomeini's ban closed the Iranian market), traffickers resorted to heroin refining, spurring heroin consumption in Pakistan and exporting the remainder to Europe and the United States.

Heroin consumption rose steadily in the Western world during the early 1980s, with heroin from Southwest Asian filling the shortage brought about firstly by the drought that had severely affected Southeast Asian production during 1978–80 (from 700 tonnes in 1971 to 160 in 1979, and 225 in 1980) and, secondly, by the successful prohibition efforts of the US Drug Enforcement Administration (DEA) in Bangkok, Southeast Asia's heroin hub (McCoy, 1991: 389–97). However, Southeast Asian 'China White' heroin quickly resurfaced on the streets of the United States, where it took over from Southwest Asian and Mexican heroin ('black tar' heroin). Afghan and Pakistani heroin ended up being increasingly exported to Europe. Alfred McCoy explains:

> by attacking heroin trafficking in separate sectors of Asia's extended opium zone in isolation, the DEA inadvertently influenced the market in ways that diverted heroin exports from America to Europe, and also shifted opium production from South West Asia to Southeast Asia and back again raising both global consumption and production with each move (McCoy, 1991: 389–97).

In perhaps the quickest rise in heroin consumption ever recorded, the number of heroin users skyrocketed in Pakistan, supposedly rising from about 5,000 in 1980 to 650,000 in 1986 (Lifschutz, 1992: 321; McNicoll, 1983: 35; Tullis, 1995: 57). In the mid-2000s, opiate consumers were estimated at 700,000 in Pakistan, including half a million using heroin (UNODC, 2006c: 74). Iran fared much worse after the 1979 revolution outlawed opium consumption. As Gerald McLaughlin notes, 'although opium has existed in Iran in some form or another for centuries, widespread addiction was not known in the country until [about 1860]' (McLaughlin, 1976: 728, quoted in McLaughlin, 2007). Iranian authorities and the United Nations estimated the number of opiate addicts in Iran at about 1.2 million in the mid-2000s (2.8 per cent of the population aged 15–64), occasional users (about 800,000) not included (UNODC, 2006c: 74; McLaughlin, 2007). Iran probably has the highest incidence of opiate consumption in the world (followed by other neighbours of Afghanistan: Central Asian countries and Pakistan), but in actual numbers Asia has many more (India: 3 million, China: 1.7 million): 'more than half of the world's opiates abusing population live in Asia, and the highest levels of opiates abuse are along the main drug trafficking routes from Afghanistan' (UNODC, 2006c: 74).

Along with the Southeast Asian drought, the Iranian revolution and Pakistani prohibition, the Afghan-Soviet war and the CIA's covert support of the Afghan resistance 'transformed Central Asia from a self-contained opium zone into a major supplier of heroin for the world market' (McCoy, 2003: 466). As Pakistan's poppy cultivation was drastically and speedily reduced (in a matter of a few years only), so opium production increased in neighbouring Afghanistan, where the war against the Soviet Union was secretly supported by the CIA:

> As in Burma and Laos, the CIA decided to conduct its war through a few local commanders, making its success contingent on their power. Under such circumstances, geographical and political, the CIA would have little leverage when its tribal warlords decided to exploit the clandestine operation to become drug lords (McCoy, 2003: 473).

Despite the earlier warning of David Musto, a Yale University psychiatrist and a White House advisor on drugs (to President Jimmy Carter) – who had advocated against going to Afghanistan 'to support the opium growers in their rebellion against the Soviets' (McCoy, 2003: 461), and who had further cautioned against repeating the mistakes previously made in Laos – the CIA funnelled its arms and money to the Afghan guerrillas by way of the Pakistan intelligence service, the Inter-Service Intelligence (ISI), who had superior intelligence and closer relations with the Afghan resistance, especially among the Pashtun groups.

According to the US Department of State, between 1982 and 1983 Afghan opium production doubled, from 300 to 575 tonnes. The figures of the United Nations differ slightly and show that while Afghan production showed a moderate increase between 1980 (200 tonnes) and 1982 (275 tonnes), in 1983 it almost doubled, to 488 tonnes. There was a further large increase between 1986 and 1987, when opium production more than doubled, from 350 to 875 tonnes, definitely setting the country on its path to becoming the world's largest opium producer by 1991, with 1,980 tonnes. Afghanistan would later reinforce its leading position by producing 3,416 tonnes in 1994, 4,565 in 1999, 6,100 in 2006, and 8,200 tonnes in 2007 (UNODC, 2006c; 2007b).

However, as the co-founder and former director of the former Geopolitical Drug Watch (OGD: Observatoire géopolitique des drogues), Alain Labrousse, explains (Labrousse, 2005), the opium economy has only played a marginal role in the financing of the Afghan resistance during the Afghan-Soviet war.

Substantial international financial and material support to the Afghan resistance came, not only from Muslim countries, such as Saudi Arabia and Egypt, but also from China, either directly or by way of CIA-ISI cooperation. In 1984, while opium production brought the equivalent of US$21 million to Afghan peasants, foreign financial and material aid to the Afghan resistance amounted to US$300 million (Labrousse, quoting Doris Buddenberg, 2005: 108). However, in 1984, due to a drought, the 160-tonne opium crop was far less than the 488 tonnes that had been harvested the previous year, when Afghan production had doubled for the first time, and farm-gate prices, as well as the overall value of the crop, had most likely abated.

Nonetheless, Afghan opium production showed a marked increase during the war against the Soviet Union (from 875 tonnes in 1987 to 1,120 in 1988), especially during the final years of the conflict, notably when the Soviets retreated to urban areas to prepare for their withdrawal. But production only significantly increased after 1989 with the Soviet Union's withdrawal from Afghanistan, as shown by a figure of 1,600 tonnes for 1990. It seems most likely that the increase in opium production in Afghanistan during the war against the Soviet Union mainly resulted from an exceptional concurrence: the Iranian revolution and simultaneous opium ban, Pakistan's prohibition and the strategic alliance between the CIA and the ISI whose arms shipments were nearly matched by imports of Afghan opium destined for Pakistani heroin laboratories. Overall, the economic imperatives of the war did not significantly spur opium production since the Afghan resistance was largely funded by the international aid provided to the mujahideen: the Afghan resistance had no need to rely on the opium economy to sustain its war economy.

The war did, however, alter agricultural production to a large extent, as 'Soviet counterinsurgency measures that targeted the rural economy destroyed local resources'; and 'in 1985 substantially more than half of the farmers in Afghanistan reported bombing of their village, more than a quarter reported the destruction of irrigation systems, and more than a quarter reported the shooting of livestock' (Rubin, 1995: 227). As a result, part of the beleaguered Afghan peasantry was pressured into the cultivation of opium poppies in order to survive. Additionally, of the 3 million Afghans who had taken refuge in Pakistan, many were returning to their fields every year and switched from growing wheat to growing poppies, thereby contributing to the increase in opium production (Labrousse, 2005: 111). As had happened in Burma's Kokang region during the Second World War, when farmers replaced a tea economy with opium, in Afghanistan the narcotic not only proved easier to market than wheat: it also proved far more profitable, at least to some.

A few mujahideen commanders also resorted to the opium economy, either because they wanted to be financially independent from the seven Peshawar-based and ISI-condoned mujahideen parties who absorbed most of the international aid, or because they favoured lucrative business interests over the Afghan cause. Barnett Rubin, a leading expert on Afghanistan, explains: 'Soviet military pressure and increasing foreign arms aid from parties based in Pakistan or Iran strengthened religious leaders against those whose power was based on property and kinship and particularly strengthened Islamists against the traditional elites'. As a result, 'sale of a cash crop to foreign markets could substitute for access to external political networks' (Rubin, 1995: 226). Gulbuddin Hekmatyar, leader of the Hezb-i Islami, was largely benefiting from the ISI-funnelled foreign aid but was nonetheless 'the only leader to exploit opium profits systematically as a basis for a hierarchically organized party and conventional army' (Rubin, 1995: 257). He made a name for himself by setting up some of the first heroin refineries in Afghanistan. Other commanders, such as Mullah Nasim Akhunzada, also favoured their own business interests by promoting opium production in the areas they controlled. In the Helmand valley, Akhunzada, who was known as the 'heroin king', devoted more energy to opium production than to fighting the invaders: he actually went as far as signing ceasefire agreements with the Soviet Army (Labrousse, 2005: 112–13).

During the warlord period (1990–4) that followed the defeat of the Soviet Union and its withdrawal from Afghanistan (from 15 May 1988 to 15 February 1989) opium production quickly increased as warlords and commanders vied for territorial, political and economic control: 'The fragmentation of the political and military structures of the resistance prevented the mujahidin from turning local victories into a national one' (Rubin, 1995: 247). Rubin also explains how, 'As in more normal times – but with more weapons – they engaged in struggles for local power [and some of them] pursued economic opportunities, especially in opium production and the drug trade while others elaborated independent political strategies' (Rubin, 1995: 247). In the meantime, in September 1991, the Soviet Union – which had installed a pro-Communist government in Afghanistan – and the United States decided to stop providing weapons to their respective Afghan clients by January 1992 (the Soviet Union itself was dissolved in December 1991). After it could no longer 'rule by redistributing externally supplied resources' (Rubin, 1995: 269), the government of President Najibullah fell, and Afghanistan slipped into warlordism and a transnational civil war, setting not only mujahideen factions but non-Pashtun and Pashtun coalitions against each other. Some of these factions and coalitions fell back on the opium economy to make up for the loss of their foreign subsidies. In the words of Alfred McCoy, after the Soviet withdrawal 'brought a slackening in CIA support, there was a scramble among mujaheddin commanders for prime opium land' (McCoy, 2003: 484).

The massive return of Afghan refugees to Afghanistan (1.3 million by the end of 1992) and the escape of many Kabulis (half a million) to safer rural areas, stimulated opium production in some areas – for example, in Nangarhar, where most of eastern Afghanistan's returning refugees settled (Labrousse, 2005: 117). According to McCoy, 'in Nangarhar province, opium cultivation spread rapidly to cover 80 percent of the arable land around the city of Jalalabad by 1992' (McCoy, 2003: 484). Some commanders took advantage of the economic needs of the returning refugees and expanded poppy cultivation to new areas. In the Helmand valley, Nasim Akhunzada offered under the *salaam* system, to pay cash for the opium crop at the time of sowing: the, opium crop was bought at the time of sowing but at half its harvest time price. Furthermore, in 1989, Akhunzada not only gave a directive that 50 per cent of the land he controlled be sown under poppy; he also established production quotas and imposed penalties on those who did not meet his terms. As many commanders turned to the opium economy to fund their private armies and to promote their business interests, opium production quickly increased in the country and led to rivalries between warlords and commanders. The growth of the opium trade gave rise to various conflicts, like those setting Nasim Akhunzada against Abdur Rahman and Abdul Wahed (Rubin, 1995: 263). Alain Labrousse also explains that although this conflict was allegedly fought along ideological lines it was in fact motivated by efforts to control the Helmand poppy fields (Labrousse, 2005: 118).

During what can be termed the 'warlord period' – i.e., from the withdrawal of the Soviets (1989) until the rise of the Taliban (1994) – Afghanistan became the world's leading producer of opium, surpassing Burma in 1991. Afghanistan's supremacy was to last well after the Taliban period (1994–2001) and was to be considerably reinforced under the administration of the new interim (2001–4) then elected (2004–9) Afghan president, Hamid Karzai. Both the Taliban regime and the Karzai government inherited an illicit drug economy that had been stimulated by two decades of war and had increasingly fuelled the country's war economy over the years. In 1999, 4,600 tonnes of opium were harvested in a country 85 per cent controlled by the Taliban: an unprecedented (though temporary) record had been set. However, just when the Taliban successfully, but counter-productively, prohibited opium production in 2001 (185 tonnes, of which only 35 tonnes were produced in Taliban held areas), they were toppled by the military intervention of the United States in response to the September 11 terrorist attack on US soil.

Following this, in a rather chaotic Afghanistan, opium production resumed and grew back to normal levels (2001–2). Subsequently, the Afghan illicit drug economy was said to be fuelling terrorism, and both the Afghan government and the United States-led coalition have considered that 'fighting drug trafficking equals fighting terrorism'. Fighting terrorism and the ongoing Taliban insurgency worked against a forced suppression of opium production in the country (whether by physical eradication or by way of alternative development measures). Indeed, in post-Taliban Afghanistan and prior to 2004, the United States has condoned opiates production both in areas traditionally controlled by the Northern Alliance (also known as the United Front) and in areas held by various local commanders whose support was deemed strategically necessary to fight the Taliban and al-Qaeda. After 2004, when the opium question was once again raised in Afghanistan, it appeared that short-term strategic advantages had been outweighed by 'unintended' strategic inconveniences and constraints: having benefited from the support of local commanders and warlords involved in the opium business, the international community and the Afghan government could not afford to lose the support of the large proportion of the Afghan population dependent upon the opium economy. In Afghanistan as in other parts of the world (in Burma, for example), opium has long been at stake in armed conflicts as its trade has allowed these conflicts to be prolonged. As the complex history of opium in Asia shows, opium production and trade have been central to world politics and geopolitics for centuries and the role of the opium economy in Afghanistan is nothing new. In many ways, history reinvents itself.

4. Opium traders, Helmand province, Afghanistan.

4

All-Time Highs and Lows

The twenty-first century started with a major disruption to Asian opium production, adding yet another phase to the long and complex history of the politics and economics of the poppy.

In the 1990s, Afghanistan's annual production increased, exceeding the 2,000-tonne threshold for the first time. By 1994 the country produced 3,416 tonnes and by 1999 this had risen to 4,565 tonnes, a record in each case (UNODC, 2006c). In Burma, meanwhile, opium production had remained fairly constant – at between 1,500 and 2,000 tonnes – and so it was that in 1991 Afghanistan's opium production overtook that of Burma.

The major disruption to Asian opium production trends occurred during the years 1998–9, when Afghanistan's poppy crop increased from 64,000 to 90,000 hectares and Burma's fell from 130,000 to 90,000 hectares. The same area under poppy cultivation in the two countries produced remarkably different yields: Afghanistan produced 4,565 tonnes of opium in 1999 (up from 2,693 in 1998) while Burma only managed 895 tonnes (down from 1,303 in 1998). But the year 1999 was notable not just for the fact that both countries had equal areas under cultivation; it also proved to be a major turning point in Asia's opium production trends. Except for the opium ban imposed by the Taliban in 2000–1 and the near complete suppression of Afghan opium production that ensued in 2001 (185 tonnes), the 2000s saw Afghanistan production attain unprecedented levels and Burma's crop fall to an all-time low.

Neither did the increase in Afghan opium production cease with Hamid Karzai's new democratic Afghanistan, despite national and international pledges, eradication threats, deals with opium farmers, and international development aid. Much to the contrary – after five years of peace-building, state-building, and economic growth, in 2006, Afghanistan set an all-time record for opium production (6,100 tonnes) and did so again in 2007 (8,200 tonnes). In Burma, meanwhile, the military junta, and most of the autonomous ethnic groups that had been tacitly authorized to grow opium, managed to progressively and significantly reduce poppy cultivation until the year 2006. Essentially, opium production exploded in a newly-democratic country backed by most of the international community while one of the world's most reclusive and repressive military dictatorships progressively abated its own production.

BURMA AND THE UNITED WA STATE ARMY: THE 'WORLD'S LARGEST DRUG-TRAFFICKING ARMY' BANS OPIUM?

In 2003 the United Nations Office on Drugs and Crime (UNODC, 2003e) estimated that 92 per cent of Burma's opium production occurred in Shan State, a mountainous and somewhat isolated area covering 155,000 square kilometres of Southeast Asia and forming the largest of Burma's seven states, along the borders of China, Laos and Thailand. Some 810 tonnes of opium were harvested on 62,000 hectares of opium poppy, down from 828 tonnes and 81,000 hectares in 2002. The United States Department of State, however, despite being heavily critical of the Burmese regime, reported a much lower figure for opium production for 2003 (only 484 tonnes – around half that reported by UNODC) and acknowledged a seven year downward trend. Yet some critics maintained that such a decrease was mainly confined to Shan State – in Burma as a whole it was much less. In fact, a 2003 report (SHAN, 2003) emanating from the Shan Herald Agency for News (SHAN) claimed that the decrease in the north of the Shan State had been more than made up by a marked escalation in the south and east of the area, thereby contesting the accuracy of the UN report. To complicate matters even further, a number of long-time observers of the region's drug trade estimate that Burma's opium production has always been largely overestimated (TNI, 2008: 6–7). What seems undeniable is that Burma's opium production, no matter how poorly known in the past, has largely decreased over the past decade, with recent UN field and satellite surveys showing that recent opium bans have been effectively implemented.

According to UNODC figures (UNODC, 2007c: 50), Burma again reduced its opium production in 2005 and in 2006 but experienced a steep increase in 2007 (in 2005: 312 tonnes of opium from 32,800 hectares; in 2006: 315 tonnes from 21,500 hectares; but in 2007: 460 tonnes from 27,700 hectares). Between 2003 and 2004, decreasing yields (from 13 down to eight kilogrammes per hectare) accentuated the impact of declining cultivation (810 tonnes off 62,000 hectares down to 370 tonnes off 44,000 hectares), while, between 2005 and 2006, increasing yields (from 9.5 to 14.7 kg / ha) had the opposite effect, downplaying the benefit of a renewed reduction in poppy cultivation (from 312 tonnes off 32,800 hectares to 315 tonnes off 21,500 hectares) (UNODC, 2006d, 2006e). In 2007, a continuing increase in yields (up 14 per cent to 6.6 kg / ha) accentuated the impact of an increasing surface area cultivated with poppies (UNODC, 2007c: 50). Overall, however, cultivated areas have drastically decreased since 2001, when poppies last covered in excess of 100,000 hectares (105,000).

The controversy over opium production in Burma worsened when the scope of involvement of the United Wa State Party (UWSP) and its 20,000-strong United Wa State Army (UWSA) in the drug trade was questioned. It deepened even further after 1998, when after four years of discussions with the UWSP, the United Nations International Drug Control Programme (UNODC after 2002) implemented its five-year pilot project in Wa Special Region n° 2 (SR2) in Shan State: the Wa Alternative Development Project (WADP), later renamed UNODC/Wa Project and extended until December 2007. In Burma, the first UN opium survey took place in 2001, covering 20 per cent of Shan State. In 2002 UNDCP launched a large-scale survey that covered (with satellite imagery) the whole of Shan State (UNDCP, 2002a), thereafter allowing the UN to establish what it referred to as a 'robust illicit crop monitoring' in the country.[1] In March 2003 UNODC additionally set up the Kokang and Wa Initiative (KOWI) to enable 'UN agencies, local organisations and INGOs [international NGOs] that provide pre- and post-emergency aid to communities in the two regions [. . .] to help local populations cope with the imposition of opium bans'.[2] After lengthy discussions between UNDCP/UNODC and UWSP, formal acknowledgement was made of the official declaration by the Wa leadership in 1995 that opium production was to be completely suppressed by 2005. Reportedly, however, the Wa leaders decided in August 1990 that the areas under their control would be made opium free by mid-2005 (Milsom, 2005: 70–1).

The UN agency had initiated contact with the UWSP in 1994 to evaluate the feasibility of an alternative development project in the Wa region and eventually decided that it had to develop this project to soften the brutal impact that the promised opium suppression would have on the people of the Wa region. However, it turned out that,

> the problematic relationship between the UNODC project and the 2005 ban has reduced the program's objectives to becoming merely the provision of humanitarian assistance to an economically opium-dependent population under severe pressure to abolish a crucial component of its survival strategy (Jelsma, Kramer, Vervest, 2005: x).

Critics of the military junta, and local ethnic-based groups opposed to both the junta and the UWSA, then believed that neither Rangoon nor the UWSP were sincere in their opium-suppression agenda. It was also argued that UNODC was being abused and that its very presence legitimized both Rangoon's ruthless dictatorship and its ally the UWSA, sensationally dubbed 'the world's largest drug trafficking army' by the US Department of State. In January 2005, the US Department of Justice indicted eight senior leaders of the UWSP/UWSA for belonging to a 'powerful criminal syndicate and worldwide narcotics trafficking organization' and, notably, 'importing over a ton of heroin with a retail value of $1 billion into the United States alone'.[3] Among those indicted, together with his four brothers, was Bao You-xiang, an ethnic Wa, former member of the Central Committee of the Communist Party of Burma, and the de facto leader of the UWSP since 1994 (officially Chairman since 2004) (Kramer, 2007; Milsom, 2005: 69). Also indicted was notorious drug trafficker Wei Hsueh-kang. Already designated (2000) as a 'Drug Kingpin' by the US 1999 Foreign Narcotics Designation Kingpin Act (along with the UWSA organisation in 2003), Wei Hsueh-kang, was a former financial aide to Khun Sa, former commander of UWSA's Division 171 and, at the time of the indictment, a special advisor to UWSP's Central Committee.

The controversy over the role and sincerity of the Wa leadership, and concerning the engagement of UNODC, grew stronger in 2003, when opium production increased by 21 per cent in Wa Special Region n° 2, i.e. on the territory administered by the UWSP and controlled by the UWSA, and, paradoxically, where UNODC had set up its alternative development project (WADP). That year, the UN reported that 34 percent of all Burma's opium was produced in SR2. However, UNODC convincingly explained that the large decrease in opium production that had taken place just north of SR2 – in the Kokang region (Special Region n° 1 – SR1), where an opium ban had already been enforced – had caused the 20 per cent production increase in the Wa region. In fact, the drastic 50 per cent drop that had occurred the previous year in the Kokang region had caused a drift of opium farmers and production into the north of the Wa region.

Among the most virulent critics of UWSP/UWSA claims to have suppressed opium production, and of UNODC projects in Shan State, is the Shan Herald Agency for News (SHAN), an 'independent media group' that published three reports on Rangoon's 'war on drugs' in Shan State (SHAN, 2003; SHAN, 2005; SHAN, 2006). SHAN is a media group related to the Restoration Council of Shan State, the political arm of the Shan State Army-South (SSA-S) – one of the very last armed groups still fighting Rangoon's military junta and still engaged in fighting against the UWSA. Thus, while clearly contributing to a better understanding of the situation in the Shan State through its valuable field surveys and reports, SHAN views are also necessarily coloured by their political objectives.

While UWSP/UWSA authorities declare their unconditional commitment to opium suppression, SHAN argues that they lack sincerity in implementing such an agenda, mentioning by way of example that one of the brothers (Bao You-hua) of UWSA commander Bao You-xiang was involved in opium production and was responsible for the temporary closure of one of UNODC's field offices (Mong Phen) in the WADP area. (Following pressure from China who also accused him of drug trafficking, Bao You-hua lost command of the Mong Phen Security Brigade.) SHAN also regrets that there has been no debate about the means by which UNODC obtained its figures, understandably so given that the survey was carried out in conjunction with Rangoon's Central Committee for Drug Abuse Control. Thus SHAN and many Burma watchers raised serious questions about both the sincerity of the UWSP/UWSA leadership and the accuracy of the UN surveys. SHAN, for instance, contended that, according to its own ground survey in the Mong Yawng township of Shan State during the 2002–3 season, poppy cultivation was 'at least four times higher than that listed in the UNODC survey' (SHAN, 2005: 5). Yet, while acknowledging that methodology could always be improved, the UNODC representative in Rangoon in 2003 declared in an interview that he 'stuck to his figures'.[4]

What is currently at stake in Special Region n° 2, however, is not just the commitment of the UWSP/UWSA leadership or the accuracy of the UN surveys: it is the fate of the people of the Wa region. It is the opium peasants who undoubtedly suffer from the implementation of an opium-suppression agenda such as that carried out in previous years. No matter how deep the Burmese socio-economic crisis is, 'critics say humanitarian aid is only supporting and legitimizing the military government and claim it is not possible to reach the target population', something international NGOs working in the country disagree with (Kramer, 2005: 49). Given that only genuine peace and sustainable political development can resolve the Burmese crisis, it is obvious that neither international aid nor economic sanctions will succeed in solving either the drug problem or the overall political and military crisis in the country. And though economic sanctions have never proved successful in bringing about regime change (except maybe in South Africa), international aid should not be denied to people already suffering from political oppression and economic underdevelopment, and whose very survival is at stake now that the opium suppression agenda has been implemented without sufficient humanitarian aid. Basically, 'community livelihoods face being crushed between the pincers of the opium ban and tightened sanctions' (Jelsma, Kramer, Vervest, 2005: viii).

The Wa: from geohistory to geopolitics

Part of the complexity of the current debate on the role of the UWSP/UWSA stems not only from the complex geohistory and geopolitics of illicit drugs in Burma but also from the history and geopolitics of the region itself and from the fact that very little is known about the Wa people and their political (UWSP) and military (UWSA) organizations. Opinions on the Wa people are mostly partial, biased and contradictory. Considerable prejudice exists: from their portrayal in British colonial literature as wild headhunters and dirty people, to more recent times when they have been described, especially in Thailand, as ruthless drug traffickers manning the largest rebel army of Southeast Asia.

The Wa are one of the least understood peoples of Asia. There are said to be about 400,000 of them in Shan State of Burma, and a further 600,000 in the Yunnan province of China. Estimates of the total Wa population (Burma and China) vary from one to two million and 300,000 of them reportedly live in Wa-controlled areas of Burma (Fiskesjö, 2000: 53; Milsom, 2005: 65, 89). Very little has been written on the Wa (except in Chinese), between Sir James George Scott's 1900–01 *Gazetteer of Upper Burma and the Shan States* and anthropologist Magnus Fiskesjö's 2000 unpublished doctoral dissertation, 'The Fate of Sacrifice and the Making of Wa History'. In fact, most of what has been written on the Wa has to do with the UWSA and is highly biased. Interestingly, in the late nineteenth century and early twentieth century, the fact that the Wa grew opium poppies was an indication of their value as hard-working agriculturalists. According to Scott's 1900 description:

> their chief crop is the poppy. The hill-tops for miles and miles are white with blossoms in February and March [. . .]. The enormous amount of opium produced shows that the Wa are not a lazy people. Indeed they are an exceedingly well-behaved, industrious, and estimable race, were it not for the one foible of cutting strangers' heads off and neglecting ever to wash themselves. (Scott, 1900–1, Part I, Volume 1: 509).

From the late twentieth century on, the Wa have been blamed for setting up Asia's most dangerous drug cartel and have consistently been referred to as former ruthless headhunters. However, Fiskesjö notes that, prior to the twentieth century, Chinese documents rarely cited the Wa as headhunters. Yet it has been this aspect of Wa culture that has since been cited more than any other, notably 'as a sign of the primitiveness of the Wa' (Fiskesjö, 2000: 3–5).

Access to Burma's tribal peripheries has always been difficult, for the Burmese, for the Chinese and even for the British and the Japanese. In 1893, Scott was the first Westerner to travel into 'so-called Wild Wa country, the central parts of the Wa outside of the control of either Burma, China or any of the Shan polities of the region, as it was a little more than a century ago' (Fiskesjö, 2000: 19–20). And, of course, Burma's protracted conflicts and political unrest has only made accessibility even harder. These difficulties go some way to explaining the lack of reliable historical and contemporary information on the Wa – one remote hill tribe among many. Thus when seeking to elicit information on the Wa and their role in the region's geopolitics and drug trade, one must always question to what extent cultural or political factors have influenced the actual facts.

The Wa – the former cannon fodder of the Chinese-backed CPB – formed the United Wa State Army (UWSA) and allied themselves to Rangoon in 1989, after signing a ceasefire with then Lieutenant-General Khin Nyunt. They then contributed militarily to the defeat of the Shan army (Mong Tai Army) of the former 'opium king' and warlord, Khun Sa, gaining in the meantime a foothold along the Thai border. From the mid-1990s onwards, the UWSA frequently clashed with the Shan State Army-South (SSA-S), made up of remnants of Khun Sa's military outfit, located along the Thai border and most likely, if unofficially, backed by Bangkok and the CIA. As a matter of fact, the Shan 'rebellion' has long been used as a proxy by Bangkok in its rather conflictual relationship with Rangoon. Wa geohistory therefore meets Wa geopolitics when one considers that the former Shan States of Burma 'served both as primary adversaries and first buffers against the shocks of the cosmic-scale events of the penetration of the Chinese state and civilization, as well as (if to a lesser extent) that of Burma' (Fiskesjö, 2000).

The Wa of the UWSA have thus emerged from a somewhat obscure history into a complex geopolitical arena, and are now in the midst of an increasingly controversial debate about the degree and scope of their involvement in the illicit drug trade. As far as geohistory is concerned, what we know for sure is that the Wa are part of the Mon-Khmer ethnolinguistic group, one of the indigenous and oldest peoples of Southeast Asia and also one of the world's least-known. It is reckoned that the central Wa territories made up 150 square kilometres in a very mountainous area between the Salween and Mekong rivers, where the UWSP/UWSA established itself and was granted control over Special Region n° 2 by Rangoon's military junta.

The Wa consider themselves autochthonous of northeastern Burma and southern Yunnan, something that can be argued by the continuous existence, over several hundred years, of an autonomous Wa centre both politically and economically independent. Wa precedence in the region is hardly contested: for instance, their Shan neighbours (Tai ethnolinguistic group) acknowledge that the Wa first inhabited the area, while, farther north, the Chinese of Yunnan also acknowledge themselves to be later immigrants. Fiskesjö stresses that in southern Yunnan, 'local Chinese still refer to the Wa as the *benren*, the "original" or "autochthonous people"'. The Lahu, from Tibeto-Burman stock, know of course that they are the latecomers in the Wa territory, having moved there only in the eighteenth and nineteenth centuries. And also agreed by both the Wa and the Shan is that the former were expelled from their old lands by the latter, their displacement from former Kengtung State (in current Shan State) and relocation farther north around Mongkha being mentioned both in the Wa oral traditions and in the Shan chronicles. Mention of this defeat and displacement of the Wa by Shan immigrants is common throughout the area, from the Kengtung area in Burma to the Menglian area in China.

Economically, the Wa are not that different from other highland ethnic tribes. As is common among such populations in Southeast Asia, the Wa have traditionally relied mainly on hill rice grown under a system of shifting slash-and-burn cultivation. Irrigated rice paddies were and still are scarce, even in those rare valleys where irrigation is possible. While Wa people in China have made use of irrigation since the 1950s, it is only in the past few years that they have employed it within Burma. As for the main cash crop of the Wa, it has been, and still is to a large extent, opium, which became widespread in Mainland Southeast Asia's northern uplands in the second half of the nineteenth century. Historically, very little opium was ever consumed in the central Wa territory, except for medical purposes. This is still the case and only 0.8 per cent of the population was found addicted to opium in 2003 in SR2.

While Burma's opium economy is clearly the outcome of a long-lasting political crisis and of a protracted internal armed conflict, where the illicit economy is both fuelled by and fuels the war economy, opium production is still seen by many as the only viable means of achieving some level of food security. Indeed, in 2002, 75 per cent of the population of UNODC's WADP area suffered rice shortages for four to six months of the year, a dire situation that UNODC determined to address through the provision of a combination of alternative income (via cash crops) and more intensive agricultural techniques, mostly through the double cropping of rice (better land use, irrigation, improved varieties of rice, etc). More recently the Wa have launched a large-scale rubber-tree plantation around Panghsang, and China, whose border runs along the outskirts of the city, and where most Burmese heroin is trafficked, has promised to allow the tax-free import of Wa rubber in an effort to help with opium suppression.

The Wa: caught between opium suppression and sanctions

Most recently, the UWSA has been said to present a challenge to regional stability in Mainland Southeast Asia, something that Thailand, the main consumer market for methamphetamine pills (*yaa baa*), produced notably in UWSA-held territory, has long been keen to claim. Thailand has repeatedly blamed the UWSA as posing the main threat to its national security. The UWSA has clearly played an active part in drug production and trafficking, as, even according to senior Wa leaders, 'the WCA [Wa Central Authorities] continued to allow drug traders to establish refineries and manufacture heroin until 1996' (Milsom, 2005: 78). Though production of heroin was supposedly banned in 1996, 'in 1997 and 1998 it [the WCA] permitted ATS [amphetamine type stimulants] factories to be set up and received some taxes'. The Wa leaders Bao You-xiang (UWSP Chairman) and Xiao Ming-liang (UWSP Deputy Secretary) claimed that ATS production was banned by decree in 1999 when they 'fully understood' the 'international implications of this trade', but opium production, trading, and taxation were allowed until 26 June 2005, when the opium ban took effect (Milsom, 2005: 79). However, some senior members of the UWSA continued to deal in drugs (production and trafficking of opium, heroin and methamphetamines) after the bans had been implemented; among others: one of Bao You-xiang's brothers, now deceased (Bao You-hua), and of course Wei Hsueh-kang, notorious drug trafficker and special advisor to UWSP's Central Committee and 'finance minister'.[5]

The Wa people already grew opium poppies when the British annexed Burma, and Wa leaders acknowledge their past involvement in illicit drug production and trafficking. They now claim to have suppressed opium production in Special Region n° 2, something attested to by UNODC, and they argue, along with Burmese authorities, that methamphetamine production is largely in the hands of Chinese producers and syndicates (Kramer, 2007; Milsom, 2005: 76–7). It must be said in defence of the UWSP/UWSA, however, that they not only inherited their governing structure from the Communist Party of Burma, after they successfully rebelled against it (1989), but that they also inherited the CPB's heavy dependence on the proceeds from opium and heroin taxes (Milsom, 2005: 70).

The Wa of the UWSA have an unmatched opportunity in Burma. The central government has granted them a de facto autonomy given to no other tribal group or political or military organization in the country. This important opportunity in a country where a ruthless military dictatorship still clings to power and makes concessions only when it has no other choice, must, however, be used most carefully by the Wa leadership if it does not want to jeopardize its stability and very existence. Seemingly willing to change both its image and its status, the Wa leadership declared its commitment to opium suppression. As we have seen, it effectively banned opium production in June 2005, although it did so with only very limited economic alternatives available to the region's peasantry.

Although the UN and various non-governmental organizations are working in the Wa Special Region n° 2 to improve the economic and health conditions of the population, such a rapid and marked change – most likely aimed at proving their alleged sincerity to the outside world – could well threaten both Wa socio-political stability and the fragile status quo that the Wa enjoy with Rangoon. UNODC, whose very presence in the area has been heavily criticized by many advocates of democracy, reportedly tried to advise the Wa leadership toward achieving what is a self-imposed goal: for example, they tried to soften the humanitarian impact of the forced relocation of opium-poppy growers from uplands to lowlands within the WADP area.

Whether or not the UWSP/UWSA leadership will succeed in ridding the territory of opium production in a sustainable way, the determination of its senior leadership to achieve such a goal is evident. In declaring itself fully committed to suppressing opium production the Wa leadership clearly hopes to be the recipient of international aid. It is also aware that it needs such aid if it is to avoid putting the livelihoods of its people in jeopardy and is not to adversely affect the already fragile regional balance of power by threatening the social, political, and military stability of the Wa Special Region. The risk is that the UWSA will not receive the much-needed aid from an international community that still imposes sanctions on Burma and views the UWSA mostly as a drug-trafficking organisation.

It should be remembered, however, that in such geopolitical issues, 'demonizing one specific player in the field, as often occurs, usually has stronger roots in politics than in evidence' (TNI, 2003: 3). In 2003, a long-time Burma watcher, journalist Larry Jagan, explained that:

> one thing that the Wa leaders, Myanmar's military chiefs and the Thai government seem to agree on now is that it is criminal gangs that are behind the production and trafficking of yaba and not the Wa. UN officials agree and say they are mainly Chinese criminals, some with connections to Hong Kong and Macau.[6]

Yet, it is worth noting here that a rare and recent survey of drug trafficking practices and networks between Burma and China, including SR2, concluded that the regional drug trade was much less integrated than commonly thought:

Drug traffickers in general do not belong to street gangs, organized crime groups, or terrorist organizations. Most are simply bold risk takers who work with family members, or form alliances with friends or other social contacts whom they come to trust. [...] Drug trafficking and street dealing in China as well as in most parts of Southeast Asia appear to remain entrepreneurial in nature and fragmented in practice (Ko-Lin Chin, Zhang, 2007: 4–5).

The same seems to be true in SR2, where the UWSP/UWSA can hardly be considered a drug cartel organizing drug production and trading, even if some of its members are undoubtedly involved in such activities, either directly or indirectly.

Although Burma's crisis is rooted in politics and will only be solved politically, the international community tends to forget about realities and issues at the local level as it is increasingly confronted with calls for stricter economic sanctions on Rangoon as well as with the military junta's struggle to cling to power. Yet, one has to acknowledge, when looking at the political and military deadlock that has characterized Burma's recent history, that current sanctions, both political and economic, have not yielded the expected results. As more sanctions have been imposed, it seems fewer levers are available to the international community to influence Rangoon's policy. This is especially true when sanctions are imposed but are not enforced by neighbouring states. For the main regional players – Thailand and China of course, but also India – it seems that the economic and geostrategic influence at stake in Burma is too great to go ahead with sanctions advocated and implemented mainly by Western countries.

In the Shan State and the Wa Special Region (SR2), millions of people struggle to survive on a daily basis. The main threat to the Wa people is a major humanitarian crisis brought about by the 2005 opium ban enforced by the UWSA without the necessary developmental aid being in place. The tight deadline, combined with international sanctions that prevent the necessary aid from reaching either the Burmese dictatorship or the so-called 'world's largest drug-trafficking army', means that the pace of opium suppression has not been matched by the ability to create alternative ways of living. Rural communities risk being sacrificed. Since the continuing programme of opium suppression is clearly unsustainable without outside economic aid, it is the Wa people who will suffer the most – both from the ban and the economic sanctions – while opium production may simply be displaced to some other area of Burma.

OPIUM PRODUCTION THRIVES UNDER THE
TALIBAN AND THE KARZAI ADMINISTRATION

When cultivation and production really began to decline in Burma (in 1999), Afghanistan produced a record opium crop, initiating a fresh upward trend that further demonized the new Taliban regime of the country. Four to five years after their 1994 appearance in southeast Afghanistan, the Taliban held sway over 85–90 per cent of the country and its poppy fields. Afghanistan and Burma were the world's leading illicit opium producers and each was home to a rather recent military regime attracting international criticism: the Taliban in Afghanistan and the UWSA in Burma. Both countries were frequently referred to as 'narco-states' by the international community, and both the Taliban and the UWSA were regularly denounced for benefiting from, or even encouraging or controlling, illicit drug production and trade in their respective territories. Just as had been the case with the UWSP/UWSA, the Taliban inherited opium production when they came to power in Afghanistan. And likewise, after the 2001 removal of the Taliban, so the Afghan Transitional Administration led by Hamid Karzai again faced the same legacy. Seemingly indifferent of political regime, opium production achieved a new record in 2006 under the presidency of Hamid Karzai (elected 7 December 2004 as the first president of the new Islamic Republic of Afghanistan). What happened was that the Taliban and Hamid Karzai not only inherited opium production – they also inherited a country ruined by war and drought.

Origins and rise of the Taliban

Originally, the Taliban were religious students educated in Pakistan's refugee camps managed by Maulana Fazlur Rehman's Jamiat-e-Ulema Islam (JUI) in Balochistan and the North-West Frontier Province. They were taught a literal and austere interpretation of Islam – Deobandism – first elaborated in 1867 in a madrassa (seminary) of the central Uttar Pradesh Indian town of Deoband. Fazlur Rehman gained important influence when Benazir Bhutto (1953–2007) was elected Prime Minister of Pakistan for the second time in 1993. Having supported her during the elections, he was appointed to a position within her government that gave him influence in Pakistan's foreign policy. Then in 1994 Bhutto's Interior Minister, General Naseerullah Babar, announced the government's plan to open a trading route between Pakistan and Central Asia, through southern Afghanistan. At this time, the ongoing conflict in northern Afghanistan together with the multiple tolls demanded by countless commanders for free passage in southern Afghanistan, rendered the roads of Afghanistan off-limits or too expensive to most traders.

This was, as Ahmed Rashid explained, 'an intolerable situation' for 'the powerful mafia of truck transporters based in Quetta and Kandahar', who could not smuggle goods between Quetta, Iran, and Turkmenistan (Rashid, 2000: 22). Mostly made up of Pashtun, the mafia of truck transporters understandably welcomed Babar's plans. When a Pakistani 30-truck test convoy was intercepted by three Afghan commanders near Kandahar in late October, and the rescue operation by Pakistan's military was ruled out as being too dangerous, Babar called on the JUI's students (*taliban*) to free the trucks, which they did before taking control of Kandahar (5 November 1994). The then new Taliban movement removed all roadblocks and set up a one-stop toll at the Afghanistan-Pakistan border post of Spin Baldak, where they had first defeated Hekmatyar's (see ch.3) men in early October. The road was finally secure and, in December, a 50-truck convoy of cotton safely reached Quetta all the way from Turkmenistan, after paying US$ 5,000 to the Taliban.

As Rashid notes: 'In just a couple of weeks this unknown force had captured the second largest city in Afghanistan with the loss of just a dozen men' (Rashid, 2000: 29). By December 1994, around 12,000 Afghan and Pakistani students had joined the Taliban in Kandahar and, by late March, twelve of Afghanistan's 32 provinces were controlled by the Taliban (Rashid, 2000: 29–30). In September 1996, they captured Kabul. The rapid territorial advance of the Taliban put them in control of most of the country's poppy fields and, in October 1997, the new regime agreed to suppress opium production from the territory it controlled if alternative development was made available to Afghan opium farmers. However, with international donors unconvinced of the Taliban's sincerity, only half of the funds requested by the UN were made available, and, as a consequence, the agreement with the UNDCP was not implemented by the Taliban. In 1999, Afghanistan produced a record 4,600-tonne opium crop.

One year later, in July 2000, the Taliban's supreme leader, Mullah Mohammed Omar, as *Amir-ul Momineen* (Commander of the Faithful), banned opium poppy cultivation and brought the country's 2001 harvest down to 185 tonnes (out of which only 35 tonnes were produced in Taliban-controlled territory), an all-time low. What caused such an unexpected move has never been explained in a satisfactory way. The Taliban claimed their act was motivated by their quest for international recognition and economic aid, while many observers argued instead, and somewhat unconvincingly, that the Taliban had large opium stocks to sell and tried to raise prices.

The farm-gate price before the edict averaged US$30 per kilogramme of fresh Afghan opium (as opposed to dry opium, which is lighter). In March 2001, during the purchasing season for recently harvested opium, the average farm-gate price suddenly reached US$700, reflecting the shortage provoked by the Taliban. After the 2001 terrorist attacks against the United States, traffickers and local traders, rightly fearing American reprisals against both the Taliban and Osama bin Laden's al-Qaeda, accelerated the sale of the 2,900 tonnes of opium that the United Nations then estimated to be stored in the north of the country.

Immediately after 11 September 2001, one kilogram of Afghan opium sold for US$ 95–120, far below the price caused by the Taliban-driven shortages. However, just before American military intervention in Afghanistan on 7 October 2001, the price skyrocketed, reaching US$500 per kilogramme. Following the 'Enduring Freedom' operation and its air strikes, opium lost some 40 per cent of its farm-gate value, a clear indication of the sensitivity of opium to market contingencies. After the defeat of the Taliban in December 2001, opium production resumed once more in Afghanistan, spurred by the brutal income shortage experienced by opium farmers in 2001, by higher (and therefore more attractive) opium prices, and because the Taliban had not renewed their ban before their defeat.

Opium production under the Taliban: from taxation to prohibition

Between 1994 and 1996, from their victory in Spin Baldak to their capture of Kabul, the Taliban progressed without the need to wage many major battles: 'local warlords either fled or, waving flags, surrendered to them' (Rashid, 2000: 30). In 1995, when they met resistance from the forces of Ghaffar Akhunzada, 'whose clan had controlled Helmand province and its lucrative opium poppy fields for much of the 1980s', the Taliban propped up smaller drug warlords against him and bribed others, eventually capturing the province in December 1995 (Rashid, 2000: 33). As explained by Rashid,

> many surrenders had been facilitated by pure cash, bribing commanders to switch sides – a tactic that the Taliban were to turn into a fine art form in later years and which was sustained by the growth in their income from the drugs trade, the transport business and external aid from Pakistan and Saudi Arabia (Rashid, 2000: 35).

The capture of Kabul (27 September 1996), which proved much more difficult than previous Taliban conquests (the first Taliban rockets were fired against Kabul on 17 December 1995, almost a year before victory), was only obtained by way of Jalalabad with Saudi and Pakistani support, and by bribing the head of the Jalalabad Shura, Haji Abdul Qadeer (Rashid, 2000: 48).

The Taliban clearly resorted to the strategic manipulation of opium warlords in their capture of most of Afghanistan and therefore benefited from some support in opium-producing areas. Moreover, as Alfred McCoy stresses, 'the Taliban's policies provided stimulus, both direct and indirect, for a nationwide expansion of opium cultivation' (McCoy, 2003: 508). For McCoy, the Taliban's ban 'on the employment and education of women created a vast pool of low-cost labour to sustain an accelerated expansion of opium production' (McCoy, 2003: 508). For Rashid, the peace and security that the Taliban established in the countryside not only 'proved to be an immense boon to opium farming', it also 'expanded trade and transport routes significantly' (Rashid, 2000: 117, 120). Of course, the Taliban also benefited financially through their taxing of both harvest and trade. This taxation was strongly denounced by the US State Department, the CIA, the DEA (Drug Enforcement Administration), and many observers of Afghanistan. However, such taxation was in accordance with Islamic principles known as *zakat* and *usher* and was indeed acknowledged by the Taliban authorities themselves. These two taxes were nothing new in Afghanistan and many warlords and commanders very likely taxed opium production and trade in such a way before the Taliban era. Indeed, during the previous years of war, some commanders who had originated (or been kept) outside the mujahideen party structures had 'launched local insurgencies initially relying on local resources: zakat and ushr' (Rubin, 1999). What changed with the Taliban is that they were the first political power to extend its writ over 85 per cent of Afghanistan after years of political fragmentation and patchy territorial control. They ended up controlling most of the country's territory in a very effective way and were therefore seen as also controlling, or at least condoning, opium production in most of the country. Basically, 'with their centrally controlled military and police, the Taliban reasserted control over what remained of Afghanistan's weak capacity for administration and revenue collection, including the taxation of opium' (Rubin, 2004: 3).

In 1997, the assistant director of the Pashtani Tjarati Bank – the Taliban's central bank in their Kandahari stronghold – was quoted as saying that 'a landowner must pay 10 percent of whatever amount he makes on his crops'. As for opium merchants, they had to pay a 2.5 per cent tax to the Taliban, as they, like any other producers, did to other rulers and regimes. These taxes are well known and are Islamic practices that predate the Taliban. *Zakat,* or purification, is the third pillar of Islam and, as a tax levied on most assets, concerns every Muslim. Once levied it is redistributed to the poor, the rulers, and the holy fighters of the jihad. *Usher,* or tithe, is the other Islamic tax that is collected on raw agricultural products. Half goes to the poor, with the other half split between the local mullahs and the rulers, at that time the Taliban.

Thus, by levying these taxes, the Taliban were doing nothing more than profiting from an economic system of production established prior to their arrival on the Afghan political scene. It is easy to see how the Taliban, who controlled as much as 96 per cent of the country's poppy fields, benefited from these taxes, which are inherent to the Islamic law, or *sharia*. Yet, as Rashid stresses, 'the Taliban had no religious qualms in collecting 20 per cent of the value of a truckload of opium as zakat' (Rashid, 2000: 118). While the Taliban 'made opium its largest source of taxation' (McCoy, 2003:508), and 'taxes on opium exports became the mainstay of Taliban income and their war economy' (Rashid, 2000:124), the real importance of the narcotics economy for the Taliban remains somehow controversial. For instance, Rashid also explained that the Afghan smuggling trade had expanded under the Taliban and that the Afghan Transit Trade agreed upon by Pakistan was 'the largest source of official revenue for the Taliban' (Rashid, 2000: 124). Estimates of the profits made by the Taliban on opium production and trade varied greatly (from US$20 million to US$75 million, depending on year and calculation methods) and it is very difficult to decide what contributed the most revenue to the Taliban: in fact it would be very complicated to prove that narcotics-derived revenues were larger or smaller than those brought by the taxation of the regional transit trade in consumer goods. To make matters worse, the Taliban did not only rely on opium and transit trade. In December 2001, Wahidullah Sabawoon, the finance minister for the Northern Alliance, declared to the *New York Times* that the Taliban had no annual budget but that they 'appeared to spend US$ 300 million a year, nearly all of it on the war'. He added that in the last years of their rule 'the Taliban had come to rely increasingly on three sources of money: "poppy, the Pakistanis and bin Laden"'.[7] In 2001, Syed Idris, the then chief of foreign intelligence for the Northern Alliance who had met with Mullah Omar in 1996 as Gulbuddin Hekmatyar's envoy, declared to the same *New York Times* journalist that the Pakistanis 'had funnelled as much as US$ 10 million a year to the Taliban, much of it hidden in the budget for the Pakistani Embassy in Kabul'. Yet, while stating that 'drugs money funded the weapons, ammunition and fuel for the war', Rashid also explained that 'unlike in the past, this income did not appear to line the pockets' of the Taliban leaders 'as they continued to live extremely frugal lives' (Rashid, 2000: 124).

Of course, the Taliban were not alone in profiting from Afghanistan's opium economy. Opium production and trade also benefited the Northern Alliance of the late Ahmed Shah Massoud, assassinated on 7 September 2001 in his Panjsher Valley stronghold. The Northern Alliance reportedly received between US$40 million and US$60 million a year by taxing the extraction and trade of precious and semi-precious stones (emeralds and lapis lazuli) from the Panjsher Valley.[8] It has been reported that the Northern Alliance was also levying taxes on opium production and trade, which would make sense considering that its own considerable war effort required significant funding. Some 30–40 per cent of the Northern Alliance's war chest supposedly came from taxes on production and trade (Chouvy, 2002: 142–4). It is worth noting that before the Taliban conquered the northern provinces of Kunduz, Balkh and Faryab, many heroin laboratories were active in areas controlled by General Rashid Dostum, as reported by the press[9] or the US State Department: 'There is evidence that heroin labs are being located close to the borders of some Central Asian countries' (INCSR, 1999: Afghanistan). The Northern Alliance outlawed poppy cultivation and heroin manufacture in June 1999, a year before the Taliban issued their ban. However, the Northern Alliance clearly failed to enforce the ban in their areas, while the Taliban impressively and unexpectedly succeeded. Indeed, according to the United Nations, up to 150 tonnes of opium were probably collected in 2001 in the areas controlled by the Northern Alliance after poppy cultivation had almost tripled between 2000 and 2001 in Badakhshan province, where the Taliban's rule did not extend. Northern Afghanistan has been a major Afghan trafficking route since Central Asian republics obtained independence in 1991, and proceeds from the opium economy therefore pre-dated the bountiful 2001 opium crop.

However, the 2000 opium ban issued by the Taliban almost completely suppressed opium production in Taliban-held areas: the 35 tonnes of opium harvested in 2001, was down from 3,300 tonnes in 2000. But the determination shown by the Taliban in 2000 to drastically reduce opium production did not, it seems, last long, for as of the beginning of September 2001 – and before the 11 September attacks against the United States – the Taliban allegedly authorized the Afghan peasants to sow opium again; or, at the very least, they are thought not to have reissued their prohibition, thus leaving the peasants one precious month to obtain the indispensable seeds before the October sowing season.

The Taliban probably banned opium production in a bid for international recognition, though, as we have seen, many observers thought and still think that the ban was only issued in order to raise opium prices and increase profit from the sale of large existing stockpiles. The year 1999 had yielded a record crop and had been followed by a lower but still large 2000 harvest. The UN then estimated that as much as 60 per cent of the fresh opium of any given year was frequently 'retained by farmers and sold at a later time as dry opium' (UNDCP, 2000: iii). In 2001 India declared, through the voice of its representative to the UN, that 'the Taliban had merely turned to their advantage three points of pressure: the drought which hampered cultivation, the international outcry against them, and the glut of opium on the market', arguing that the Taliban had not destroyed 'the stocks in their possession', 'estimated at 2,800 tons'.[10] In 2002, the UN mentioned the 'existence of significant stocks of opiates accumulated during previous years of bumper harvests' (UNDCP, 2002b: 2). As some have observed, 'production in 2000–2001 decreased by 94 percent, but cross-border seizures of trafficked opiates decreased by only 40 percent, indicating continued trafficking of accumulated stocks' (Rubin, 2004: 4).

In September 2000 the Taliban sent a delegation to the UN in an attempt to obtain international recognition in exchange for its opium ban. But, 'in December, the United States led the UN Security Council in additional sanctions against the regime for harbouring Osama bin Laden' (McCoy, 2004: 518). Yet the United States and the United Nations later recognized the extent of opium suppression in Afghanistan and, in May 2001, US secretary of State Colin Powell announced 'US$ 43 million in new humanitarian assistance for the people of Afghanistan', including 'those farmers who have felt the impact of the ban on poppy cultivation, a decision by the Taliban that we welcome'. Powell, however, made clear that US aid would bypass the Taliban 'who have done little to alleviate the suffering of the Afghan people, and indeed have done much to exacerbate it'. He further explained, 'We provide our aid to the people of Afghanistan, not to Afghanistan's warring factions.' Afghanistan's humanitarian crisis had motivated the delivery of supplementary US aid despite the 'number of fundamental issues' still separating the United States from the Taliban: 'their support for terrorism; their violation of internationally recognized human rights standards, especially their treatment of women and girls; and their refusal to resolve Afghanistan's civil war through a negotiated settlement'.[11]

The opium ban proved very successful but short-lived, as production resumed in 2002, after the December 2001 demise of the Taliban. Worse, production and prices actually increased in the following years, due in part to the profound economic crisis that the ban had provoked. The ban and its implementation clearly proved counterproductive and the economic crisis they engineered would undoubtedly have made the situation intolerable for the Taliban had they stayed in power and prolonged their prohibition. For Barnett Rubin, 'that the Taliban defeated warlord forces in the areas they controlled and used centrally managed revenue to finance a single army and administration helps account for their success in enforcing the ban'. Yet, in order to obtain their brief success the Taliban 'had to negotiate with and provide hefty subsidies to major tribes, and it is unlikely that they could have continued the ban without significant international development assistance, which they would not have received' (Rubin, 2004: 3–4).

In any case, the opium ban ended along with the Taliban. After the terrorist attacks of 11 September against the United States, US President George W. Bush delivered an ultimatum to the Taliban to hand over al-Qaeda leaders based in Afghanistan and to close terrorist camps. On 7 October 2001, after the ultimatum expired, Operation Enduring Freedom started with US and British forces conducting air strikes against Taliban positions and al-Qaeda camps. Supported by US and British air power, Northern Alliances troops eventually marched on Kabul, driving the Taliban out of the city on 12–13 November 2001. The Taliban nevertheless held the southern town of Kandahar until they were able to negotiate their surrender with the United States on 6 December 2001, one day after the Bonn agreements were signed and a transitional Afghan government was established, led by the royalist Hamid Karzai, a Durrani Pashtun who became head of the Popalzai tribe (Kandahar) after his father was killed in 1999, most likely by the Taliban (Anderson, 2005: 65).

Opium production increases despite new state and new regime

The new Afghanistan emerged from more than twenty years of war and economic collapse. Yet the transition from war to peace was to prove very difficult, for, although the Taliban had been toppled, they had not been entirely defeated. In fact, the Taliban supreme leader, Mullah Omar, had evaded US forces in 2001 in Kandahar and, by 2003, the Taliban insurgency had gained strength, further complicating (if not compromising) the peace-building and state-building efforts of the new Islamic Republic of Afghanistan, as aid workers (reportedly the highest death toll of aid workers worldwide) and troops (both foreign and Afghan) suffered growing casualties. Worse, suicide attacks, which were unknown in Afghanistan, increased from two in 2003 to 123 in 2006 and 160 in 2007 (not including thwarted attempts: HWR, 2007: four, UN GASC, 2008: five). In June 2007, Pierre Krähenbühl, director of operations of the International Committee of the Red Cross, the only organization present across all of Afghanistan, denounced the situation, remarking how it had become 'incredibly difficult for ordinary Afghans to lead a normal life' as 'civilians suffer horribly from mounting threats to their security' (including from regular aerial bombing raids) and 'lack access to basic services'.[12] He also mentioned how it had 'become increasingly challenging to carry out humanitarian work outside major cities', as, 'the

conflict pitting Afghan and international forces against the armed opposition
has significantly intensified in the south and east of the country and is
spreading to the north and west'. In March 2008, a report by the Secretary
General of the United Nations on 'The situation in Afghanistan and its
implications for international peace and security' stated that out of the 376
districts of the country, 36 (including most districts in the east, south-east
and south), remained largely inaccessible to Afghan officials and aid workers.
The report further explained that, 'owing to insecure conditions', United
Nations agencies were 'unable to operate in 78 districts in the south of the
country' and that United Nations road missions 'to almost all districts in
the south' had been suspended for several months (UN GASC, 2008: 1; 12).

Against such a background, opium production not only resumed after
2001 but increased, reaching an all-time high in 2007. This increase has
been caused by a number of factors, among which has been the strategic
manipulation of local warlords and commanders by the US military, Special
Forces, and intelligence services. Between 2001 and 2004 the United States
condoned opiates production both in areas traditionally controlled by the
United Front (Badakhshan) and in areas held by various local commanders
whose support was deemed strategically necessary to fight the Taliban and
al-Qaeda (Chouvy, 2004d). As a matter of fact, the demise of the Taliban
happened 'under a covert-warfare doctrine first developed in Laos during
the 1960s' as 'Washington fought this war deploying massive air power, CIA
cash, and Special Forces as advisers to Afghan warlords – providing arms
and money that reinvigorated local commanders long eclipsed by the Taliban'
(McCoy, 2004: 520). Whether in northern, eastern or southern Afghanistan,
the CIA mobilized and supported, often financially, Afghan warlords long
involved in drug trafficking: among others, General Abdul Rashid Dostum
in northern Afghanistan, Haji Abdul Qadeer and Hazrat Ali in Nangarhar,
and the pre-Taliban Governor of Kandahar, Gul Agha Shirzai, who in
November 2001 had launched 3,000 troops on Kandahar along with Hamid
Karzai. In fact 'only weeks after the Taliban's fall, all of Afghanistan's key
opium-producing regions – Helmand, Nangarhar, and Badakhshan – were
again under the control of powerful drug lords' (McCoy, 2004: 522).

After their contribution to the demise of the Taliban, commanders from
the Northern Alliance gained formal political position in the interim
administration of Hamid Karzai. Meanwhile, in the Pashtun belt of southern
and eastern Afghanistan, 'strongmen linked to tribal structures continued
to exert political control both locally and nationally, and continued to
dominate the local political economy' (Lister, 2007: 3). As Sarah Lister
explains, during more than twenty years of war, 'decentralised power, which
had rested largely in the structures of customary institutions, shifted to those

who controlled the military and financial resources generated by participation in the conflict and the war economy', until after the fall of the Taliban when 'many of these same powerholders also gained formal political power at both the national and subnational levels in the newly emerging "state"' (Lister, 2007: 3–4). This power shift, which compromised state-building and peace-building efforts, was made possible notably because 'for several years, a contradictory policy was pursued by different parts of the US administration – with some actors actually undermining efforts by others to curb the powers of regional strongmen' (Lister, 2007: 11). The US General Accounting Office's 2004 report mentioned that while 'the criminality of the warlords' private armies continued to destabilize the country and impede reconstruction' by fostering 'an illegitimate economy fuelled by the smuggling of arms, drugs, and other goods', the United States continued using 'warlord-commanded militias in its continuing counterinsurgency effort against the Taliban' (Lister, 2007: 11).

Yet, on 17 January 2002, the transitional Afghan government declared poppy cultivation, together with the sale and consumption of opium, prohibited in Afghanistan, notwithstanding the fact that poppies sown in the fall of 2001 were about to bloom and to yield an unexpectedly high 3,400-tonne opium crop. Of course, the new ban deeply upset those Afghan peasants who, under the *salaam* system, had traditionally borrowed significant sums or who had received advance payments in order to be able to feed their families until the harvest season. It is in this delicate context that, on 3 April 2002, the transitional government launched a UK devised eradication program and offered US$250 compensation for eradication of each *jerib* (0.2 hectare) of poppies (i.e. US$1,250 per hectare). The eradication processes met strong resistance from opium farmers as the poppy growers declared that they could obtain from US$1,700 to US$3,500 per *jerib* if they collected their opium and sold it at market prices. The dispute between the government and the peasants caused some disorder and even led to armed confrontation. In April 2002, one such clash killed eight peasants and wounded 35 others in the Kajaki district of Helmand province (Chouvy, 2003c). Despite these incidents, and others – including tractors exploding on mines while eradicating poppy fields in Helmand province – the UN estimated that 16,500 hectares of poppies, a third of the total surface planted in 2001–2, had been destroyed during the eradication program undertaken by the transitional government (mainly in the provinces of Helmand, Uruzgan, Nangarhar, and Kunar).

The Afghan government also estimated that its eradication campaign had included more than one-third of the cultivated areas, even though many observers argued that, for various reasons, only 10 per cent had really been eradicated. In fact, it seemed that, in many cases, financial compensation was pocketed by local commanders and governors without ever reaching the peasants. In other instances, peasants were reportedly compensated after having only partially eradicated their opium poppy fields (Chouvy, 2003c). However, in 2003, poppy cultivation increased by 8 per cent and nearly matched the surface area cultivated in 2000. Opium production also slightly increased (by 6 per cent, to 3,600 tonnes) and became at the time the second highest ever recorded in Afghanistan. While production largely decreased in two of the three traditional and main opium-producing provinces of the country (decreasing in Helmand and Kandahar provinces but not Nangarhar), it largely increased in others (especially in Uruzgan and Badakhshan). The number of provinces where cultivation was reported (Ghor, for example) also increased, for the sixth consecutive year – from eight in 1994, to 15 in 1998, 18 in 1999 and 28 in 2003 (out of a total of 32) (Labrousse, 2005: 179–80; UNODC, 2003b: 7).

Yet, the expansion of poppy cultivation and the increase in opium production were not over in Afghanistan. As Antonio Maria Costa, Executive Director of UNODC, commented in the preface to the Office's 2004 opium survey: 'Afghan annals will record 2004 as contradictory'. He added:

> On the one hand, the political progress towards democracy culminated in the near plebiscite election of President Karzai – the country's first-ever leader chosen by the people – whose courage and determination I salute. On the other hand, opium cultivation increased by two-thirds, reaching an unprecedented 131,000 hectares (UNODC, 2004a: Preface).

Opium production had *only* increased by 17 per cent, due to drought and disease, but had still reached 4,200 tonnes, a second consecutive record for Afghanistan. Poppy cultivation had also expanded, now occurring in 32 of the 34 Afghan provinces (two provinces were added in 2004, making a total of 34). In the same document, Costa also warned that if the 'drug problem' were to persist in Afghanistan, then 'the political and military successes' of the past three years would be lost. The following year, 2005, Costa lauded an 'important and encouraging' 21 per cent decline in cultivation (104,000 hectares), and stressed the fact that 'one field out of five which was planted with an illicit opium crop in 2004, was planted with a licit crop in 2005' (UNODC, 2005a: Preface). However, more favourable weather conditions and less disease than in 2004 yielded almost the same crop: down only 2.5 per cent from 4,200 to 4,100 tonnes, i.e. 87 per cent of the world's total.

Optimism was to be short-lived, however, as Afghanistan's opium production increased by 49 per cent in 2006, in spite of a slight decrease in average opium yields (down 6 per cent). Of the 28 provinces in Afghanistan involved in opium production, Helmand province alone produced 42 per cent of Afghanistan's 2006 output. As Costa acknowledged, 'there was considerable alarm when it was announced that cultivation in Afghanistan rose to 165,000 hectares in 2006, a 59 per cent increase over 2005'. The contrast between the 2005 three-page preface and the 2006 half-page preface of the UNODC opium surveys is obvious. The 2005 optimism gave way to despondency in 2006 as Costa warned that 'major traffickers, warlords and insurgents' were 'reaping the profits of this bumper crop to spread instability, infiltrate public institutions, and enrich themselves'. 'Afghanistan', he wrote, 'is moving from narcoeconomy to narco-state' (UNODC, 2006b: Preface). At that time, both Karzai and Costa reckoned that 'either Afghanistan destroys opium or opium will destroy Afghanistan' (CARE, 2006: 1).

Efforts aimed at reducing and even suppressing opium production have been numerous and diverse. In 2003, Afghanistan launched a five-year National Drug Control Strategy (NDCS) the overall goal of which was 'to eliminate the production, consumption and trafficking of illicit drugs in Afghanistan'. The government strategy, as set out in the NDCS, 'focuses on interdiction and law enforcement against traffickers and processors while investing in licit livelihoods for those, especially the poor, who now depend economically on narcotics'. The NDCS identified eight 'pillars' through which to implement its strategy: demand reduction, alternative livelihoods, eradication, public awareness, law enforcement, criminal justice, international and regional cooperation and institution-building.[13] As many observers have stressed, the counter-narcotics scene is highly complex in Afghanistan as 'there are a myriad of different organisations involved with overlapping responsibilities' and as there is 'competition within the Afghan government, as well as within the international community, over how to deal with the drugs problem' (TNI, 2006: 17).

The Afghan government implements its counter-narcotics policies through the Ministry of Counter-Narcotics and the Ministry of Interior, although the former clearly has the dominant role. The complexity of counter-narcotics organizations and procedures can be understood from the number and the variety of counter-narcotics agencies and bodies: the Ministry of Counter-Narcotics controls the Counter-Narcotics Police of Afghanistan who operate the National Interdiction Unit. A provincial-level Poppy Elimination Programme also reports to the Ministry of Counter-Narcotics. The Ministry of Interior runs the Afghan Special Narcotics Force, a paramilitary unit. There is also a Criminal Justice Task Force, created to bring cases before a Central Narcotics Tribunal. In accordance with the Bonn agreement (2001), responsibility for different areas of Afghan stabilization was divided between various countries: Germany is the lead nation for police programs, Italy is the lead nation for justice programs and the United Kingdom is the lead nation for counter-narcotics. However, the United States created an Afghan Eradication Force (formerly Central Poppy Eradication Force) to push forward its eradication and crop-spraying agenda. The United Kingdom therefore created the Central Eradication Planning Cell within the Ministry of Interior, 'to ensure that eradication by the CPEF is targeted in a way which takes account of alternative livelihoods' (B. Rammell quoted in: TNI, 2006: 18).

Yet, cultivated areas and production increased by 120 and 80 per cent respectively between 2002 and 2006 (2001 cannot be used as a reference year). Most observers explain this 'inability of the international community to counter the opium sector effectively in Afghanistan' by 'three main problems: the United States' continued alliance with warlords and militia commanders involved in trafficking; the inadequate overall level of international security and reconstruction aid; and flaws in analysis, strategy, and counter-narcotics policies' (Rubin, 2004: 10). The increase of the overall size (absolute value) of the opium industry in Afghanistan, however, was not matched by an increase in relative value (much to the contrary), at least not before 2007 when expanded cultivated areas and increased yields produced another all-time high (8,200 tonnes of opium). In fact, the Afghan opium industry was equivalent to 61 per cent of licit GDP in 2004, to 52 per cent in 2005, 46 per cent in 2006, and 53 per cent in 2007 (UNODC, 2006b: 9; 2007bb: iii). Therefore, in 2006, 32 per cent of the country's overall economy (opium economy added to the GDP) was generated by the opium industry. It must be understood, though, that most of the proceeds from the opium industry do not remain in, or alternatively, are not repatriated into, the Afghan economy. Of course, such a high proportion reflects not only the importance of the opium industry but also the extreme poverty of Afghanistan, whose GDP is very low (US$6.7 billion in 2006). However, the regular growth of the licit Afghan economy (average 17 per cent GDP annual growth since 2001) and the decline in farm-gate prices of opium (reflecting the increase in production) limited and (at least before 2007) lowered the relative value of Afghanistan's opium economy. Nonetheless the absolute and relative values of Afghanistan's opium industry are much higher than what they would be if farm-gate opium prices were three to four times lower, as was the case before the ban of 2000–1.

Given the importance of the drug economy, 'the combination of credit, extension services, cash income, and security guarantees from local warlords who share in the profit could not be matched by the meagre resources offered by the Hamid Karzai government and its foreign backers' (Rubin, 2004: 8). Additionally, a growing Taliban insurgency and deteriorating security compromised and sometimes halted development projects in parts of the country and prevented eradication operations. Where development projects were too dangerous to implement for development workers (at least 31 non-governmental organization (NGO) staff members were killed in 2006, up from 24 in 2004, when Afghanistan had the world's highest death toll amongst NGO staff), eradication operations were even riskier and largely avoided for fear of pushing opium farmers into the Taliban ranks. As noted by Jonathan Goodhand, a political scientist, 'although the transitional authority staged a number of high profile crop destructions, it had few resources, was too compromised and had limited leverage in relation to regional warlords to enforce a drug eradication programme' (Goodhand, 2005: 201). This is still relevant: 2007 yielded the highest opium crop ever in the country, and major, development projects (repair of the Kajaki dam in the upper Sangin valley of Helmand province, for example); and eradication operations (as around Tirin Kot, in Uruzgan province) were still stalled by insurgency.

5. Opium bales, Nangarhar province, Afghanistan.

5

In and Out of the Golden Triangle and the Golden Crescent

Asian opium has always been exported, whether by early traders, colonial powers, or modern drug trafficking criminal networks. But it was with the advent of *heroin* that drug trafficking became truly global.

Before 1990, heroin from the Golden Triangle and the Golden Crescent almost invariably travelled via the southern routes, and Thailand, Iran and Pakistan, former opium producers, were the first to face growing narcotics trafficking and rising narcotics addiction. Then, as the Cold War came to an end and borders were opened and trading and customs agreement signed, the traffic was suddenly and partially reorientated towards China, Central Asia and Russia, enabling drug traffickers to diversify their shipping routes and to push for the development of new markets. Afghanistan – still mainly a producer but likely to become an important consumer – has increasingly shipped opium and heroin through Central Asia because Iran, previously the primary trading route, has fought a large-scale and costly war against drug trafficking. Thailand, Burma's neighbour, has long faced the same problems and has, to some extent, diverted trafficking routes toward China, Laos, and Vietnam.

THE OLD DRUG TRAFFICKING ROUTES OF MAINLAND SOUTHEAST ASIA (Maps 2, 3, 4, 5)

With the emergence of the Golden Triangle, opiates trafficking followed the main caravan axes of Southeast Asia and Southern China. Indeed, Chinese opium was already exported to Southeast Asia at the end of the nineteenth century. And the migration of the Haw, the Hmong and other tribal populations, from China to Southeast Asia played an important role in spreading opium production within the Indochinese peninsula, aiding the emergence of the Golden Triangle by perpetuating some of the trafficking and contraband routes. The caravan tracks of the Haw, which criss-crossed Siam very early on, largely contributed in turning Thailand into a privileged hub of opium and heroin trafficking.

Mya Maung (Mya Maung, 1991) has described the diverse commercial routes that feed Burma's black market from Thailand, China and India. The towns of Mae Sai, Mae Sot and Ranong respectively in northern, western and southern Thailand, have long been the main cross-border points along Burma's eastern border. Most of the trading between Burma and Thailand occurred between Tachileck and Mae Sai until cross-border commerce began to be disrupted by ethnic rebellions and Communist guerrilla activities. Present-day trading routes, whether legal or illegal, basically follow the invasion routes used by the Burmese when they invaded and raided Siam (in the sixteenth and eighteenth centuries, for example). The route from Moulmein to Myawaddy and Mae Sot is one of the most famous of these routes, Similarly, the route followed by the Mongols when they invaded Burma in the thirteenth century has long been the main trading route between Burma (Muse) and China (Ruili). The famous Jade Road was developed at the end of the seventeenth century by Yunnanese merchants (it would later become known as the Burma Road during the Second World War) and was used to export the highly-coveted and extremely expensive imperial green jade (jadeite) from Kachin State to China, where it was known as the Stone of Heaven and is still highly prized (Mya Maung, 1991: 210–15; Walker, 1995; Frey, Lintner, 1995; Levy, Scott-Clarck, 2002). The jade mines are located in Hpakan, in Kachin State, but, after the Chinese Communist revolution, trade in the precious material was diverted from China to Thailand, through Mae Sai and on to Hong Kong, which quickly became the world's most important trading town for green imperial jade. Not long after, Hong Kong became one the world's main heroin hubs.

Thailand is regarded as the traditional outlet for Burmese opium and heroin and has long been the main outlet in Southeast Asia, at least since the emergence of the Golden Triangle and until Laos and China began to attract increasing amounts of Burmese opiates towards Hong-Kong, Macao, or Vietnam. With the emergence of the Golden Triangle after the Second World War, there were in fact two main routes that could be considered 'traditional', both much affected by historical and geopolitical developments in Southeast Asia, and both more or less replaced by new routes. The first was an air route that has largely disappeared today. The second, a ground route, changed very recently and is today of decreased importance. As for other routes, they were originally of minor importance but have since been recently and profoundly modified.

In his seminal work, *The Politics of Heroin in Southeast Asia* (1972), historian Alfred McCoy has shown how the secret wars and covert operations carried on in Laos and Vietnam first by the French and then by the United States, have stimulated opium and heroin trafficking at both the regional and global level. He reveals the role played by the CIA and its airline company, Air America, in the anti-Communist war effort of the United States as well as in the spread of heroin addiction among their own fighting troops in Vietnam. The opiates were transported by Air America (which in 1965 had replaced a French network of Corsican airmen), Continental Air Service, and Lao Development Air Service, which flew from the Long Tieng and Vientiane airports, where the heroin was supplied by Hu Tim-heng, a partner of General Ouane Rattikone, one of Laos' major opium traders and the commander in chief of the Laotian Army between 1965 and 1971. In Vietnam, the well-connected Ma brothers dealt with the Vietnamese Air Force's Vice-Marshal Ky. Later, it was General Dang Van Quang, the intelligence adviser to Vietnamese President Nguyen Van Thieu and the commander in chief of the Vietnamese navy, who took over opiates trafficking from Cambodia to South Vietnam and Hong-Kong (McCoy, 1991: 226–34; Booth, 1999: 198).

Within the context of its anti-Communist operations, the CIA played a positive if indirect role, if not in northeastern Burma's opium production then at least in the organization of its commerce by the KMT troops, which it supported in its fight to reclaim China from the Communists. The great majority of the opium traded from Burma to Thailand or Laos was handled by KMT troops after their flight from southern China to Burma's Shan State, and was secretly supported by the CIA. The caravans that transported the Burmese opium under the control of the KMT troops were largely made up of Panthay and Haw caraveners, whose mules and networks allowed such traffic in the hills and mountains of eastern Burma and western Thailand. After the 1967 'opium war' that led to the defeat of Chan Shi-fu, alias Khun Sa, in Ban Houay Xay, Laos, the KMT – according to the CIA operative William Young – controlled about 90 per cent of Burma's opium trade from its bases in northern Thailand, while the Shan caravans then only transported approximately 7 per cent of Burma's opium and those of the Kachin Independence Army (KIA), which were mostly loaded with green imperial jade, 3 per cent (Booth, 1999: 198).

The KMT established itself in the north of Thailand after its headquarters in Mong Pa Liao, along the banks of the Mekong River in Burma, were attacked by five thousand soldiers of the Burmese Army and by twenty thousand soldiers of the Chinese Communist troops, in January 1961. The nationalist troops first fled to Laos, in Luang Namtha province, but their repatriation to Taiwan, arranged by the US Department of State (whose embarrassment increased as its support for the KMT became public knowledge), was organized via Thailand. (Some of them, however, stayed in Luang Namtha until 1962, before they settled down definitively in Thailand, along Burma's border – in Mae Salong for example.) From that moment on, the KMT, which had been manipulated by the CIA, could play a similar role for and from Thailand while being in a privileged geographical position to resume its drug trafficking activities.

Thailand's history helps us to understand how the kingdom became the region's first heroin outlet after the Second World War. Thailand has long been home to the world's largest community of Teochiu peoples, or Chiu-Chao,[1] following the Chinese diaspora from Swatow, in Guangdong province of southern China. The Teochiu make up what is probably the richest and most powerful underground network in the world (Seagrave, 1995). One of the most successful of the overseas Chinese's networks, they achieved a dominant economic position in Siam as a result of the part they played in the history of the Thai kingdom, for the role of economic adviser to the Thai monarchs had long been awarded to Chinese merchants and especially to Teochiu people. General Taksin (1734–82), whose father was Teochiu, first assured his people a leading position in Siam's political and economic life by ennobling many of them after he had reunited the kingdom which the Burmese had invaded in 1767. When Taksin the Great became king of Siam in 1768, he moved the capital from Ayutthaya to Thonburi (Bangkok grew out of Thonburi) and his Teochiu advisers, be they noble or merchant, followed him en masse.

Later, during the Second World War, the Teochiu managed to secure the rice monopoly, thereby affirming their economic influence over the Hokkien Chinese[2] who, in spite of the fact that they are the world's most numerous and most widely dispersed overseas Chinese group, had significantly – as we shall see later – failed to ally themselves to the Japanese. This privileged position in the Thai politico-economic system also allowed four or five of the most important Teochiu syndicates to achieve a quasi-monopoly over the Golden Triangle's opium and heroin trafficking. Three leaders from among the main Hong Kong-based Teochiu triads of the 1970s invested largely in trafficking heroin from the Golden Triangle: Ma Sik-yu (alias White Powder Ma), Ma Sik-chun (Golden Ma), and Ng Sik-ho (Limpy Ho). Ma Sik-yu began trafficking heroin in 1967. He quickly gained direct access to the source supply, i.e. to the Golden Triangle, where he struck a deal with KMT General Li Wuen-huan, who employed him as an intelligence agent for Taiwan. Southeast Asian Teochiu triads controlled by Ma Sik-yu infiltrated the Communist groups of the region, while considerably increasing their drug trafficking activities. Thailand thus found itself at the centre of the system, benefiting both from the importance and the connections of the Teochiu community as well as from its central geographic position. Laos was also included in this system after the Ma brothers allied themselves with General Ouane Rattikone, who was supplying them with the infamous '999' or 'Double UO Globe' heroin (Booth, 1999: 195–8). It would in some ways seem that the Teochiu were almost predestined to become the main suppliers of the Golden Triangle's opium and heroin, since one of their Siamese commercial associations had very early on obtained an official licence for opium retail sales in Shanghai's French concession: the first opium retail store of Shanghai, Hongtai, was owned by Teochiu merchants.

This impressive Chinese presence, especially the importance of the Teochiu in Siam, created a climate that was ready for political change. In 1910 Rama VI came to the throne (born in 1881, he ruled until his death in 1925). Educated in the United Kingdom, far from the established customs and ways of the kingdom, he questioned the place and the role attributed to the Chinese in an iniquitous system: not only did the Chinese have a disproportionate influence over the kingdom's economy and politics but they were also taxed less than the poorest of the Thai. Rama VI directly confronted the Chinese community by publishing a pamphlet entitled 'The Jews of the East' and by abolishing the ennoblement of the Chinese (Seagrave, 1995: 191). His death, and the awkward attempts of his successor Rama VII (born in 1893, ruled from 1925 until 1932, died in 1945), to restore a bygone order, led to the 1932 coup d'Etat and spurred a Thai nationalism that eventually fully unfolded during the Second World War with the support of the Japanese invaders.

Associated with Thai nationalism, irredentism, and militarism, these developments in the history of Siam, which became Thailand in 1939, facilitated the extraordinary importance of drug trafficking in the kingdom. During the Second World War, Thailand, supported by the Japanese and motivated by a rising Thai linguistic nationalism nurtured by strong anti-Chinese feelings, annexed Burma's Shan States, where Tai languages are spoken (Shan for instance). General Phin Choonhavan[3] acted as the military governor of the Shan States, making Kengtung the headquarters of the Thai Northern Army (or Phayap Army). Phin had been part of the 1932 coup d'Etat that eventually installed Field Marshal Phibun Songkhram in power (1938–4 and 1948–57). He not only controlled the heart of what was yet to be called the Golden Triangle; he also had privileged connections with some of the most powerful of Thailand's Teochiu syndicates.

Another fundamental component of the Thai drug trafficking equation is the Japanese occupation of the region. Some of those involved in the Japanese Army's southern strike in Southeast Asia had been involved in the marketing of Manchuria's opium in eastern Asia. In the 1930s, Japan was already funding part of its Chinese military expeditions by producing and trading opium from Manchuria (Meyer, Parssinen, 1998: Seagrave, 1995; Kobayashi, 2000). During the Second World War, the Japanese traded low-grade heroin bought from the Chinese Nationalist government in order to finance their occupying army in Guangdong (Booth, 1999; Meyer, Parssinen, 1998; Seagrave, 1995). Of course, the Japanese Army had a direct interest in supporting the occupation of the Shan States by the Thai Northern Army and in encouraging its commander, General Phin, to build durable and lucrative relations with the KMT.

As a consequence, the role of the KMT in the development of the opium trade grew considerably. The Japanese had established financial links with the Chinese nationalists, and the Thai followed suit after General Phin met with General Lu Wi-eng, commander of the KMT's 93rd Division, in Yunnan, in April 1944 (Seagrave, 1995). The meeting included the ruthless Japanese colonel, Tsuji Masanobu, an Imperial Army tactician and key figure in the Japanese occupation of Southeast Asia. It had been organized in order to divert to the Japanese Imperial Army material aid from the United States (in the form of Lend-Lease Supplies) that had been intended to help the KMT in its fight against Chinese Communist troops. Five years later, when the Communist victory forced the KMT to flee to Burma, the 93rd Division took refuge in Shan State, along with its new commander, General Li Mi. The links that had been established between the KMT and General Phin proved useful, for the exiled KMT troops 'seized control of the best opium-growing areas in the Golden Triangle, and resumed a lasting military and commercial alliance with General Phin in Thailand – all made possible by Japan's wartime' (Seagrave, 1995: 159–61).

After the war, and two years of democratic transition, Phibun and his military clique returned to power. Phin became commander-in-chief of the armies, Marshal Sarit Thanarat became the commander of the First Army (thereby controlling Bangkok), and the son-in-law of Phin, General Phao Sriyanond, was made deputy director of the national police force. Phin, Phao and Sarit monopolized opium and heroin trafficking for years and turned Thailand into a regional drug-trafficking hub. Indeed, Phin and Phao won control of two of the five main Teochiu syndicates of Thailand that handled most of the opiates trade: from northern Thailand down to Bangkok's warehouses, and all the way to Singapore or Hong Kong and Taiwan. After 1948, when Phin seized power and became Prime Minister, Sarit was made commander-in-chief of the armies and Phao director-general of the police. Two rival camps formed and both men engaged in a fierce rivalry over opium and heroin trafficking.

Thus opiates trafficking became all the more important after Burma's Shan State sheltered the defeated troops of the KMT. The 93rd Division assured the transport of opium and heroin to Thailand, where Teochiu syndicates, the Thai Army and the Thai police safeguarded the shipments to their final destinations. Twenty years after Chiang Kai-shek's KMT had shared the proceeds from the Green Gang's drug trade in 1930's Shanghai, the Generalissimo and his son, General Chiang Ching-kuo, ordered General Li Mi to turn to drug trafficking.

The United States also played a notorious role in the development of the drug trade between Burma and Thailand, for the CIA chose to favour the most eager of the two competing Thai camps and supplied Phao and his police force with about US$35 million worth of equipment between 1950 and 1953. Through its front organization, known as Sea Supply Corporation, the CIA delivered material aid not only to Phao and his police but also to the KMT. In fact, the CIA provided Phao's police with the modern equipment that Sarit and his Thai Army were denied, and Phao and his Thai police protected the military shipments that the CIA was also sending to the KMT to support its hopeless attempts at reclaiming Yunnan and China (McCoy, 1991: 184). As Alfred McCoy explains:

Since Sea Supply shipments to KMT troops in Burma were protected by the Thai police, Phao's alliance with the CIA gave him extensive KMT contacts, through which he was able to build a virtual monopoly on Burmese opium exports (McCoy, 1992: 184).

However, in 1957, when General Sarit and his troops seized power from Phibun, Phao fled to Switzerland (where he died in 1960) and the opium and heroin trade fell into the hands of his long-time rival.

Post-war Thailand, therefore, emerged as a major trafficking corridor for opiates produced either in Burma or, despite Sarit's 1959 ban on opium production, in its own territory. The growing importance of drug trafficking in Thailand is clearly the direct consequence of a combination of several factors: on one hand, the deep penetration of the Thai politico-economic system by Teochiu syndicates and their use by the Thai leaders; on the other hand, the role of the Japanese occupation forces, and the evolution of the role of the KMT, firstly in China, then in Burma and in Thailand. Also, the emergence of a nationalistic and irredentist Thailand during the Second World War allowed the kingdom to play a privileged intermediary role between the KMT and Japan. This position, that Thailand's Teochiu made possible, eventually benefited their own networks and those of the Taiwan-based Hokkien, for these two Chinese communities have played a major role in the region's drug trafficking (Chouvy, 2002a: 182).

MODERN DRUG TRAFFICKING ROUTES OF MAINLAND SOUTHEAST ASIA (Maps 2, 3, 4, 5)

Thailand remained the main heroin trafficking route in Southeast Asia until the early 1990s, when a number of factors contributed to a reorientation of drug trafficking routes within Southeast Asia and to the development of new routes to other parts of the continent. The Thai crackdown on heroin trafficking after the 1984 nation-wide opium eradication campaign considerably reduced the use of its well-developed road system by smugglers and traffickers from the Thai-Burma border. Subsequent patrols of the north and northwestern Thailand borders by the Thai Third Army and the Border Patrol Police also disrupted the routes used by opium and heroin traffickers to cross the Thai-Burma border (Chouvy, 2002a: 173–99; Chouvy, 2002c).

Yet, since the mid-1990s, the old routes of the former Communist Party of Thailand (CPT) through the mountain range stretching from Chiang Mai to Lampang, as well as outposts of KMT within Thailand (Haw Division 93, for example, in Mae Hong Son province), have been widely used by traffickers mainly carrying methamphetamine. Since 1999, Thai authorities have responded to these new trends by turning their Internal Security Operations Command from an anachronistic and ineffective anti-Communist task force into an anti-drugs unit. In 2000, they also set up a Territorial Defence Training Scheme that turned about 600 border villages into anti-drug trafficking outposts (Chouvy, 2002a: 173–99; Chouvy, 2002c).

The commercial opening up of both southern China and northeast India since the mid-1980s has also allowed the emergence of new trafficking routes. Heroin trafficking has followed the famous Burma Road since at least 1985, passing through the Burma-China border posts of Muse and Ruili and continuing on through Baoshan, a nineteenth-century Yunnanese hub of opium trafficking, then through Dali and Kunming (Lintner, 1998: 172; Malik, 1995, Zhou, 1999: 115). The Chinese border, spanning 1200 km, has been increasingly traversed since Burma's junta legalized cross-border trading in 1986, and since the 1989 fall of the CPB and the subsequent appearance of the United Wa State Army (UWSA) (Renard, 1996: 62). A decade later, in May 1998, Chinese authorities estimated that at least 100 kg of heroin passed daily through Bose, in Guangxi province (Chouvy, 2002a: 173–199; Chouvy, 2002c).

Other drug trafficking routes include those through the Kambaiti Pass or, farther south, through Loije. From Yunnan, Burmese heroin can then reach eastern China and Hong Kong, to be eventually exported overseas to Australia and North America. However, large quantities of Burmese heroin are also bound for the Southeast Asian market, entering Laos through its Luang Namtha and Phongsaly provinces. China is prone to drug trafficking from Burma since its southern neighbour has an important Chinese population that consists of, among others, Panthay caravan traders, former KMT as well as CPB members and local Kokang Chinese, all of whom are involved to a greater or lesser extent in illicit cross-border activities and drug trafficking. The powerful attraction of both Hong Kong and Taiwan as major international heroin trafficking hubs is also likely to add to the appeal of the Chinese route (Chouvy, 2002a: 173–99; Chouvy, 2002c; Ko-lin Chin, Zhang, 2007). According to the results of a rare field study of drug trafficking activities between Burma and China:

> Over the past few decades, drug trafficking between Burma and China has evolved in several directions. Shipments of drugs in large quantities have largely disappeared (or perhaps are better concealed) and most drugs are moved in small quantities by large numbers of individuals, or 'mules', who know little about the organizers behind the scene. Between drug manufacturers and end users are multiple and often overlapping layers of transportation and distribution networks, each involving only a few people. These groups of 'mules' and their organizers work much like ants moving the contraband piece by piece successively from one location to another (Ko-lin Chin, Zhang, 2007: 4).

This phenomenon is not restricted to the drug trade between Burma and China: it has also been witnessed between Burma, Thailand, Laos and India.

While China is certainly the main transhipment destination for heroin from Burma, it is not the only one, as northeast India also draws some of the traffic. From poppy fields in northeast Burma, opium and heroin are transported by road, through Bhamo, Lashio and Mandalay to northeast India, which shares a 1,463 km border with Burma. Heroin trafficking across the India-Burma border was first noticed in the early 1990s, and six heroin laboratories were discovered in western Burma in 1992 (Lintner, 1998: 175). There are two main drug trafficking routes leading from western Burma to the Indian states of Nagaland, Manipur and Mizoram. The foremost route begins in Mandalay, continuing through Monywa and Kalewa, where it splits: northward, to the Tamu–Moreh border crossing and the Indian Road 39, in Manipur; and southward, to Hri–Champhai, into Mizoram (SAIN, 1998; Tarapot, 1997). Farther north, Homalin is reached via Bhamo and serves as a springboard into Nagaland, from where the heroin goes to Assam and, through Dispur, joins other shipments bound for Calcutta and the rest of the Indian subcontinent.

From Mandalay, however, Burmese heroin also goes to Rangoon, Burma's capital until 2005 and the country's largest town, either by road or by way of the Irrawaddy River. This upsurge in drug trafficking across the India-Burma border occurred in the context of a thriving contraband economy centred around Tamu/Moreh and Hri/Champhai since 1965, despite the fact that cross-border trading was finally legalized in 1995. Political and social instability, armed violence linked with autonomous rebellions as well as state repression and endemic underdevelopment and poverty, make a long and poorly manned border prone to drug trafficking as well as to the smuggling of precious stones, hardwoods (teak), gold and a variety of consumer goods (Tarapot, 1997).

'New' routes for a 'new' drug – yaa baa

The late 1990s, saw increased diversification of drug trafficking routes and illicit drug production. The explosion in methamphetamine production in Burma has led to resurgence in the use of the Thai route, since Thailand is by and far the leading consumer market of methamphetamine, or *yaa baa* as it is known. *Yaa baa* traffickers differ from others in that they are more numerous and carry small quantities of pills across the Thai-Burma border. They form what Thai authorities have referred to as an 'ant army', criss-crossing the border along countless hill paths and using small tribal villages as staging posts. The strong crackdown led by the Thai army and the police in the early 2000s in the northernmost part of the country has more recently diverted the flow of methamphetamine, pushing traffickers to use new itineraries. *Yaa baa* (but also heroin), therefore started entering Thailand from Laos through border towns such as Chiang Khong, Nan, Loei, Nong Khai, Nakhon Phanom, Mukdahaern and Ubon Ratchathani. The roads of Laos are frequently used for transporting illicit drugs bound for Thailand, even though drug trafficking using speedboats along the Mekong River, which demarcates the international border between the two countries, is the first choice. Many villages straddle the border, such as Ban Ahi in Laos – 50 km north of Loei – from where methamphetamine, locally grown cannabis, and weapons enter Thailand (Chouvy and Meissonnier, 2004).

Farther south along the Thai border and lower on the Mekong, Cambodia is also increasingly used as a staging point for trafficking methamphetamine, via Trat and Chanthaburi, into Thailand. East of Laos and Cambodia, Vietnam has similarly been turned into a drug trafficking route, either from or to China. Overseas trafficking is frequently organized from Vietnamese seaports such as Hoi Anh, Danang, Vinh and Haiphong or from the Cambodian Koh Kong province or Pochentong airport (Phnom Penh). Vietnam is also a destination for Burmese heroin, the Hekou–Lao Cai border crossing being one of the most frequently used. Even though drug trafficking routes in Southeast Asia are multiplying, traffickers continue to diversify their itineraries, some of them sometimes taking national authorities by surprise.

After the Second World War, Thailand was initially avoided by drug traffickers coming from Burma because its police and army, as well as its leaders, were notoriously corrupt: it cost the traffickers too much in bribes. Laos was thus originally used. Now, however, it is the tough anti-drug policy of the Thai authorities that is driving traffickers towards alternative routes, such as Laos and Cambodia. In 1999, for example, Thai authorities increased the number of border checkpoints along its Laotian and Cambodian borders from 100 to 269, again encouraging the traffickers to find other routes.

In recent years, routes through southern Thailand have been on the agenda of both traffickers and anti-drug forces, particularly since March 2000, when several million methamphetamine pills were seized in Prachuap Khiri Khan, having been trafficked from Kawthaung, or Victoria Point, in Burma, to Ranong province, Thailand. In January 2001, another seizure confirmed this reorientation of drug trafficking through southern Burma and Thailand. Close to eight million pills and 116 kg of heroin were seized aboard Thai fishing boats west of the Ko Surin islands, pointing to the Andaman Sea as a major drug route. Allegedly, most (80 per cent) of the drugs entering Thailand still come across the northern part of the Thai-Burma border, but the continual strengthening of Thai anti-drug initiatives has clearly fostered a wide diversification of drug trafficking routes as well as a diminution in the quantity of drugs being transported at any one time (Chouvy and Meissonnier, 2004).

Drug trafficking in post-2003 Thailand

Upon taking office in February 2001, Thailand's Prime Minister, Thaksin Shinawatra, vowed to eradicate both drug trafficking and drug consumption from the kingdom. Past efforts to do so had failed, as methamphetamine had become the country's drug of choice. One consequence of this was a rapid increase in the prison population: 'Over 7 years from 1996 to 2002, Thailand's prison population increased by 250 percent. At the end of this, in Bangkok 70 percent of prison sentences were drug-related. For the whole country the percentage was 53 percent' (Pasuk, 2003). The Thai Government launched public campaigns to reduce demand and established the death penalty for dealing in or using *yaa baa*. However, trafficking and consumption of *yaa baa* continued to increase and, on 1 February 2003, Thaksin launched a nationwide 'war on drugs' aimed at making the country drug-free within three months.

Thaksin set the tone of his anti-drug campaign when he declared, in his 28 January speech: 'Because drug traders are ruthless to our children. So being ruthless back to them is not a big thing . . . It may be necessary to have casualties . . . If there are deaths among traders, it's normal'. Pasuk Phongpaichit stresses: 'He also quoted a famous saying of a 1950s police chief known to have masterminded several political assassinations: "There is nothing under the sun which the Thai police cannot do"' (Pasuk, 2003). The Thai Government and the Thai police drew arbitrary lists of drug suspects, establishing a climate of fear that drove injecting drug users, in particular, underground. In a June 2004 report, Human Rights Watch explains: 'the government crackdown has resulted in the unexplained killing of more than 2,000 persons, the arbitrary arrest or blacklisting of several thousand more, and the endorsement of extreme violence by government officials at the highest levels' (Human Rights Watch, 2004: 1). Many of those named on government 'blacklists' and 'watchlists' had been mistakenly included or reported by personal rivals and many were killed for no reason or for reasons other than related to drug trafficking.

The 2003 Country Reports on Human Rights Practices of the US State Department criticized the Thai government for the 'excessive use' of 'lethal force against criminal suspects' and denounced the many 'extrajudicial, arbitrary and unlawful killings' that took place during Thailand's war on drugs. The report stated: 'According to official figures, there were 1,386 narcotics-related deaths between February 1 and April 30, 2003. No arrests were made in 1,195 of these cases, which led many observers to believe police were responsible for most of these deaths' (US State Department, 2004: Thailand). In answer to Thailand's human rights activists, who accused the government of unleashing a 'shoot to kill' policy and condoning the killings of suspected-only drug dealers, the government replied that many of the killings resulted from dealers fighting each other. The campaign, however, has been popular in Thailand despite the fact that only a few key drug traffickers were arrested and at least a dozen managed to flee to Burma, Laos, or even China.

Most observers agreed on the fact that 'the violence unleashed by the Thai government on 1 February 2003 created terror and confusion among drug traders and users, which – not surprisingly – had a genuine impact on the supply of methamphetamines' (Roberts, Trace and Klein, 2004: 7). Some also warned: 'the 'ya ba' problem may have – to a certain extent – been temporarily suppressed, but that it has not gone away' (ibid.). Human Rights Watch concluded in its report:

> The clearest outcome of the war on drugs was not to curb Thailand's illegal drug trade, but simply to make it more dangerous. Most drug users interviewed by Human Rights Watch reported continuing to use heroin or methamphetamines during the drug war, albeit at a higher cost and less frequently (Human Rights Watch, 2004: 1).

In late 2003, the Thai government claimed that the operation had been a 'victory beyond expectation'. However, after *yaa baa* seizures increased again in Thailand,[4] Thaksin called for a second war on drugs in October 2004, this time with much less violence and publicity, despite a few heated declarations: 'Drug dealers and traffickers are heartless and wicked. All of them must be sent to meet the guardian of hell, so that there will not be any drugs in the country'.[5] In 2005, methamphetamine was still widely produced in Burma and in the rest of Mainland Southeast Asia, where consumption continued to increase. Still, in May 2006 (a few months before he was ousted by a military junta on 19 September 2006), Prime Minister Thaksin Shinawatra 'pledged to step up the government's crackdown on drugs following complaints about the re-emergence of drugs in several Bangkok districts'.[6]

Drug trafficking and HIV/AIDS

The existence of the Golden Triangle has contributed to the considerable increase in opiates consumption among Southeast Asian populations and, even farther afield, along all Asian drug trafficking routes. In Asian countries, a correlation exists, in both time and space, between the spread of opiates trafficking, the increase in their consumption, and the surge, only slightly later, in the HIV/AIDS epidemic. The HIV/AIDS outbreak in Asia occurred between 1988 and 1990 and coincided with the multiplication and diversification of Asian drug trafficking routes – from Southeast Asia as well as from Southwest Asia – and their re-orientation towards the north, as well as with the spread of heroin addiction throughout the Asian continent.

North of Burma, the Chinese province of Yunnan has not only become the region's main drug trafficking route but also accounted for 80 per cent of all China's HIV-positive individuals in 1990. The area is now awash with Burmese heroin, and two-thirds of the injecting drug users in the Chinese border town of Ruili are HIV-positive, as is also the case in Guangxi, the next stop on the traffickers' route (SAIN, 1998).

The correlation in Yunnan between the development of heroin trafficking, the emergence of intravenous injection – nowadays the main mode of heroin use – and the near-simultaneous waves of heroin addiction and HIV/AIDS infection, can now be seen all over Asia. A similar process occurred in northeast India, where heroin trafficking from Burma quickly increased. As in China, 80 per cent of the heroin addicts in Manipur, the main drug trafficking gate, are currently infected with HIV (SAIN, 1998; Beyrer et al., 2000). Manipur is the Indian state with the largest HIV/AIDS epidemic, and it appears that the disease began to spread at a particularly rapid rate after the bilateral Indo-Burmese border agreement came into effect. Apart from law and order issues, the upsurge in heroin addiction and the raging HIV pandemic that have accompanied the development of the drug trafficking routes in southern China and northeast India now constitute one of the main challenges facing Asia, the second most affected continent as regards HIV/AIDS and the only one where HIV/AIDS first spread through injecting drug use (UNAIDS, 2000; Beyrer et al., 2000).

OLD DRUG TRAFFICKING ROUTES OF SOUTH AND SOUTHWEST ASIA (Maps 2, 6, 7, 8, 9)

Southwest Asia produced opium before Southeast Asia and its involvement in opium trading is even earlier. Opium was probably one of the many goods traded on the so-called Silk Road that linked the Greek, Arabic, Persian, Indian and Chinese worlds. Despite its name – suggested in fact only in the nineteenth-century by German geographer and geologist Ferdinand von Richthofen, who called it *seidenstrasse* (Wild 1992) – trading on the Silk Road was far from limited to silk. And neither was the Silk Road a single road, as might be imagined. In reality it was made up of a series of ancient trade routes with numerous branches that parted and re-joined, bypassing mountains and deserts, linking together oases and trading centres. The Taklamakan Desert, still one of the world's most formidable deserts, was one of the main obstacles to be avoided. The southern and the northern routes of the Silk Road, that sought to achieve this, separated and reunited from the region's main hub – the town of Kashgar, now known as Kashi, where one the largest weekly markets of all Central Asia is still held. From Kashgar, several roads led to Samarkand, the Caspian Sea via the Pamir Mountains, and even to India through the Karakoram.

Kunduz, Kabul, Peshawar and, by way of the Indus valley, the Makran Coast, all served as major relays for the early traders, who very likely contributed to the spread of opium, in the same way that pilgrims of various religions spread their faith. Christianity spread this way in its early years and Nestorianism, banned from Europe in 432 CE, spread eastwards with Persian merchants, reaching as far as China. Manichaeism, a religion born in the third century CE and preached by Mani in Persia, also spread along what would later be called the Silk Road. Of course, Islam is the religion that spread most successfully. Arab traders and sailors, who controlled the spice trade as early as 950 BCE, had visited places as far off as China and Southeast Asia long before the birth of Islam. Later, after the seventh century, the old trading links of the Arabs helped considerably the spread of their new religion. While Islam had spread to North Africa and the Middle East by military conquest, it spread to sub-Saharan Africa and to Asia, including to Southeast Asia, through the movements of Muslim traders and merchants. As Xavier de Planhol put it, Arab tribes spread Islam along caravanning routes by effectively acting as a spearhead for the Muslim faith (Planhol, 1993: 165–7).

In Asia, the spread of Islam largely occurred by way of the spice trade, and opium could well have been among these spices. It is worth noting that the term 'spices' in earlier times included far more products than it does today. Spices included incense but also ointments, flavour enhancers and many substances supposed to have medicinal or even magical properties, either to prolong life or to act as antidotes. It seems likely, therefore, that opium, long known to the Egyptians as a panacea, was traded both by the earliest Arab traders and merchants and, later on, by their descendants who had become adherents to the Muslim faith.

In the thirteenth century, the Mongol invasions momentarily but profoundly disrupted commerce along the Silk Road. Ultimately however, the unification of the many different regions achieved by the Mongol Empire gave a new boost to the trans-Asian trading and, until the empire collapsed in the second half of the fourteenth century, a number of European merchants and missionaries, such as Marco Polo and William of Rubruck, travelled all the way to China (Di Cosmo, 1999). Meanwhile, the Ming Dynasty (1368–1644), in accordance with its isolationist policies, began to reduce considerably the trade along its part of the Silk Road. As a result, after 1400, trade in silk along the Silk Road virtually stopped and the only oases and routes that remained were located in what had become Muslim areas. Western interest in these routes decreased significantly after the fall of the Mongol Empire and the isolationist policies of the Ming Dynasty.

In 1488, Bartolomeu Dias became the first European to reach the Persian Gulf by a maritime route and, in 1497, Vasco de Gama was the first European to reach India by sea. In doing so, ninety years after the Chinese Muslim eunoch Zheng He (first voyage in 1405–1407) and his sixty-two ship fleet, the Portuguese were set to initiate seaborne trading between Europe and Asia. They conquered Malacca – Southeast Asia's most prominent trading centre – in 1511, which opened up the long-coveted route to China. Canton was reached in 1513 by the Portuguese, who then turned Macao into a trade depot in 1557. From that time on, modern large scale opium trading was made possible, and especially so after the British East India Company was given trading rights by the Mughal Emperor Jahangir (reigned 1605–27) in 1617, and after the Company gained a monopoly in opium trading in Bengal in 1773.

If the Silk Road was slowly abandoned after the late fourteenth century, trading along Asia's countless caravan routes continued to develop south of the Himalayas, and opium was only one of the numerous commercial goods that were transported in South and Southwest Asia. In India, the Mughal emperors had established an opium monopoly by the end of the sixteenth century and a few of them had even become addicted to the substance. Later on, Persia became the largest opium producer and consumer market west of the Indian subcontinent. Persia was famous for its long sticks of rather low quality opium, or *trebizond*, known in England in the early nineteenth century, and, after 1870, Persian opium was exported in large quantities from Bushir and Bandar Abbas to London. The Ottoman Empire, however, also produced some of the world's most renowned opium. Opium from Constantinople was 'sold in small lens-shaped cakes covered with poppy leaves' (Booth, 1996: 10) and looked like the flat cakes of Yunnanese opium (Hodgson, 1999). Thus opium, it would appear, has been traded for a very long time along the caravan routes of Southwest Asia, Central Asia and South Asia. The importance of nomadism and the presence of numerous caravan hubs, such as the ones between Kashgar and the Makran Coast (Kunduz, Peshawar or Kabul), allowed the development of a trans-regional commerce among which opium is likely to have been included on a regular basis.

After the thirteenth century and the Mongol invasions, a characteristic feature of Southwest Asia had been its extensive and diverse nomadism, ranging from transhumant pastoralism to long-distance caravanning. In Persia, for instance, major caravan routes developed, with countless tracks criss-crossing its deserts, and connecting up with the routes of Central Asia and Asia Minor. Very early on, such caravan routes linked Meshed, in northeastern Persia, to either the Persian Gulf port of Bandar Abbas – by crossing the Dasht-e Lut desert between Birjand and Kerman – or to the cities in the foothills of the Zagros Mountains, via the oases of the Dasht-e Kavir desert (Planhol, 1993: 518; Cressey, 1960: 527).

East of Persia, the road from Mazar-i Sharif to Herat had been one of the main trading routes of the region since Greek antiquity: fresh and dried fruits, china, silk and karakul skins (a Central Asian sheep whose breeding and export provided most of Afghanistan's foreign currency in the 1970s) are among the goods that have long been traded from what is now Afghanistan. From Persia and from the Ottoman Empire, the opium trade actually developed both by land and by sea. In 1546, French naturalist Pierre Belon visited Asia Minor and Egypt and observed the extent to which Egyptians and Turks abused opium but also noticed at least one forty-camel caravan loaded exclusively with opium on its way from Egypt to Europe (Booth, 1996: 25). Caravans loaded with opium, whether exclusively or not, must also have left from Asia, at least from the Ottoman Empire, as the caravan observed by Belon suggests that a European opium market already existed as early as the sixteenth century. As far as Asia is concerned, Turkish opium was much more potent than Indian opium and most of the nineteenth-century imports made by Britain were from Turkey: opium 'could easily be exported through Smyrna, which had long been an important trading centre, used particularly by the British who had established commercial links with Turkey since the founding of the Levant Company in 1581' (Booth, 1996: 51).

Opium has also been exported from the Persian coast, where many caravan routes end – for example, in Bushir. Arab merchants in their traditional dhows plied their trade in the Persian Gulf long before they had reached Chinese ports in the sixth century, and long before they bartered 'silks and silver in exchange for "drugs of cambray, afiam, which we call opium, wormwood and saffron"' as Duarte Barbosa recorded in 1516 (Booth, 1996: 103). Later, Persian opium was traded by Arab dhows travelling from the Persian coast to Southeast Asia's European colonies, notably French Indochina.

Southeast of the Zagros Mountains, the regions of Sistan va Balochistan in Iran and Balochistan in Pakistan are inhabited by the Baloch people. The Balochi region has long been renowned as unsafe, and the early Arab geographers already spoke of its marginal groups and dreaded bandits. Here, donkeys preceded camelids as pack animals, and the Bashkard country of the Bandar Abbas region continues to use them. As for the Baloch, they opted for the dromedary, the one-humped camel of the great caravanning nomads that is still used today for trading and drug trafficking across the Balochi region (opium-loaded camel caravans are often intercepted by the Iranian soldiers and police). But, in Iran, donkeys have not been completely replaced by dromedaries, as was shown in July 2000 in the northeastern part of the country, when a donkey caravan carrying 470 kilos of opium was intercepted. For the sake of comparison, a train of 40 camels can carry up to seven tonnes of opium and there have even been stories of caravans of camels addicted to opium so that they could be sent without guides on routes they knew!

Camelids used to traffic opium, or to smuggle consumer goods between Afghanistan, Pakistan, and Iran, are extraordinarily well adapted to the sand and stone deserts of the region. From Anatolia to Afghanistan they mostly result from cross-breeding, between the two-humped Asian camel (*Camelus bactrianus*), or Bactrian camel, very well adapted to rocky surfaces and steep mountainous slopes, and the one-humped Arabian camel (*Camelus dromedarius*), or dromedary, more at ease on sandy surfaces and in desert dunes (Planhol, 1993: 51–4). Benefiting from three means of transportation particularly well adapted to their environment – the donkey, the horse and the dromedary – the Baloch very early proved to be highly mobile, migrating to the Sindh region in the fourteenth century, to the southern Punjab in the fifteenth century and eventually settling around the khanate of Kalat, in current Pakistani Balochistan, in the eighteenth century. Over the centuries the Baloch spread from the south of Central Asia (some say from Syria), to Pakistan's Makran Coast, eventually concentrating themselves in southwest Pakistan (70 per cent of the total Balochi population now live in Pakistan), southeast Iran, and southern Afghanistan (Planhol, 1993: 547–53).

Balochistan has been a region of commercial transit since at least Greek Antiquity, maybe not a major one but at least one permitting trading between the Turkish, Persian and Arabic worlds. The Arabs turned Balochistan, or more exactly the Makran Coast, into an artery of trans-regional commerce. Then, the Mughals, the Afghans, the Persians and the British – each succeeding the other in Balochistan strove to control the region by restricting access to the routes and most strategic passes that linked northern Balochistan to Central Asia: the Bolan, Khojak, Gomal (between Afghanistan and Dera Ismail Khan), Tochi (between Ghazni and Bannu) and Mula passes. The Bolan Pass is to Balochistan what the Khyber Pass is to the North West Frontier: a several-thousand-year-old invasion and trading gate.

Significantly, the Great Game started in and around Balochistan, after the British feared a Russian invasion of India by way of Herat and the Sistan region, the 'terra media' of Lord George Curzon, the youngest ever Viceroy of British India (1899– 1905) who created the North-West Frontier Province

(NWFP) in 1901 (Ispahani, 1989: 39). In 1876, in order to protect Balochistan, the British occupied and fortified Quetta (from *kwatkot*, fort, in Pashtu), a strategic town between the Khojak (west) and Bolan (east) passes that led to and from Kandahar and Herat. As for the Gomal Pass, it was protected by Fort Sandeman, formerly known as Apozai and renamed Zhob in 1970: Fort Sandeman proved strategic to the British not only because it controlled access to the Gomal Pass but also because the Zhob valley was the shortest route between the NWFP and Quetta (Elliot, 1968: 55).

To the west of British-ruled India and its North West Frontier, Russian-British rivalries focused on the two main roads crossing the area that would become known as Afghanistan after the mid-nineteenth century. At the time, these roads were renowned historically as invasion and trade routes; now they have become avenues for smuggling and trafficking, notably for consumer goods and opiates. They both start from Herat and either cross the Hindu Kush to reach Peshawar by way of the Khyber Pass, or skirt round its southern foothills to reach Quetta, by way of Kandahar and the Bolan Pass. However, if the region's early opium commerce most likely occurred along the so-called Silk Road of Central Asia, the closing of lower Central Asia after the 1873 Russian conquest of the Khanate of Khiva and the ensuing rivalries between the Russian and the British brought all exchanges between Central and South Asia to an end. By 1894, with an imposed customs union between Russia and Bukhara and the deployment of Russian garrisons on the southern borders of the emirate, Central Asia became isolated from South and Southwest Asia. Borders were not only drawn but long-standing traders of the silk roads, such as the Turkmen, were forced to abandon their nomadic way of life and to settle (Choukourov, 1994: 51). Later, when Communist China sealed off Chinese Turkestan (present-day Xinjiang), the closing of the high passes of Kan Kuch Kach and Khotgaz interrupted the centuries-old trading and communication between Kashgar and Yarkand (Dichter, 1967: 27).

However, in the nineteenth century, Central Asia was not producing opium in significant quantities and its commercial isolation had no significant impact on the rapidly growing world trade in opiates. From the Pontic Mountains to the Pamir Knot, the south of the Caspian Sea and the Yunnan Plateau, the opium trade was limited to South Asia in the broad sense (from Turkey to Vietnam by way of India), with its only northern extension being in China. Indeed, the Russian southward push to the north of Turkey, in the Caucasus and in Central Asia, had interrupted the commercial and cultural links which had long existed between northern Asia and southern Asia, reorienting commerce and trade along East–West axes of communication by ground and even more by sea. That part of Asia under Russian influence increasingly differed from that under British influence, where commerce and trade in Indian opium grew rapidly. The three zones of the Asian geopolitical system that would later be described by Alastair Lamb were already taking shape: the Russian Zone, the Chinese Zone and the Southern Zone extending from Iran to the European colonies of Southeast Asia (Lamb, 1968: 17–18).

Afghanistan, this buffer state created by the Great Game played by the Russian Empire and the British Empire, is the country that suffered the most from this imposed east-west caesura across Asia. Imperial politics of access, or rather, of its denial, had Russia and England terminate their railways exactly at Afghanistan's northern and southern borders, therefore isolating a landlocked country. South of the Himalayas, the opium trade has been influenced by the closing of what has been called the 'soft under-belly' of the Russian Empire: from the Ottoman Empire, later Turkey (1923), and from Persia, opium trading developed southward, eastward and westward, to feed the consumption of the Europeans themselves (England, France) or of their colonial empires (French Indochina). Later, during the Cold War and the Soviet-Afghan war, Afghanistan would not only become a leading opium producer but would also contribute to the fall of the Soviet Union. Eventually, the Central Asian republics would become independent and the opiates trade would, at last, spread northward, all the way to Moscow and Siberia.

MODERN DRUG TRAFFICKING ROUTES OF SOUTH AND SOUTHWEST ASIA (Maps 2, 6, 7, 8, 9)

Afghan heroin and the drug trafficking routes that bring it into Europe are becoming an increasingly serious problem, especially given that the European Union is extending membership to eastern European states through which Afghan heroin transits. After the fall of the Taliban regime, and more than five years into a new democratic Afghanistan, Afghan production and trafficking has reached unprecedented levels (Chouvy, 2006c). An examination of the trafficking routes taken by Afghanistan's opiates suggests that the task of curbing the entry of Afghan drugs into Europe is a complex one. Since the fall of the Taliban, the pattern of opium production has undergone significant change within Afghanistan and trafficking routes have evolved to reflect these changes. The post-2001 rise of the northeastern province of Badakhshan as a major production centre, for example, clearly put more pressure on Central Asia as a main drug trafficking route, especially after the estimated 200 per cent increase in volumes traded in 2002. The Pakistani and Iranian routes are also still plied by drug traffickers, in spite of close monitoring and patrols along the Afghanistan-Pakistan border, US Special Forces included.

The Pakistani route

Heroin and opium have long been exported to Pakistan through the North-West Frontier Province and Balochistan. One of the main opium markets in eastern Afghanistan was, until it was closed down in April 2002, in the village of Ghani Khel, southeast of Jalalabad, the capital of Nangarhar, one of the main opium-producing provinces of Afghanistan. Less convenient, at least until the closure of Ghani Khel, were the two other regional markets of Achin and Kahi, located farther away than Ghani Khel from the Kabul-Jalalabad-Peshawar road. According to the UN, in southern Afghanistan, where most of the opium production is concentrated (in Kandahar and Helmand provinces), the opium market was less centralised than in the north (Nangarhar), where the Pashtun tend to monopolize the trade (the Shinwari tribe in Afghanistan and the Afridi in tribe in NWFP). In the south, Sangin, in Helmand province, was the largest opium market in 2002, followed by Musa Qala, north of Sangin (UNDCP 1998; Chouvy, 2002a: 210–12).

Northern Afghanistan's regional market has long been dominated by the heroin trade, mainly because of the leading role taken by both the Shinwari and the Afridi in heroin production. In the south of the country, the principal trade has been in opium and morphine base (which is converted into heroin using acetic acid anhydride), mostly conducted by Balochi and Pashtun merchants who are not members of the Afridi and Shinwari tribes. The result has been heroin trafficking on a larger scale in NWFP and Central Asia than in southern Pakistan (Balochistan) and Iran, where seizures have tended to relate to opium and morphine base. Heroin was easily trafficked in NWFP from Afghanistan across Afridi territory and the Khyber Pass, through what has been termed a 'drug pipeline' (UNDCP 1998; Chouvy, 2002a: 212–13). However, matters evolved after 2003 as the political normalization process in Afghanistan (as we shall see later) increasingly involved individual warlords and commanders, concentrating and consolidating the networks and organization of opium trading and trafficking.

The closing of the opium markets in the south, significant international and law enforcement pressure in the east, and the greater secrecy under which opium trafficking and trading now operate, have led to important shifts in the last few years in how and by whom the illicit drug market is controlled (Shaw, 2006: 204).

Among other changes, one of the most significant has been the influence of drug traffickers from southern Afghanistan in the north of the country, where poppy cultivation strongly increased during 2005 (Balkh, Sari Pul, and Samangan). Opium produced in the north of Afghanistan, but not in the northeast (Badakhshan), is now sent to the south by traffickers from the southern provinces who refine it into heroin to be sent to Iran, either directly or by way of Pakistan (Shaw, 2006: 207).

Balochistan province, in southern Pakistan, shares a 1,200km border with Afghanistan including two of that country's largest opium-producing provinces, Helmand and Kandahar. Significant quantities of opiates go through Balochistan to the Makran coast, where thousands of fishing boats and cargo and passenger vessels navigate. However, opium, morphine base and heroin also cross into Iran from Balochistan. Balochistan is thus at the crossroads of Afghan opiates trafficking and is plied by countless caravans of camels, crossing the deserts of Afghanistan, Pakistan and Iran by night. Groups of drug traffickers form relays; for example, from Afghanistan to Panjgur in Pakistan, then to Turbat and eventually to Mand, Pasni or Gwadar. Dalbandin, in the Chagai Hills, is a major centre of regional drug trafficking from Afghanistan to the Makran Coast or to Iran, with the Balochi said to take a leading role in the trade (Chouvy, 2002a: 212–13).

The Indian route

Heroin is imported into Pakistan either to supply its large domestic market or for despatch to destinations farther afield. India is one such destination, with heroin arriving into the country through Punjab, Rajasthan and Gujarat: the districts of Jaisalmer and Barmer, in Rajasthan, have long been among the traffickers' favourite crossing points as the Thar Desert offers many hideouts for illicit drugs, which are often buried in the sand before being retrieved and moved about within the country. The single train link between the two countries – the Samjhauta Express between Lahore (in Pakistan), and Amritsar (in India), has largely been used by drug and counterfeit currency traffickers. Amritsar, in Punjab, has long been an important node in the drug trafficking routes to India – or at least since it emerged as such in the context of Pakistani secret services support for Sikh separatism. After 1992, when Sikh militancy died down and insurrectionary violence increased in Kashmir, Indian drug seizures revealed a sudden increase in Afghan and

Pakistani heroin moving through Jammu and Kashmir, mainly via Ranbirsingh Pura, Samba and Akhnoor. Acetic acid anhydride also goes through these areas, although in the opposite direction: from India – an important industrial manufacturer – to Pakistan and Afghanistan (Chouvy, 2002a: 208–20).

The Iranian route

Iran is arguably the main route for Afghan opiates trafficking, across its Khorasan and Sistan va Balochistan provinces. In Khorasan, opiate seizures by Iranian authorities usually account for about 40 per cent of all such seizures worldwide, with the country as a whole accounting for 85 per cent of such seizures (UNODC). Iran shares borders with both Afghanistan and Pakistan and is a strategic outlet for Afghan opiates on their way to the main consumer market: Europe. A 2,440 kilometre-long coastline also makes Iran a natural springboard for maritime drug trafficking, towards the United Arab Emirates and East Africa. Iran's borders with Afghanistan and Pakistan, are manned by 30,000 law-enforcement personnel, who have a wide variety of means at their disposal to help counter trafficking – such as patrol roads, concrete dam constructions, ditches, sentry points, observation towers, barbed wire, electrified fences and electronic surveillance devices. Iran says it spends US$ 400 million annually on anti-drug operations and has, so far, invested over US$ 800 million in efforts to improve control over the Afghan border (Chouvy, 2002a: 208–20).

In Iran, as well as in Pakistan, trafficking and anti-drug trafficking operations are characterized by their extreme violence: drug traffickers are typically armed with weapons such as rocket-propelled grenade launchers, and large-scale battles are regularly waged with Iranian law-enforcement authorities. In Khorasan alone, in 1999, some 285 drug traffickers and 33 members of the Iranian armed forces were killed during such engagements. In November of the same year, 35 policemen were killed in Sistan va Balochistan during a single engagement with Pakistani drug traffickers. Overall, in twenty years of anti-drug operations, Iran has lost more than 3,500 men on active duty.

Iran's anti-trafficking efforts have been subsidized by the United Kingdom, Germany and Switzerland. For years now, the USA has recognized in its annual International Narcotics Control Strategy Report (INCSR) that, although Iran is 'a major transit route for opiates smuggled from Afghanistan and Pakistan', it is pursuing 'an aggressive border interdiction effort' (US State Department, 2005). Despite its efforts, Iranian authorities estimate that

65 per cent of the trafficking in Afghan opiates goes through their territory. As opium production is concentrated in southern Afghanistan, the Iranian route remains the major route through to Turkey and Eastern Europe, where heroin laboratories are known to operate, and thence to the European Union (Chouvy, Labrousse and Koutouzis, 2003).

It also seems that heroin has been increasingly shipped across the Iran–Iraq border since the fall of Saddam Hussein. More than a decade of economic sanctions helped create efficient smuggling networks in the country and even the dictator's security apparatus in Basra was allegedly involved in smuggling activities and drug trafficking. The demise of Hussein's regime and the ensuing civil war and internal chaos led to a weakening of border controls and a rise in illicit trading. In Jordan, seizures of illicit substances significantly rose after Iraq's 2003 US-led invasion. Seizures of Captagon pills – the trademark name of fenetylline, a central nervous system stimulant similar to amphetamine – rose in Jordan after 2003. According to the US State Department, Syrian traffickers used Iraq's weak borders to ship Captagon to Jordan and to Saudi Arabia and the Gulf states where the drug is very popular among rich party crowds. Seizures of heroin and marijuana, but also of cocaine, have increased in Iraq since 2003 and officials of Iraq's Ministry of Labour and Social Affairs are said to have also noticed rising consumption trends within the country, thereby echoing concerns by UNODC officials. In 2007 and 2008, anecdotal reports also suggest an emerging opium production inside Iraq, on well-irrigated lands along the Euphrates and north-east of Baghdad, along the Iranian border.[7]

The Turkish route

Afghan opiates enter Turkey mostly from Iran, through the provinces of Igdir, Agri, Van and Hakkari. In August 1999 Turkish authorities seized 500 kg of heroin in Agri. However, Turkey is not only an entry point and transit route for heroin: it is also home to many heroin refineries. In March 2000 three tons of morphine base were seized in Iran, between Yazd and Kerman, supposedly on the way to Turkey. In May 2000 the Turkish police found 250kg of morphine base in Baskale, in the province of Van, close to the Iranian border, while drug traffickers were arrested in Istanbul with 80 kg of heroin destined for the UK. Such shipments of morphine base or even opium from Afghanistan to Turkey via Iran are increasing, reinforcing the belief that heroin production occurs in Turkey as well as eastern European countries, before being traded on the European consumer market (Chouvy, 2002a: 217–18).

The Central Asian route

In the 1990s, the UN estimated that Central Asia was the outlet through which 65 per cent of Afghan opiates passed. This estimate was largely exaggerated and the UN now estimates that only 15 per cent of Afghan opiates are trafficked through Central Asia, entering the region mostly through Tajikistan. With the demise of the Soviet Union in 1991, Afghanistan saw its northern border split three ways, between Turkmenistan, Uzbekistan and Tajikistan. The old silk roads were revived and Afghan opiates were quickly taken through this northern outlet. In the late 1990s, Rashid Alimov, then Tajikistan's UN representative, went as far as saying that his country was a victim of an 'opium tsunami' and 'narcotic aggression'. Tajikistan claimed to have witnessed a 250 per cent increase in drug trafficking between 1998 and 1999 alone. His Uzbek counterpart, Kamol Dusmetov, reported a 600 per cent increase for the same period, while in Kyrgyzstan the interior minister reported a 1,600 per cent increase in illicit drugs seizures between 1999 and 2000, including an 800 per cent increase in heroin alone (Chouvy, 2002a: 208–20).

Tajikistan, – in the throes of civil war between 1992 and 1997 – became the main corridor for Afghan opiates intended for the emerging Russian market and the traditional European market. From Ishkashim to Nijni Pandj, drug trafficking was fast developing across the Amudarya (formerly Oxus) River, turning Khorog into the main transit town from where heroin reaches Dushanbe, the Tajik capital, Osh in Kyrgyzstan and the Ferghana valley. Afghan opiates then go west, to the Caspian Sea, Azerbaijan and Georgia, or north, through Kazakhstan and on to Russia.

Turkmenistan has also become a major passageway for Afghan opiates. Many major seizures have occurred in Kushka, the main border post between Afghanistan and Turkmenistan. In the second half of the 1990s, the re-opening of the Quetta-Kandahar-Herat-Ashgabat road by the Taliban, partially financed by the Pakistani (Pashtun) mafia, considerably helped the development of drug trafficking in Turkmenistan. However, it is through Tajikistan that trafficking has increased most in the immediate post-Taliban years. Indeed, after the Taliban proscribed opium production in 2000, the 2001 harvest was a mere 185 tons, and of this, only 35 tons were produced in Taliban-held areas, while 150 tons came from Northern Alliance-controlled regions. In northeastern Afghanistan – mainly in Badakhshan – opium poppy cultivation more than doubled between 2000 and 2001.

Increased drug trafficking through Central Asia and opium production in Afghanistan has encouraged heroin consumption along drug trafficking routes. Intravenous heroin use has surged both in Central Asia and Russia, as far as Novosibirsk and Irkutsk in Siberia, where heroin first appeared in

1999. Russian and Kazakh authorities mention the leading role of Tajik drug traffickers in the regional trade: one-third of traffickers arrested on the Dushanbe-Saratov train are Tajik, and Russian police forces in Irkutsk have declared that they seized heroin in trucks driven by traffickers suspected of being Tajik special services personnel. According to the Russian interior ministry, in 2000 half the heroin entering Russia was arriving through Kazakhstan: shipments crossed via Troitsk (in Chelyabinskaya oblast) to go to Iekaterinburg, or via Orenburg and Oral, to Samara. Further east, Barnaul is a trafficking relay before Novosibirsk and, eventually, Irkutsk (Chouvy, 2002a: 221–39).

OF ROUTES, FRONTIERS AND BORDERS: THE POLITICS OF ACCESS

Many of the trafficking routes of the Golden Triangle, the Golden Crescent, and their peripheries are major axes of the caravan trade of former days, which have been maintained despite long and complex political and territorial changes. Although some of these routes have been regularly used since antiquity, others have fallen from use at different times. Crowded or abandoned, roads, tracks, trails, paths, all kinds of communication channels, wherever they run (dried up river beds, hilltops, mountain slopes, rivers, etc.), are potential trading routes and, therefore, drug trafficking channels. Routes provide access and are fundamental not only to travellers and traders but also to smugglers and traffickers. Routes and access prove fundamental, indeed, not only to drug trafficking but also to drug production. In the overall context of the global prohibition of certain drugs, agricultural drug production (i.e. drugs that are produced through agriculture – such as cocaine, opium, heroin, hashish, etc. – which is very different from synthetic production) has increasingly been concentrated in remote regions where the writ of the states does not extend or is limited: hilly and mountainous areas, naturally, but also far more accessible areas of countries or states at war that lack the will, means or ability to renounce or to forbid illicit agricultural drug production. While few routes and limited access tend to play in favour of illicit agricultural drug production, traffickers still need to get the opium and heroin to market, whether national, regional, or global. Drug production and drug trafficking therefore depend upon a fine balance between inaccessibility and accessibility.

Mahnaz Ispahani explains: 'since routes perform in both the crucial spheres of state activity, security and development, they are an ideal instrument by which also to reveal the qualitative relationship between these two facets of state policy' (Ispahani, 1989: 2). Insecurity, violence, and economic underdevelopment often characterize areas of illicit agricultural drug production. Quite significantly, the relative lack of routes leading to or coming from these areas reveals, and also explains, the negative relationship between security and development. Ispahani further explains how a route is 'both a geographical and a political idea, both an end and a means'. Her study of the politics of access in the borderlands of Asia draws on the work of the French geographer Jean Gottmann, who stated that 'one of the major aims of politics is to regulate the conditions of access'. Ispahani then contrasts the antiroute – that is, 'any natural or artificial constraint on access' – with the route: 'antiroutes create pressure against movement – they limit, restrain, or 'channel' it – where routes facilitate broader movement' (Ispahani, 1989: 2–3). Antiroutes, whether determined by relief features, climatic conditions, border regulations, customs tarrifs, political enmities, or armed conflicts, 'may serve the same human purposes as routes', that is, to regulate the conditions of access. Indeed, 'what routes move, and what antiroutes prevent from moving, are people and goods within and across frontiers' (Ispahani, 1989: 2–3). And routes are consubstantial with borders, since 'without land routes, borders cannot be defined and secured'. Ispahani continues: 'Whereas states cannot come into existence without the ability to deny access, they cannot be physically consolidated and politically sustained without the ability to expand access – without the extension of the authority and the legitimacy of the center to the peripheries' (Ispahani, 1989: 7).

Trading and, of course, trafficking and smuggling have always largely depended on routes and borders, that is, on access, whether granted or denied. A border, through its definition and its delimitation processes, modifies the very nature of any traditional trading that preceded its imposition. In fact, for many merchants, activities suddenly termed smuggling or trafficking are nothing else than traditional trading turned illegal or traditional goods turned illegal; for instance 'what is now called smuggling was normal among the Pashtun nomads of eastern Afghanistan for many generations' (Canfield, 1986: 97). Indeed, according to a Pakistani Afridi from the North-West Frontier Province (NWFP) of Pakistan: 'You might call what we do smuggling. But to us, it's just trade' (Edwards and Baumann, 1977: 122). Between Afghanistan and Pakistan, as well as between Burma and Thailand, imposed boundaries cut through frontier zones and tribal land, changing frontiers into borders and creating de facto jurisdictions – in effect, bounded legal territories. But boundaries also affect the very nature or existence of routes. For example, 'a road through tribal territory is much more than an avenue of mobility. Here the laws of the state intersect with the laws of the tribe' (Ispahani, 1989: 141). As David Ludden puts it, since 'modernity consigned human mobility to the dusty dark corners of archives that document the hegemonic space of national territorialism [. . .] we imagine that mobility is border crossing, as though borders came first and mobility second' (Ludden, 1994).

As Lord Curzon, Governor General and Viceroy of India remarked, 'the earliest frontiers "erected a barrier or created a gap": that is, restricted movement and access' (Ispahani, 1989: 3). What was true in the borderlands of Southwest Asia, and for its borderlanders, can also be observed in the frontier area that stretched between Burma and Siam in the nineteenth century. When the British raised the question of the western frontier of Siam, in the early nineteenth century, no document or treaty identifying and delimitating the boundary could be provided by the local chiefs: 'as these were friendly neighbors who shared understanding and trust, one local chief replied, the boundary did not forbid people to trespass or to earn their living in the area' (Thongchai, 1994: 73). The borders were even said to be 'golden, silver paths, free for traders' and 'the tribal people wandering in the mountain forests were subjects of no power' (Thongchai, 1994: 73). Far from being boundaries, borders were then frontiers. Lord Curzon depicted this 'widely diffused type of ancient Frontier' as 'the intermediary or Neutral Zone': 'This may be described as a Frontier of separation in place of contact, a line whose distinguishing feature is that it possesses breadth as well as length'.[8]

Despite the fact that Southeast Asian frontiers had long been areas linking policies rather than separating them, boundaries were imposed on trans-frontier routes (Chouvy, 2002a). Colonialism and, later, nationalism, required having boundary lines clearly demarcated: 'The major principle behind the Asian frontier system was recognition of the desirability of avoiding direct contact between the administered territories of the various colonial empires concerned' (Lamb, 1968: 62–3). In Asia, where the power over individuals was traditionally separated from the power over land, since a subject was bound first and foremost to his lord rather than to a state, modern boundaries have 'violently and arbitrarily' divided 'ethnic peoples into different nationals' (Thongchai, 1994: 164). Hence, the 'external', or alien, may not really be external, 'while the "internal" can be made alien or external' as evidenced in Thailand, where many tribal people have spent decades waiting for Thai citizenship and thus have never 'belonged' to any state or nation (Thongchai, 1994: 170).

As far as the symbiotic relationship between routes and borders is concerned, Willem van Schendel and Itty Abraham explain how 'the act of enforcing a selected flow of people and objects across a border, from border patrols to customs, immediately allows for the possibility of rents to be charged for circumventing these rules and by the same token provides opportunities for smuggling of people and objects across these borders'. Of course, 'The weight of enforcement is directly related to the prices that can be charged for getting around it – the risk, uncertainty and demand for these flows 'across the border' all go into making the border a site for illicitness, from an economic point of view'. But, it is also important to understand that 'making borders also makes illicit the life activities of border communities' (Schendel and Abraham, 2000).

Not surprisingly, all kinds of smuggling and trafficking flourish in these old frontier areas that often became buffer zones, as is still the case between Burma and Thailand: the border not only affords some protection (from political oppression, economic distress, or even law enforcement) for the refugees who cross it, it can also help enrich those who do not travel 'empty-handed'. Thus, a route and an antiroute can engender one another: a closed border can engender a route to transgress it and the rules and restrictions it implies; the presence of a route can call for an artificial antiroute (a checkpoint for example) to monitor or restrict access. Hence the ever-growing diversity of smuggling and trafficking routes and techniques that arise as a consequence of growing markets and increased controls.

If routes are a means of physical access which make communication and transport possible, if they are vectors of integration, or of assimilation, sometimes even of alienation, then antiroutes are the opposite: they hinder access, either naturally or artificially. Antiroutes are a means of isolation, of exclusion, or alternatively of preserving autonomy. Routes and antiroutes have in common the fact that they are strategic and political tools that reveal past and ongoing power struggles. Access is granted or refused but only very rarely is it a given. Drug trafficking thrives according to such geographical and political dimensions. In the context of illicit economies, antiroutes, natural or artificial (customs, police, relief, natural environment), call for routes (avoidance or crossing routes), and routes call for antiroutes (checkpoints, fences, etc.) because, according to the words of Schendel and Abraham, 'making borders engenders illicitness' and, according to Janet Roitman, whom they cite, 'transgression is productive' (Schendel, Abraham, 2000). Hence the diversification and increasing complexity of unlikely or unexpected drug trafficking routes that result from artifical antiroutes. Hence, also, the increase in human and material means devoted to anti-trafficking activities along national borders (checkpoints and border patrols) and at strategic crossroads (harbours, airports, railway and bus stations). Traffickers and state authorities vie for control of routes and antiroutes (corruption may allow traffickers to avoid checks and controls) in their respective attempts to secure territories. Thus, trafficking and anti-trafficking activities depend on, and call for, two conflicting territorialization agendas and processes. Of course, the level of territorial control is constantly adjusted, as it depends on the human and material means deployed by each side and, therefore, on the overall power balance between them (Chouvy, 2002a: 259–64).

6. Naresuan Task Force outpost on the Thailand-Burma border, Chiang Rai province, Thailand.

6

War, Drugs, and the War on Drugs

In Burma and in Afghanistan the opium economy has been partly responsible for financing the war efforts of some of the opposing factions, and the strong synergies that exist between civil war economies and drug economies have weighed heavily upon the two countries' potential for political and economic development. As well as allowing and even encouraging a prolongation of conflict and making any resolution of crises all the more difficult, the conflict/drug 'synergy' has also laid the foundations for a criminalization of these countries' peace economies, so potentially compromising their internal peace and security.

These links between the war economy and the opium economy have certainly had a destabilizing effect in the recent histories of Afghanistan and Burma. But while the opium economy has surely helped perpetuate the Afghan and Burmese conflicts, it was not the cause of them, and the two countries' ongoing politico-territorial and economic crises do not result from it – at least, not directly. Neither was it simply a matter of the opium economy bankrolling the warring factions: it also enabled some of the countries' farmers to survive as best as they could during long periods of economic depression. As Jonathan Goodhand writes, 'opium is simultaneously a conflict good, an illicit commodity and a means of survival' (Goodhand, 2005: 211).

Synergies between war economies and drug economies are nothing new and the oldest documented case of an Asian civil war financed (at least to some extent) by proceeds from opium dates back to China in the late 1910s when Yuan Shikai, the second president (1912–16) of the Republic of China, carried on the opium suppression campaign started by his predecessor. After his death in 1916, however, and the subsequent breakdown of the central government, former warlords-turned-military governors split into countless factions and warlordism emerged once more. During this period, 'narcotics provided a means to finance the expensive arms and ammunition required to survive as a warlord', and 'opium revenue became a major financial resource for warlords, mainly through "fines" on cultivation, trafficking, selling, and smoking' (Meyer and Parssinen, 1998: 143; Zhou, 1999: 40). In the late 1920s, 'the escalating cost of warfare forced even the most reluctant and high-minded politicians to turn to the opium business for revenues' and even Chiang Kai-shek, despite his hostility to morphine and heroin, was forced to 'acknowledge opium's significance' in order to consolidate his power in the country (Meyer and Parssinen, 1998: 158, 154). Later, in the mid-1930s, the Nationalists – confronted with increasing international and national pressure – launched a nationwide anti-drug campaign that eventually failed. However, as historian Zhou Yongming stresses, such a move was again strategically motivated, as it was in part designed to 'consolidate the power of the central government nationwide by cutting off the revenue sources of regional powers' (Zhou, 1999: 78). Then, as historians Kathryn Meyer and Terry Parssinen explain:

> It was in this hothouse, created by China's disintegration and the League's successes, that gangsters and politicians molded the modern international narcotics trafficking industry. The symbiotic relationship between trafficker and politician that has become the dominant feature of the contemporary drug trade has its roots in Asia in the early twentieth century. The men in the shadows succeeded because they structured their careers with webs of smoke at the point where profits and power converge' (Meyer and Parssinen, 1998: 12).

However, symbiosis between drug traffickers, politicians and other power holders, and synergies between war economies and drug economies, only developed fully during the Cold War.

THE COLD WAR AND THE RISE OF OPIUM PRODUCTION IN ASIA[1]

The Cold War played a direct and prominent role in the production and trafficking of illicit drugs. Indeed, the financing of many anti-Communist covert operations, such as those led by the CIA, derived from the drug economy that existed in various proxy states where trafficking was often condoned and even encouraged. Specific historical examples illustrate how the anti-Communist agenda of the CIA played a decisive role in stimulating the global illicit drug trade. These include the French Connection and the role of the Corsican mafia against Communists in France and in Southeast Asia (Laos and Vietnam), the propping up of the defeated KMT in northern Burma, the Islamic mujahideen resistance in Afghanistan and, on another continent, the Contras in Nicaragua (McCoy, 2003).

The United States, as the leader of the global struggle against communism, made extensive use of its special services and intelligence agencies to conduct covert operations worldwide. In the global struggle to contain communism, local aid was needed and widely found in the form of local criminal organizations. The first such case dates back to the early 1930s, when New York's organized crime kingpins – Salvatore Lucania, aka Charles 'Lucky' Luciano, and Meyer Lansky – trafficked heroin exported from China to support Chiang Kai-shek's KMT in the civil war there. Luciano was jailed in 1936 in the United States, not long before trafficking in Chinese heroin was considerably disrupted by World War II.

It was during World War II that the American Office of Naval Intelligence cooperated with Luciano: he was to be freed after the war so long as he ordered his thugs to watch US docks and ports to protect them from Nazi saboteurs. Then, the Office of Strategic Services (OSS), the precursor to the CIA, used mafia assistance in the Allied invasion of Sicily. Such activities initiated what was to become a long-term feature of covert operations led by United States intelligence services when consent of the United States Congress could not be obtained: the enlistment of nefarious groups engaged in illicit activities in order to wage secret wars through both proxies and alternative funding. Basically, drug traffickers were useful to special services and politicians, and in turn relied on such connections to expand their activities.

Luciano was freed in 1946 and sent to Sicily where he was to cooperate with the CIA. Indeed, to counter the growing communist influence in France and Italy, the CIA turned to the mafia and condoned its drug trafficking activities. The CIA soon asked Luciano to use his connections in France to break the strikes led by socialist unions in Marseille's docks, from which arms and supplies were sent to Indochina. The sometimes violent assistance of Corsican mobsters in cracking down on the unions was especially motivated by their involvement in the opium business in Indochina and by the smuggling of raw opium from Turkey to Marseille, where it was refined into heroin for export to the United States. Luciano took advantage of such high refining capacities and helped turn Marseille into the heroin capital of Europe. These Marseille syndicates, dubbed the 'French Connection', supplied the United States heroin market for two decades.

But it is in Southeast Asia, Southwest Asia, and Latin America that the CIA most significantly influenced the illicit drug trade. Its anti-Communist covert operations benefited from the participation of a number of drug-related combat units who, to finance their own struggle, were directly involved in illicit drug production and trafficking. The CIA's backing of different groups in the drug trade (for example, the Hmong in Laos, the KMT in Burma and the mujahideen in Afghanistan), inferred that the agency condoned the use of drug proceeds and the increase in opiate production in Asia. However, no evidence has surfaced to suggest that the CIA condoned or facilitated the export of heroin to the United States or Europe, as clearly happened with cocaine and the Nicaraguan Contras.

In October 1949, the Communists defeated the KMT in China, and in the years that followed they cracked down on what was then the world's largest opium production network. Opium production then shifted to the mountainous and frontier areas of Burma, Laos, and Thailand, where KMT remnants had fled and become deeply involved in drug trafficking. Beginning in 1951, the CIA supported the KMT in Burma in an unsuccessful effort to assist it in regaining a foothold in China's Yunnan province. Arms, ammunition, and supplies were flown into Burma from Thailand by the CIA's Civil Air Transport (CAT), later renamed Air America and, still later, Sea Supply Corporation, created to mask the shipments. The Burmese Army eventually drove KMT remnants from Burma in 1961, but the latter resettled in Laos and northern Thailand and continued to run most of the opium trade.

CAT not only supplied military aid to the KMT: it also flew opium to Thailand and Taiwan. There is no doubt that the CIA sanctioned both the KMT's involvement in the opium trade and the use of CAT (and later Air America aircraft) in that trade. The KMT would eventually enlarge its role in the opium trade after the CIA's withdrawal of financial and logistical support. Burma eventually became one of the world's two main opium producers.

Following the French defeat in Indochina in 1954, the United States gradually took over the intelligence and military fight against Communism in both Laos and Vietnam. It also took over the drug trafficking business developed by the French by buying the opium produced by the Hmong and Yao hill tribes in return for help with counterinsurgency operations against the Viet Minh. To meet the costs of this war, the French secret intelligence service, the SDECE (Service de documentation extérieure et de contre-espionnage), had allied itself with the Corsican syndicates, trafficking opium from Indochina to Marseille in order to gain control of the opium trade that the colonial government had outlawed in 1946. The CIA ran its secret army in Laos, composed largely of Hmong tribesmen led by General Vang Pao. Air America would fly arms to the Hmong and fly back their opium to the CIA base at Long Tieng, where Vang Pao had set up a large heroin laboratory. Some of the heroin was then flown to South Vietnam, where part of it was sold to US troops. After the Americans pulled out of Vietnam in 1975, Laos became the world's third largest opium producer and retained this rank until the mid-2000s.

However, Vietnam was not the only battleground of Cold War drug operations. The CIA launched a major new covert operation in Southwest Asia in the early 1980s to support Afghanistan's mujahideen guerrillas in their fight against Soviet occupation. United States President, Ronald Reagan, was determined to counter what he viewed as Soviet hegemony and expansionism, a goal shared by his CIA director, William Casey. To support the mujahideen with arms and funds, the CIA turned to one of Pakistan's intelligence services, the Inter-Services Intelligence (ISI). The ISI chose which Afghan leaders to back and used trucks from Pakistan's military National Logistics Cell (NLC) to carry arms from Karachi to the Afghan border. However, the ISI not only chose Gulbuddin Hekmatyar, an important Afghan opium trafficker, as its main beneficiary: it also allowed NLC trucks to return from the border loaded with opium and heroin. After the Soviet withdrawal from Afghanistan in 1989, United States aid to the mujahideen stopped, and the internecine conflict that ensued in the country favoured an increase in opium production in order to maintain rival warlords and armies. Afghanistan eventually became the world's leading opium-producing country.

As Jill Jonnes puts it:

> In the years before World War II, American international narcotics policy had been extremely straightforward. The United States was righteously against anything that promoted or sustained the non-medical use of addicting drugs. But the Cold War created not only new national security policies, but a new shadow world that accepted a far more ambivalent attitude toward drugs and drug trafficking (Jonnes, 1996: 164–5).

Illicit drug production and trafficking increased during the Cold War. During this period, the United States government was less interested in waging the 'war on drugs' begun in 1971 by Richard Nixon than in using drug traffickers to support its wars and proxies abroad. Indeed, had the CIA cracked down on drug trafficking during the Cold War, it would have forgone valuable intelligence sources, political influence and much needed funding for its covert, and sometimes illegal, operations. Ironically, there is no evidence that the Soviet Union or its secret intelligence agency, the KGB (Komitet

Gosudarstvennoy Bezopasnosti), resorted to drug sales to fund activities during the Cold War.

Thus, after the modern international narcotics trafficking industry emerged in pre-Second World War China, and after communism had enabled the People's Republic of China to suppress local opium production, trafficking and consumption, it was the Cold War fight against communism that provided the justification for using proceeds from opium production and trafficking to finance covert operations and secret wars. In the third edition of *The Politics of Heroin*, Alfred McCoy writes:

> Rhetoric about the drug evil and the moral imperative of its extirpation has been matched by a paradoxical willingness to subordinate or even sacrifice the cause for more questionable goals. The same governments that seem to rail most sternly against drugs, such as Nationalist China in the 1930s and the United States since the 1940s, have frequently formed covert alliances with drug traffickers (McCoy, 2004: 459).

In his effort to reveal the extent of the 'CIA complicity in the global drug trade' McCoy then explains that 'nowhere is this contradiction between social idealism and political realism more evident than in the clash between prohibition and protection during the cold war' (McCoy, 2004: 459). However, the end of the Cold War would not reduce illicit opium production in Asia, as the end of foreign subsidies to warring Afghan factions largely stimulated opium poppy cultivation in Afghanistan. During most of the twentieth century, wars and conflicts fostered illicit opium production and made peace-building more difficult, as war economies and drug economies fed each other in a vicious circle.

WAR AND ILLICIT AGRICULTURAL DRUG PRODUCTION

Of course, illegal agricultural drug production is not restricted to Asia. Vast expanses of coca and of cannabis, but also of opium poppies, exist in the Americas (including large-scale outdoor and indoor cannabis cultivation in the United States and Canada) and in Africa (widespread but as yet unestimated – except in Morocco – cannabis cultivation). Of course, illicit cash crops are usually more profitable than local food crops or even other possible licit cash crops, and it is tempting to suggest that people resort to them simply out of economic considerations. But the fact is that illicit cash crops proliferate, above all, at times of armed conflict (Afghanistan, Burma,

Colombia) or times of social and political upheaval (sub-Saharan Africa, Bolivia, Morocco and Peru), which compromise the controls necessary to enforce the rule of law (Chouvy and Laniel, 2006). Illicit cash crops are thus not only – and perhaps not mainly – the result of economic problems. Instead they thrive in political contexts marked by the use of force and violence (and its consequences), and by complex and often trans-national power struggles. This is precisely how opium production was first commercially developed in Asia: in the context of colonialism and of early globalization.

War played a very early role in the spread of opium production and consumption in Asia, as evidenced by the two 'opium wars' waged in the nineteenth century by the British against Imperial China. Later, opium economies largely contributed to sustaining war and even to making it profitable; in turn, war, and the political and territorial disruptions it caused, made illicit opium production easier and, sometimes, necessary. In Asia, opium production clearly thrived in the two countries that underwent the continent's longest-lasting wars: Burma and Afghanistan.

It seems, therefore, that war best explains the success of Afghanistan's and Burma's illicit drug economies. But what of economic problems? In fact, simply to suggest that illicit drug crops prosper on the ruins of under-development proves much harder. It is easy to observe that economic underdevelopment and poverty are not burdens endemic to areas of illicit agricultural drug production and that they cannot explain its emergence and perpetuation in a systematic way: in Asia as well as in Latin America (mostly Colombia and Mexico) illicit opium production is much more concentrated and localised than poverty. Concurrently, illicit agricultural production is far from being restricted to the developing world or to countries at war – Canada and the United States are among the world's leading producers of illicit marijuana (both indoor and outdoor cultivation). Reportedly, the market value of US-produced marijuana exceeded US$35 billion in 2005, which is more than the country's most profitable staple crop – corn – for the same year (US$23 billion) (Gettman, 2006).

The overlap that may be observed between areas of underdevelopment and areas of illicit agricultural drug production is not of itself a satisfactory explanation of the latter. Indeed, if economic underdevelopment were to be the main cause of illicit opium production many more countries would resort to the production of illicit drugs, especially in Asia, where history and ecology would make Central Asian, Chinese and Indian production all the more easy.

Equally, it does not seem that the other argument frequently advanced to explain the appeal of the opium economy – that of an economic strategy designed by dominated and marginalized ethnic minorities – has any more validity than that of poverty. While opium production in Asia is almost exclusively undertaken by tribal people, opium farmers differ greatly in Burma, Laos and Thailand, where they all belong to ethnic minorities, and in Afghanistan, where it is the largely dominant (politically, culturally and demographically) Pashtun people, one the world's largest tribal groups, who resort to opium poppy cultivation (other ethnic / tribal groups also produce opium).

Economics and ethnicity, therefore, do not survive examination as unique causal factors leading to illicit agricultural production. And even ecological or more classic geographical factors fail to explain why specific groups/peoples in some countries resort to opium production and why it is not more widespread. In Southeast Asia, opium production occurs in ecological milieus and geographical environments that are very different from those of Afghanistan. The heavily rain-fed highlands of Southeast Asia where opium is produced lie in the far peripheries and borderlands of Burma, Laos and Thailand, while the main opium-producing areas of Afghanistan are largely, but not exclusively, located in much drier lowlands, irrigated or not. Ecological and geographical constraints are definitely worse in Southeast Asia's hills and mountains, where most people rely almost exclusively on rain-fed agriculture, suffer from a lack of access to regional markets and do not have many other cash crop opportunities than the one offered to them by opium.

What changed the 'hill tribe economy from subsistence agriculture to cash-crop opium farming' (McCoy, 1991: 119) in Southeast Asia in the 1940s is similar to what spurred large-scale commercial opium production in Afghanistan in the 1980s and 1990s: war. Whether through the strategic use of opium and opium producers (the Hmong in Laos and the mujahideen in Afghanistan), or through physical destruction (of orchards, irrigation channels, landmines in Afghanistan), or both, war has turned opium production into a source of funds for military commanders and warlords faced with financial shortages, and into a coping mechanism for farmers confronted with a new war-driven market and with war-induced physical and economic disruption.

There clearly exists, therefore, a strong correlation between war economies and drug economies, most notably in Burma and in Afghanistan. Although opium production predated the Burmese and Afghan conflicts, the wars and internecine conflicts that plagued both countries clearly stimulated opium production. In return, opium production helped perpetuate the Burmese and Afghan conflicts by making them economically viable. However, as the polemologist[2] Gaston Bouthoul warned, long before the World Bank economist Paul Collier argued that 'greed considerably outperforms grievances' in triggering and perpetuating civil wars, 'one should not confuse the economic aspect of conflicts with their necessity or their economic fatality.' (Collier and Hoeffler, 2001; Bouthoul, 1991: 226). Indeed, the Burmese and Afghan conflicts obviously did not start because of opium production, for their causes were much more complex and deeply rooted. The key causes of large-scale illicit opium production in Burma and Afghanistan lie in the pre-existence of opium production in both countries, in the trans-nationalization of their conflicts (mainly by the Soviet Union, the CIA, China, the CPB, and the KMT), and finally in the necessity of both countries' belligerents to find alternative financial resources after foreign subsidies and support were cut off.

War alone, however, cannot satisfactorily explain the emergence or the development of illicit opium production. While the cost of war may explain such recourse in Burma and in Afghanistan, the case of illicit cannabis production urges some caution. Cannabis cultivation and hashish production developed considerably in Morocco during the last decades of the twentieth century until, interestingly, the 2003 crop equalled that of the opium poppy in Afghanistan in 2004: 134,000 hectares of cannabis were reportedly cultivated in 2003 in Morocco (UNODC, 2003d), while opium poppies covered 131,000 hectares in Afghanistan a year later. The comparison is all the more striking since both countries hold almost the same area of arable land (Afghanistan holds 12 per cent of arable land (7.8 million ha) and Morocco, whose territory is smaller, holds 19 per cent of arable land (8.5 million ha)).

Yet, hashish production in Morocco differs greatly from opium production in Afghanistan and Burma, or even from coca production in Colombia, for no armed conflict challenges the writ of the Cherifian kingdom over its territory (Chouvy and Laniel, 2006). Although cannabis cultivation is illegal in Morocco, a complex set of colonial, political and economic factors has resulted in an entrenched tolerance of hashish production in the northern region of the country, the Rif Mountains. The Rif is one of the poorest regions in Morocco and its tribal Berber population has long resisted foreign and even Arabic rule, eventually obtaining a de facto tolerance of cannabis cultivation by the Moroccan state that obviously saw the large hashish econ-omy as an alternative to regular economic development (Chouvy, 2005c). Both ecologically and economically, cannabis cultivation and its rapid increase in the Rif Mountains during the last decades are understandable. The Rif is densely populated and is one of the most unsuitable regions of Morocco for intensive agricultural production: a rugged relief of steep slopes and poor soils, with heavy but irregular rainfall compounded by a lack of irrigation infrastructure, make most crops other than cannabis not worth much.

Though war cannot explain Morocco's large-scale illicit agricultural drug production, other features previously identified in Afghanistan and in Burma are also present in Morocco: poverty, geographical and ecological constraints and problematic inter-ethnic relations make up a complex set of factors highly favourable to the production of an illicit cash crop. And although Moroccan cannabis cultivation has not developed in an armed conflict context, it is (at least to some extent) the consequence of tense and violent relations, and there has been at least one full-blown war (the Rif War: 1921–6) between the Cherifian state and the Riffian Berbers. What the Moroccan example shows is that a crop whose production benefited both the French and the Spanish Moroccan Protectorates (economically and strategically) became entrenched in one of the poorest and most restive areas of the country (Chouvy, 2005c). Cannabis cultivation was only really prohibited in 1954 in the French Protectorate and in 1956 in the Spanish Protectorate, at independence.

Long term consequences of war and low intensity conflict have made the Rif perhaps the largest region of hashish production in the world. Without an ongoing war in the Rif to explain its current existence and importance, illegal cannabis cultivation appears to be tacitly tolerated by the state, whatever the reason: either because the state benefits economically and strategically from it, or because it does not have the means to control its own territory and to impose its writ over it. Most likely, the reality lies somewhere in between: since independence, the Moroccan state has not had the political and economic means to prohibit and/or eradicate cannabis cultivation in the Rif, nor has it had the means to promote economic alternatives to a rapidly-growing and profitable hashish industry. Corruption has, of course, played a large role in the development of cannabis cultivation, and many drug-related scandals have rocked the state's administration in the past years. Ultimately, what explains the huge extent of illicit cannabis cultivation in a country at peace – such as Morocco – is the failure of the state to control its territory, by economic development, political integration and law enforcement. Most likely, the Moroccan state has lacked the authority, legitimacy and capacity to impose the rule of law over its entire territory, or to formulate adequate strategies and carry out reforms.

In Burma and Afghanistan war has played a fundamental role in the development of illicit opium production and it is highly doubtful whether their output would have reached such levels if they had not been at war for so long. Although under-funded wars clearly favour a resort to informal and illicit economies (both by civilians and the military), it is not war per se that makes large-scale illicit agricultural production possible – it is the lack of state territorial control that war implies. While opium production preceded war in Burma and Afghanistan, and developed as its drug economy helped to perpetuate war, it does seem, if we draw upon the experience of Burma, Afghanistan and Morocco, that illicit agricultural production has a tendency to outlive war and to complicate the transition from war economy to peace economy. Worse, it is likely that the forced suppression of illicit agricultural production without adequate compensation and alternatives may well threaten the old status quo, as in Morocco, or compromise peace-building and state-building, as in Burma and Afghanistan.

DRUGS AND WAR: THE 'WAR ON DRUGS'

In 1971 United States President, Richard Nixon (1969–74), launched a 'war on drugs' that, after it successfully addressed the issue of Turkish opium production, 'defined the character of subsequent drug wars by applying the full coercive resources of the United States government to eradicate narcotics production at its source' (McCoy, 2004: 47). However, this extremely expensive US-led war on drugs, denounced at length by McCoy (2004) and many others, not only failed to achieve both US and UN objectives of global interdiction and suppression of certain drugs, it produced many 'unintended consequences' (Tullis, 1999) and even proved counterproductive. As McCoy stresses,

> after 30 years of failed eradication, there is ample evidence to indicate that the illicit drug market is a complex global system, both sensitive and resilient, that quickly transforms suppression into stimulus (McCoy, 2004: 96).

Reduction and even suppression of drug supplies in producer countries have been the guiding ideals as well as the ultimate goals of the global prohibition regime and of the war on drugs (Bewley-Taylor, 2001). Yet almost forty years of war on drugs have in fact been accompanied by expansion of illicit opium poppy cultivation in Asia and Latin America, of coca in South America and of cannabis cultivation worldwide.

Acknowledging this failure has proved difficult for national and international agencies and other bodies involved. Thus, in the 2006 edition of its annual *World Drug Report* the United Nations stated: 'there is less land under coca and opium cultivation today than a few years ago, and significantly less than a century ago' (UNODC, 2006c: 1). Indeed when Charles Henry Brent in 1906 called for an international conference to enforce anti-opium measures in China (convened in Shanghai in 1909), the Middle Empire contributed 85 per cent of the 41,624 tonnes of opium reportedly produced worldwide. Yet, at that time, a nationwide opium prohibition campaign was just about to start in China and the size of the Chinese crop was still a direct consequence of the opium trade imposed during previous decades by colonial powers. Prohibition and forced suppression were yet to come. Thus, in comparing the 2005 global opium crop to the 1906 global opium crop, the United Nations did nothing more than compare the results of one hundred years of global prohibition – i.e. of the accumulated efforts of the League of Nations, its own efforts and more than thirty years of a US-led war on drugs (since 1971) – with the results of two 'opium wars' (1839 and 1856) and the unequal treaties they imposed upon China. Comparing the outcomes of decades of coerced Chinese opium production with a century of coerced suppression in order to claim success in the global prohibition of drug production could be easily viewed as misleading.

Of course, comparing the 2005 global output of illegal opium (4,620 tonnes) to that of 1970 (1,066 tonnes) would have made much more sense, as 1970 can be said to be a significant year in the history both of prohibition and of the war on drugs: the Single Convention on Narcotic Drugs had already been adopted (in 1961) and the Nixon administration was to launch its global war on drugs only one year later. Yet, it would have proven much more difficult for UNODC to claim that 'drug control is working' and that 'the world drug problem is being contained' (UNODC, 2006c: 1). Rather than address what the Transnational Institute denounced in 2006 as 'scientific insults',[3] UNODC reiterated its claims of success in 2007, when its Executive Director, Antonio Maria Costa, asserted: 'there is a clear correlation between UN-led drug control efforts and a perceived 'recession' in the drug economy', even though the *World Drug Report* 'fails to document the existence of a recession'.[4] Meanwhile, the International Drug Policy Consortium (IDPC), a global network of NGOs and professional networks specializing in issues related to illegal drug use, stated in a briefing paper that, 'in keeping with previous World Drug Reports', the 2007 edition 'contains much useful data and analysis, but its credibility is undermined by the selective use of the available evidence to support questionable claims for the success of the UN track record in tackling illegal drug markets' (IDPC, 2007: 1).

Obviously nothing has changed since 2000, when the US anti-narcotics annual budget was much lower than it is now, and when historian Ted Galen Carpenter, among others, was already drawing attention to the fact that 'as is so often the case with failing wars, fanatical proponents prefer escalation to surrender or even a compromise settlement', notably by seeking 'additional increases in an already bloated budget' (Carpenter, 2000). In fact, as many observers have noted, 'the Drug war has achieved a self-perpetuating life of its own', for 'rather than reassess the failure of US prohibition policies, [US] federal officials blame smaller countries with meagre resources for the problems in their inner cities and suburbs' (Blumenson and Nilsen, 1998: 38; Davenport-Hines, 2001: 348). This is why drug war politics have been described as a 'politics of denial' (Bertram, Blachman, Sharpe and Andreas, 1996). Despite its gigantic yet unmeasured global cost (around US$ 50 billion spent annually by the United States alone in the 2000s), the war on drugs has not only failed to reduce both the surface area dedicated to illicit drug crops and the quantities produced; it has also encouraged their spread worldwide, and done much to contribute to the militarization of many countries and areas of production (Chouvy and Laniel, 2006).

The war on drugs indeed 'precipitated a qualitative shift toward the militarization of police power, making it difficult to say where domestic policy ends and foreign policy begins' (Marez, 2004: 4). After Richard Nixon launched his war on drugs – what he termed America's 'second civil war' – a large bureaucratic apparatus was established, developed and funded by successive US presidents. In 1973, the Drug Enforcement Administration (DEA) was created and took over federal drug enforcement policies in the United States from the multiple law enforcement and intelligence organizations previously responsible. Not unexpectedly, as both a product and a means of a largely failing war on drugs, the DEA also failed in its mission, both nationally and globally. Yet, as the war on drugs failed so the DEA became larger and richer. As illicit opium production increased from 1,066 tonnes in 1971 to 6,610 tonnes in 2006 (UNODC, 2007a: 40), so the DEA grew from 1,470 special agents in 1973 to 5,320 in 2006 and its budget increased from US$65 million to US$2.4 billion (1 billion in 1995).[5] The case of the DEA alone shows how the war on drugs 'keeps a vast military and bureaucratic machine humming' and demonstrates how 'source control' has an addictive quality in itself' (Naím, 2005: 80). As of 2007, the DEA had 86 foreign offices in 62 countries: therefore, as a 'hybrid of a national police agency and an international law enforcement organization' that has a 'mandate and a mission effectively authorized by international conventions and the United Nations', the DEA 'plays a unique role in international politics', notably as a tool of US foreign policy (Nadelmann, 1993: 129). In fact, since the early 1970s and the beginning of the war on drugs, 'the United States has made overseas source control an explicit and central part of its foreign policy' (Naím, 2005: 80), promising and delivering military, technical and financial support to those countries cooperating in the US-led war on drugs, whilst chastising and imposing sanctions upon the countries that do not.

The cooperation of foreign countries is sought, and sanctioned, by the United States through a yearly certification process that (supposedly) influences its foreign policy and international commercial relations according to the anti-narcotics policies and efforts of foreign governments. Mandatory sanctions are applied to 'major illicit drug producing countries' and to 'major drug-transit countries'. Sanctions take the form of the withdrawal of most US foreign assistance not directly related to counter-narcotics programs and of US opposition to loans to these countries from multilateral development banks. Major illicit drug producing countries are those with 1,000 or more hectares of illicit opium poppy or coca under cultivation and 5,000 hectares or more of illicit cannabis under cultivation. However, inclusion in the list, or the implementation of the so-called mandatory sanctions, may be reconsidered if 'substantial efforts to address the problem' are asserted or if assistance to a given country 'is vital to the interests of the United States'.[6] Enacted by Congress in 1986 under the Reagan administration, the certification process has been largely denounced as ineffective (along with the war on drugs, the DEA, etc.) and highly hypocritical. Beyond the fact that the United States is one of the world's leading consumers of illicit drugs and is home to large-scale production of cannabis and methamphetamine, its certification process is clearly biased along dubious foreign policy lines. Mexico, for example, 'to date . . . has always been fully certified, although the degree of its actual cooperation with the US and commitment to drug control were questionable' (Spencer and Amatangelo, 2001). David Bewley-Taylor, the author of *The United States and International Drug Control*, explains how 'US narcotic diplomacy can ultimately be understood as the product of oscillation between two forces', which he terms as 'American moral idealism' and 'political realism': 'despite the rhetoric and fundamental assumptions of the moralistic American approach to the foreign policy concerning narcotics, realist concerns for national interest influence the contours of drug control abroad' and have often 'eclipsed the desire for international drug prohibition' (Bewley-Taylor, 2001: 11, 12). Of course, one of the most obvious conflicts between moral idealism and political realism occurred during the Cold War, with the 'subordination of US narcotic foreign policy to a desire to contain communism' (Bewley-Taylor, 2001: 13).

Interestingly, the world's foremost illicit opium producer – Afghanistan – has been certified since the fall of the Taliban, notwithstanding its rapidly increasing poppy cultivation and despite numerous allegations of government corruption and the alleged funding of terrorism by the illegal Afghan opium economy. On the other hand, Burma, where illicit opium poppy cultivation had fallen by 85 per cent between 1993 (the year of Burma's record high opium crop) and 2006, was said by Presidential Determination n° 2006–24 to continue posing 'a threat to Asia'. No mention is made of the large reduction in illicit opium poppy cultivation documented by both UNODC and the US Department of State (International Narcotics Control Strategy Report) in recent years. Instead, Burma is blamed for methamphetamine production and for failing 'demonstrably to make sufficient efforts during the last 12 months to meet its obligations under international counter-narcotics agreements and US domestic counter-narcotics requirements'.[7] Afghanistan is part of the democratization, state-building agenda and counter-terrorism efforts of the US administration, while Burma – a military dictatorship with a long record of human rights violations, and an ally of China – remains a pariah state. It would seem that strategic, geopolitical and economic considerations carry greater weight than strict counter-narcotics objectives in the US certification process.

While such cases further erode the credibility of a certification process that is largely denounced as ineffective in the first place, they nevertheless legitimize and reinforce the US-led war on drugs, since certification 'allows the US government to place the blame abroad without taking a serious look at the failure of US efforts to curb demand' (Spencer and Amatangelo, 2001). The certification process also plays an important role in increasing the funding of national and international prohibition programmes. According to the White House Office of National Drug Control Policy (ONDCP), 'the budget for prevention programs increased by only 33 per cent between 1994 and 2001 while funding for international drug control programs increased by 175 per cent, and spending on interdiction increased by 68 per cent' (Spencer and Amatangelo, 2001). The failure and adverse effects of the war on drugs are not only felt in producing countries where it is waged as part of US foreign policy: they are also felt within the United States, where the 2007 US Conference of Mayors adopted a resolution not only denouncing the fact that a drug war that costs US$40 billion annually has failed to cut drug use or demand, but also calling for a 'new bottom line' in drug policy.[8]

THE MILITARIZATION OF THE WAR ON DRUGS

The war on drugs took on full significance during the mandate of US President Ronald Reagan (1981– 9), i.e. when investment in police and military action was increased and made easier. The war on drugs really deserved the label 'war' after Reagan further militarized it. The Posse Comitatus Act barred the military from involvement in domestic law enforcement, so in 1981 amendments were adopted in order 'to enable the military to assist law enforcement agencies in the enforcement of the drug laws' (Carpenter, 2000). Later, in 1986, Reagan added substance to the 'war on drugs' metaphor 'by issuing a presidential directive that drug trafficking constituted a national security threat' (ibid.). The militarization of the war on drugs increased considerably during the Reagan years though it did not abate (much to the contrary, in fact) under succeeding US administrations. In fact, this militarization of counter-narcotics operations occurred not only in the United States but also abroad, where billions of US dollars were, and continue to be, spent, especially in Latin America but also in Asia. From the US Marine Corps patrolling the border with Mexico to prevent illegal drugs entering the United States, to the delivery of military helicopters to the Burmese military dictatorship (prior to the bloody put down of street protests in 1988), to the US-financed Plan Colombia, and finally to the setting up and funding of Afghan paramilitary counter-narcotics units, the US-led war on drugs in reality became a war waged with weapons.

Yet many observers of the militarization of the war on drugs have questioned the semantics and the conduct of such a war. Commented Milton Friedman in 2000:

How can there be a war on drugs? Can there be a war on stones, on buildings, on aspirin? Surely, wars are on living, not inanimate, objects. And this war is being waged on people' (Friedman, 2000).

The war on drugs is indeed a war waged not against drugs but against people, among them the cannabis, coca and opium farmers – people who, understandably, are likely to resist forced eradication of their crops. Coercion, source-supply reduction and suppression programmes are essentially violent in nature, requiring as they do police and/or military force for implementation. Being far more than simply a metaphor, the war on drugs implies suppressing illicit agricultural drug production rather than understanding and addressing its very causes. The war on drugs does not target the causes of illicit agricultural drug production but, in reality, illegal farming and 'incriminated' farmers – in accordance with what Nixon called for in 1967 when he declared that 'the country should stop looking for root causes of crime and put its money instead into increasing the number of police' (Davenport-Hines, 2001: 338).

The militarization of the war on drugs is therefore a direct consequence of the criminalization of the cannabis, coca, and opium farmers that prohibition brought about. Illicit farmers are only one of the enemies that Nixon referred to when he called for 'a total war against drugs': i.e. 'a war on all fronts against an enemy with many faces' (Davenport-Hines, 2001: 339). While the war on drugs is therefore clearly a misnomer, it is also an ill-designed, inefficient and counterproductive policy: illicit cropping is an economic activity that should be addressed through economic and political measures and not through military means. Worse, as illicit agricultural production occurs mostly in the context of war economies, the war on drugs increases violence and the availability of its means (arms and weapons), and potentially reinforces the nexus between the drug economy and the war economy instead of promoting peace and development.

Militarization of drug-trafficking interdiction in Southeast Asia

In Asia, prior to the most recent developments in Afghanistan, the US-led war on drugs had been located mainly in Burma and in Thailand. The United States gave economic aid to Burma after independence in 1948, when the country was no longer a British preserve and when anti-Communist sentiments and fears motivated United States foreign assistance to Asian countries (Burma was the first country to recognize the People's Republic of China). However, the United States was not only concerned with the 'perceived threat of Chinese expansion' but also – at least after the CIA supported the KMT – with the trade in heroin produced from Burmese opium: 'stopping the production and supply of opium [. . .] became a US priority' (Steinberg, 2006: 224). Between 1974 and 1978, the United States provided Burma with eighteen helicopters to intercept opium caravans (McCoy, 2004: 429). Although 'the equipment was to be used solely for antinarcotics activities [. . .] it became apparent that it was used against the Karen rebels, who shot one down, and also used to transport military officials on non-narcotics-related trips' (Steinberg, 2006: 224). Between 1974 and 1988, the United States concluded fifteen bilateral agreements with Burma and attributed US$86 million to Burmese counter-narcotics programmes, 'including fixed-wing aircraft and communications equipment that supported Burmese military operations, called Mohein, which were directed against [heroin] refineries and base camps near Tachileck, just opposite Thailand's northernmost point' (Renard, 1996: 51–2).

Between 1985 and 1988 the United States supported the use of 2,4-D, a common systemic herbicide, in the Kokang region of Burma, one of the earliest instances of aerial spraying against drug crops. (Mexico's aerial fumigation started in 1977.) The experience proved problematic and controversial (as it would do later in Columbia and Afghanistan), since 'in 1987 Burmese pilots were unwilling to fly over opium-growing areas in the Trans-Salween areas (such as Kokang), apparently because they feared anti-aircraft fire' (Renard, 1996: 68). Although the spraying programme was over a very limited period of time, controversies relating to health issues arose and rumours spread of pilots being bribed to spare certain fields. Additionally, people from Upper Burma who were affected by the aerial spraying (and whose insurgents had a history of conflict with the Burmese military) reportedly perceived it as being an 'act of war' – hence, understandably, the fears of pilots involved in crop spraying. In fact, many observers believe that the efforts made by Burma in the 1970s and 1980s 'were made more to impress the international community and facilitate resistance against insurgents than they were to fight narcotics' (Renard, 1996: 53). In 1988, the United States cut off all aid to Burma, including counter-narcotics aid, after the violent suppression of street demonstrations in Rangoon. Since then, however, 'some funds contributed by the United States to the UNDCP central budget' have been 'meant specifically for the purpose of freeing up other funds for use in Burma' (Renard, 1996: 105).

After 1988, the US Drug Enforcement Administration responded to the difficulties of implementing supply-reduction programmes in Burma. It did so by building up its partnership with Thailand's counter-narcotics and security forces along Thailand's border with Burma, although this actually did more to diversify and complicate drug trafficking itineraries than it did to stop the inflow of heroin (and later of *yaa baa*) into Thailand. Large-scale corruption of the Thai police and military, however, thwarted US drug interdiction and suppression efforts during the 1970s and 1980s as the DEA was forced 'to outbid the traffickers for police services' (McCoy, 2004: 413). Yet Thailand's strategic imperatives also played a major role in allowing the development of opium production and trade in the region, for until 1990 the Thai military used opium warlords and their armies as proxies for securing its rather volatile border with Burma. Thus, in Thailand, the war on drugs suffered from the strategic imperatives of the Cold War and the containment of Communist insurgencies, and from the strategic imperatives of the centuries-old hostility towards Burma.

Thailand's counter-narcotics programme had started in 1969, although forced eradication was not brought in before the 1980s, once highland development projects had been implemented in poppy growing areas (Renard, 2001: 169–70). Alongside this development-orientated 'thirty-year journey' toward opium reduction (Renard, 2001), an enduring war on drugs nevertheless took place in Thailand, although it started more as a war against insurgents than as a war on drugs. This war against insurgents had started as a war against communism, and the Thai military set up alliances with the Nationalist Chinese of the KMT who had settled in Thailand after having been pushed out of Burma (1961), but also with Khun Sa's Shan United Army (SUA). In fact, in 1977, ten years after the Opium War that had set Khun Sa and General Li Wen-huan's KMT troops against each other, the Thai military tried to counter the threat posed by the Burmese Communist Party (BCP) by extending its support of General Li's opium trafficking KMT troops to Khun Sa's SUA, and by fostering an alliance between both armies.

Under an agreement reached with the Thai military, 'Khun Sa was allowed to maintain a caravan camp just inside Thailand, at Ban Hin Taek, a base that he used to control about 40 percent of Burma's opium exports' (McCoy, 2004: 428). However, Khun Sa became an international embarrassment for Thailand after he dubbed himself 'King of the Golden Triangle' in the Thai press (1977) and boasted that he was able to 'stop the drug flow' (1978). Under orders from Thailand's Prime Minister, Prem Tinsulanonda (1980–8), the Thai air force first tried to dislodge Khun Sa by bombing Ban Hin Taek in July 1980. Eventually, 1,500 elite Thai Rangers, backed by the air force, expelled him from his Thai stronghold in January 1982. Within a year, however, Khun Sa 'had rebuilt his heroin redoubt just across the Thai border from Mae Hong Son at Homong, a bastion where he would remain for the next fourteen years', that is until his 1996 negotiated surrender to the Burmese military (McCoy, 2004: 429).

After the demise of Khun Sa and the surge in methamphetamine trafficking from Burma, Thailand's war on drugs evolved toward interdiction and the interception of heroin and methamphetamine trafficking, as Thailand's opium poppy cultivation came under control in the 1990s and was almost suppressed in the 2000s (Chouvy and Meissonnier, 2004). In November 2000, the head of the Thai National Security Council identified drug trafficking as the major threat to Thailand's national security, and various Thai officials blamed the situation on neighbouring Burma and denounced Rangoon's 'narcotic aggression' against Thailand. Methamphetamine seizures had doubled between 1996 and 1997 (1.5 tonne), between 1997 and 1998 (2.8 tonnes), and again in 1999 (4.5 tonnes). During the same period, heroin seizures had declined by almost 30 per cent, with only 511 kg confiscated in 1998. This increase in methamphetamine trafficking coincided with an increase in violence along the Thai-Burma border, where numerous incidents of differing intensity led to major crises between the two countries. The northern portion of the border area was the scene of repeated armed confrontations between the pro-Rangoon UWSA and the Shan State Army-South (SSA-S), one of the last armed resistance movements opposing Rangoon's authority. Farther south, a war was being waged between two factions of the Karen insurgency movement: the pro-Rangoon Democratic Karen Buddhist Army (DKBA) and the Karen National Union (KNU). Fighting between the UWSA, the SSA-S, and the Burmese military, but also between the DKBA, the KNU and the Burmese military led to an increased militarization of the border region by the Thai military.

Efforts to protect Thai territory overlapped with the war on drugs, as complex relationships between cross-border violence, drug trafficking and insurgency exacerbated one another. As Thailand saw matters, drug trafficking had replaced communism as the main security threat, a view that was reinforced when traffickers actually started using paths formerly used by the Communist Party of Thailand in order to cross illegally into Thai territory. In keeping with their view, Thai authorities turned their main anti-Communist body, the Internal Security Operations Command (ISOC), into a dedicated counter-narcotics unit (Chouvy, 2002a: 183–4). In the early 2000s, this unit became the final component of a large defence system made up of the ISOC, the Border Patrol Police (set up by the CIA in the early 1950s), the Third Army[9] and the National Security Council (Chouvy, 2002d).[10] In the meantime, the Third Army launched its Territorial Defence Training Scheme, a programme intended to strengthen the Thai-Burma border, by arming 592 border villages and training them for self-defence against incursions of armed groups and drug traffickers. In 2001, the Thai government, which hosts the annual Cobra Gold military manoeuvres with the United States Army, set up a special fighting force dedicated to counter-narcotics operations along the border. Task Force 399, based in Mae Rim (Chiang Mai) and made up of 200 men from the Thai Special Forces and Border Patrol Police, was assisted by twenty instructors from the United States Special Forces 1st Group. Allegedly used by the United States to supply military equipment and covert drug interdiction training to Yawd Serk's SSA-S (opposed to Rangoon and the UWSA), Task Force 399 was dismantled in October 2002 after Rangoon complained about its 'provocative actions' and denounced it as an impediment to friendly Thai-Burmese relations. However, as it does elsewhere to support its global war on drugs, the United States not only offered technical and financial aid to Thailand's counter-narcotics programmes but also directly improved the drug-interdiction capacity of the Thai military by providing it with military equipment, such as expensive Black Hawk helicopters. Yet, in the early 2000s, the UWSA reportedly acquired Chinese surface-to-air HN-5N missiles (Chouvy, 2002a: 170–1), thereby increasing the militarization of drug-trafficking and drug-interdiction groups on each side of the border.

Despite its heavy militarization and incarceration rate, Thailand's war on drugs failed to reduce – or even contain – drug trafficking and drug use in the country. Despite this, the war continued, reaching a climax in 2003, when the country's Prime Minister, Thaksin Shinawatra (2001–6), vowed to eradicate both drug trafficking and drug use from the kingdom. In 2003, Thailand's war on drugs in reality became a war on people, for about 2,000 were killed in extra-legal shoot-to-kill police operations that led even the US State Department to denounce the many 'extrajudicial, arbitrary and unlawful killings'. Yet, the terror that the 2003 war on drugs provoked throughout the country only temporarily disrupted the drug trade, pushing Thaksin to call for a second, smaller war on drugs in 2004, despite – or because of – the ineffectiveness of the first war. The Thai war on drugs 'crossed lines that should never be crossed in a civilised society' (Roberts, Trace and Klein, 2004: 7).

Militarization of supply reduction: Afghanistan and the Colombian model

In Colombia, as in post-Taliban Afghanistan, the United States has favoured a military approach to the issue of illicit cropping, devoting most of its counter-narcotics direct and indirect aid to the military, leaving only a small share for economic development. In the year 2000 as its contribution to Plan Colombia (originally devised by Colombian president, Andrés Pastrana), the United States earmarked 75 per cent of its aid (total aid US$860 million) for the military and for counter-narcotics (interdiction and eradication) thereby further involving the Colombian military in counter-narcotics operations. Over the longer 2000–5 period, the United States allocated no less than 80 per cent of its US$4 billion aid to Colombia to the military and the police, while only 8 per cent went to alternative development (Isacson, 2005: 170–1). While United States contributions to Plan Colombia failed to reduce coca production (it mostly modified the geography, methods and techniques of coca cultivation), it considerably increased the involvement of the Colombian military in counter-narcotics operations (virtually absent before Plan Colombia) and encouraged forced eradication through aerial crop spraying of a glyphosate-based herbicide (marketed in the United States by Monsanto under the brand-name 'Roundup') (Isacson, 2005: 172). Plan Colombia illustrates how the militarization of the war on drugs not only fails to suppress or even reduce illicit agricultural drug production[11] but also shows how it fails to extend in any significant way the state's writ to unruly regions where guerrilla activities and drug production occur (Isacson, 2005: 183). The failure of the military solution in Colombia, however, was not enough to lead to a re-think on the war on drugs and its repressive, military solutions: William Wood, aka 'Chemical Bill', the former US ambassador to Colombia (2003–7), was transferred to Afghanistan in 2007.

The United States has been calling for aerial spraying of Afghanistan's poppy crop since 2004, when it really grasped the extent of Afghan opium production and its implications. The Afghan president, Hamid Karzai, however, has so far always opposed such a solution and has instead favoured 'manual' eradication, i.e. conducted on the ground. (This may not always be manual – it may, for example, be mechanized, using tractors.) Yet, despite this, William Wood, then US ambassador to Colombia, became US

Ambassador to Afghanistan in 2007, and five Afghan policemen from the National Interdiction Unit (operated by the Afghan Ministry of Counter-Narcotics) were sent to Colombia on a US-sponsored training programme run by Special Forces within the Colombian police. In a statement on 26 June 2007 – International Day Against Drug Abuse and Illicit Trafficking – Ambassador Wood complained about the limited eradication conducted in Afghanistan in 2006 and mentioned that work was being undertaken 'to shape an international consensus to fight the drug trade more effectively', notably by 'exploring new techniques' that were to be coordinated with the Government of Afghanistan and the international community.[12] The so-called 'new techniques' are in fact not new, at least not in Colombia, where they were widely used in the 2000s. But in Afghanistan, aerial spraying, while clearly favoured by the US State Department and Congress, has not yet been implemented, mostly through lack of 'international consensus'.

Yet, in spite of increased militarization and growing budgets, the war on drugs has so far utterly failed to reduce, or even to stabilize, opium poppy cultivation in Afghanistan and, as a result, aerial spraying was promoted as the central component of a new eradication strategy. The US Central Command (CENTCOM) budget for counter-narcotics operations in Afghanistan grew from US$1 million in 2002, when the 'war on terror' was still being prioritized over the 'war on drugs', to US$73 million in 2004,[13] when the United States really decided to stop turning a blind eye to opium production and began to view alleged links between the Taliban insurgency and terrorism as strategic threats to state-building and reconstruction in Afghanistan. When the 2006 Afghan opium crop set a new world record, some US$700 million were allocated by the US Senate to 'counter-narcoterrorism' operations conducted by the Department of Defence in Afghanistan in 2007.[14] However, CENTCOM made it clear that its 'roles include intelligence support, helicopter transport, logistical and administrative assistance for counter-narcotics operators in country, rescue and close air support operations' but that US troops are not to be involved in forced eradication, whether manual or aerial. It was therefore suggested by US lawmakers that the 2007 counter-narcotics funds 'be spent mostly on supporting the DEA, buying or leasing helicopters and gunships to support enforcement action against drug kingpins, heroin chemists, narcotics convoys and heroin labs'.[15]

As Ted Galen Carpenter already noted in 2000,

> to its credit, the military hierarchy has generally tried to resist the pressure for deeper involvement [in drug eradication], even though in the immediate post-Cold War period it seemed that the drug war was one of the few

missions that might prevent the downsizing of the Pentagon's budget and force structure (Carpenter, 2000).

Historian Richard Davenport-Hines confirms such a post-Cold War shift when he writes that 'the fight against drugs has replaced the fight against communism as the principal moral imperative of US foreign policy' (Davenport-Hines, 2001: 348). The US military has always been reluctant to intervene directly in counter-narcotics operations, whether in Colombia or in Afghanistan, which explains why DynCorp International, one of the world's largest private security firms, is in charge of some of the US-funded counter-narcotics operations both in Colombia and in Afghanistan. DynCorp International contracts with more than thirty US government agencies, including the State Department, the Department of Defence, the DEA, the FBI and the Office of National Drug Control Policy (the ONDCP's former director and US 'Drug Czar', General Barry McCaffrey, is on DynCorp's board of directors). In Colombia, where the United States started outsourcing its war on drugs to DynCorp in 1997, the contract linking DynCorp to the US Department of State mentions that the company 'participates in eradication missions, training, and drug interdiction, but also participates in air transport, reconnaissance, search and rescue, airborne medical evacuation, ferrying equipment and personnel from one country to another, as well as aircraft maintenance'.[16] In Colombia, DynCorp conducts aerial spraying operations by operating several State Department aircraft, including armed helicopters (UH-1H Iroquois) and crop dusters (T-65 Thrush).[17]

DynCorp's first contract in post-Taliban Afghanistan dates back to 2002, when it handled Hamid Karzai's personal security: the original six-month contract was extended until January 2006. Since then, all of Karzai's bodyguards have been Afghans. Yet it was only in 2004 that DynCorp-led Afghan troops began eradicating opium poppies, leading to violent encounters with opium farmers (opposed to the forced eradication) but also to gun battles with Afghan insurgents. By December 2005, DynCorp had eradicated only 220 hectares of poppies out of a planned 10,000–15,000 hectares, but instead of blaming DynCorp for failing to meet its objectives the US Department of State mentioned only that 'the effort lacked coordination, communication, and the will on the part of some Afghan government officials to commit' (Nawa, 2006: 20). At this point, the United States put increased pressure on Hamid Karzai to accept aerial spraying of Afghan opium poppy fields. Yet, to date, the Afghan president has made it clear that he opposes aerial spraying. In the meantime, DynCorp still operates in Afghanistan and often has to fight its way out of forced eradication operations without achieving much by way of its suppression objectives, as occurred for example in Uruzgan province in the spring of 2007 (Anderson, 2007).

Whether in Colombia, where aerial spraying is authorized by the Colombian government and is conducted by DynCorp, or in Afghanistan, where only non-chemical, 'manual' eradication is conducted, the war on drugs has proven expensive and ineffective. Christopher Alexander, former Canadian Ambassador to Afghanistan (2003–5) and Deputy Special Representative of the Secretary General of the United Nations for Afghanistan in 2007, declared, during an eradication operation in Uruzgan (2007), that 'the per-acre cost of forced eradication is excruciatingly high' (Anderson, 2007). Alexander criticized manual eradication only to stress that aerial spraying would be easier, faster and cheaper to conduct. Yet, the limitations on the effectiveness of eradication are more pronounced in Afghanistan than in Colombia, for the opium poppy is an annual plant that would need to be eradicated every year, while the coca plant is a perennial plant whose eradication cuts production for years. And even in Colombia, the aerial spraying programme comes at a price that could also be described as 'excruciatingly high', since it costs an estimated US$34,000 to effectively eradicate one hectare of coca (Laniel, 2007: 135). But of course, despite official claims, cost-effectiveness is not a guideline, nor even a goal, of the war on drugs. Indeed, as argued above, the ineffectiveness of the war has only resulted in budget increases, in spite of – and maybe because of – its counterproductivity. Given the Colombian and Afghan results, the war on drugs clearly appears to be counterproductive since coca cultivation has spread in Colombia (figures for cultivated areas are highly controversial), and in post-Taliban Afghanistan poppy cultivation has increased considerably.

FROM THE 'WAR ON DRUGS' TO THE 'WAR ON TERRORISM': 'NARCO-TERRORISM'

In Afghanistan, opium production is frequently described as one of the most serious security threats to the country's state-building and reconstruction processes. Insurgents and terrorists are said to be benefiting directly from opium production and pressuring Afghan farmers into producing the crop. While the funding of terrorist groups and activities through illicit drug trafficking (at least to some extent) is likely to be nothing new, the so-called 'narco-terrorist' threat has been increasingly denounced since the terrorist attacks on the United States of 11 September 2001 (Laniel, 2003). Of course, the situation in Afghanistan, where Osama bin Laden and his al-Qaeda terrorist training camps were hosted by the Taliban, offered reasonable grounds for such narco-terrorism links to be suspected. Indeed, despite the near-nationwide suppression of poppy cultivation by the Taliban in 2001, Afghanistan had previously been the leading opium producing country in the world for some years, producing its highest ever opium crop (4,581 tonnes) in 1999 under Taliban rule. However, much larger crops were to be produced (in 2004, in 2006, and again in 2007) after the US-inspired fall of the Taliban, thus raising concerns that the country was becoming a 'narco-state' and was at risk of succumbing to 'narco-terrorism'. During a conference held in Kabul in February 2004, Antonio Maria Costa, UNODC Executive Director, warned of 'mounting evidence of drug money being used to finance criminal activities, including terrorism', and claimed that 'fighting drug trafficking equals fighting terrorism'.[18] Even before that, it seems to have been widely accepted that 'narco-terrorism' was a major threat where Afghanistan was concerned. Former French Defence Minister, Michèle Alliot-Marie (2002–7), for example, declared in January 2003 that drugs were 'the principal source of funding for Osama bin Laden's al-Qaeda network' (Chouvy, 2004d ; Sedra, 2003). However, no definition was offered of what 'narco-terrorism' might be: surely a prerequisite to understanding the nature of the threat it – allegedly – represents.

Defining 'narco-terrorism'

Although the term 'narco-terrorism' has only recently been applied in the Afghan context, it seems that it was first used by former Peruvian President, the late Fernando Belaúnde Terry (1912–2002), when, in 1983, he used the term to describe terrorist-type attacks against his nation's counter-narcotics police by the Shining Path Marxist rebels (Davidson, 1991). Later, in 1986, former US President, Ronald Reagan, also spoke of 'narco-terrorism' when referring to purported links between international drug trafficking and terrorism among allies of the Soviet Union (Cuba, Nicaragua) (Labrousse, 2002).

In May 2003, Steven Casteel, the DEA Assistant Administrator for Intelligence, told the US Senate Judiciary Committee, that 'the nexus between drugs and terrorism is perilously evident', thereby justifying that 'the war on terror and the war on drugs are linked'. He also gave the DEA definition of a group involved in 'narco-terrorism':

> an organized group that is complicit in the activities of drug trafficking in order to further, or fund, premeditated, politically motivated violence perpetrated against non-combatant targets with the intention to influence (that is, to influence a government or group of people).[19]

According to such a definition – and disregarding the fact that defining terrorism alone has always proven very controversial – a narco-terrorist group would be any terrorist group resorting to illicit drug proceeds in order to fund its activities. Targeting funding procedures of terrorist groups is of course a crucial objective for counter-terrorism agencies, but the DEA definition lumps together terrorism itself with its alleged financial means, instead of characterizing the specific motivations and goals of particular terrorist groups. According to such a definition there would be as many types of terrorism as there would be different ways of financing them. Terrorism is illegal, politically motivated violence and has little to do with specific funding resources, especially when such resources are known to be diverse and quickly changing. Targeting 'narco-terrorism' by associating the 'war on drugs' with the 'war on terrorism' (or worse, the 'war on terror' as it eventually became known), falls short of explaining why illicit drug production and terrorism are resorted to. Fighting an alleged 'narco-terrorist' threat implies fighting the consequences, rather than the causes, of two phenomena that have nothing to do with each other – one being a means of coping with economic difficulties; the other being a violent way to register political – and sometimes economic – claims. Additionally, in the same way that the logic of waging a war on drugs can be questioned – drugs are objects/products and as such do not make enemies – so waging a war on terrorism raises questions about how a war against what is basically a violent means of coercion can be won. In September 2001, Daniel Warner, then secretary general at the Institute of International Studies in Geneva, wrote: 'Wars against poverty and drugs have not succeeded. War is a legal term used between states with formal declarations. A war against terrorism makes no sense'.[20] Jason Burke, a journalist with the British newspaper *The Observer*, who has written on Islamic extremism and has covered the war in post-Taliban Afghanistan and in Iraq, explains that 'terrorism is after all a tactic' and that 'the term "war on terrorism" is thus effectively nonsensical' (Burke, 2004: 23). Burke goes further when he states: 'As with the term "al-Qaeda", "Islamic terrorism" is a catch-all of dubious use in helping us comprehend a phenomenon, and address the threat, confronting us' (Burke, 2004: 23). Moreover, the war on drugs and the war on terrorism make no sense as they result from an attempt to find military solutions to problems rather than solve their complex political, economic, and social causes.

Despite its apparent narrow meaning, the term 'narco-terrorism' appears too vague and counterproductive to address either drug trafficking or terrorism, since it brings very different actors into too broad a category. As explained by the Council on Foreign Relations, some experts think that 'while terrorists and drug traffickers often share some short-term goals, they have different long-term objectives (political goals for terrorists, greed for drug lords) and shouldn't be conflated'.[21] If the term is not to become hackneyed, therefore, narco-terrorism should not refer to terrorist groups that have been only partly funded by illegal drugs – since any terrorist outfit is likely to at least try to benefit from such a resource. Rather, it should be used to identify organized drug traffickers who try to affect the policies of a government by terrorist means, i.e. by the systematic threat or use of terror. In the same way that 'narco' does not politically define a state, neither does it politically define terrorism. States are defined and categorized according to their political regimes (monarchy, democracy, military dictatorship, etc.) and not according to their economic resources, except sometimes for rentier states. Neither Afghanistan nor Burma can be said to be 'narco-states' as they are far from fitting any definition of rentier states and as illicit opium production is far too limited in terms of cultivated areas to justify such a designation (between 1 and 5 per cent of arable land in Afghanistan).

Terrorism is the use by the weak against the strong of illegitimate violence to reach a political goal through terror (in a radically asymmetrical distribution of power) and can also be said, according to Peter Waldmann, to be an attempt to occupy the mental space of a society; by contrast, guerrillas aim to conquer territories and riches (Waldmann, 2002; Labrousse, 2002). Terrorist actions have regularly been perpetrated in Afghanistan since the fall of the Taliban, notably against civilian targets such as foreign and national NGO personnel and most likely by Taliban remnants, al-Qaeda-affiliated groups and Gulbuddin Hekmatyar's Hezb-i Islami: i.e. by opponents of the Afghan government and those opposed to a foreign military presence in the country.

An unbiased look at terrorism in Afghanistan reveals that many of these 'terrorist' individuals or groups were once 'freedom fighters' struggling against the Soviets during the 1980s. Not only were they fighting what Ronald Reagan had dubbed an 'Evil Empire', they were also, to some extent at least, availing themselves of the already growing Afghan opium economy. At the time, both the CIA and the ISI played a direct role in funnelling weapons and money to the 'freedom fighters' – the Afghan mujahideen – and at least an indirect role in the local nascent trade in narcotics. Thus, the involvement of the CIA and the ISI in the drug trade further complicates the adequacy of a category such as 'narco-terrorism'. Use of this term would require comparing how different actors like resistance guerrillas, intelligence and counter-insurgency agencies and terrorist organizations use the drug economy and illegal violence.

Although some former United States allies in the war against communism were clearly engaged in the illegal drug economy, and some of these have since turned 'terrorist', most recent allies in the 'war on terrorism' have also been said to have turned to opium and heroin for funding. In post-Taliban Afghanistan, and prior to 2004, the United States condoned opiates production both in areas traditionally controlled by the United Front (Badakhshan) and in areas held by various local commanders whose support was deemed strategically necessary to fight the Taliban and al-Qaeda. However, more official allies of the US 'war on terrorism' also seem to have been engaged in the drug economy (or to have benefited from it). Indeed, as Wendy Chamberlin, former US Ambassador to Pakistan, testified under oath in March 2003 before the Subcommittee on Asia and the Pacific of the House Committee on International Relations, the ISI's involvement in opium trafficking across the Afghanistan-Pakistan border had been 'substantial' during the past six years.[22]

Thus opium, having played a significant role in the counter-insurgency war on communism, was also used during the 'war on terrorism'. And now it seems that the long-failed 'war on drugs' has been called to the aid of a 'war on terrorism' that has not proven much more successful. The war on 'narco-terrorism' would, then, seem to be some new kind of integrated approach to the security problem facing Afghanistan, regardless of whether or not a war can effectively be waged on either drugs or terrorism, regardless of whether it could be won, and regardless of whether or not narco-terrorism really does exist in Afghanistan (or anywhere else). The military approach to drugs and terrorism that is obviously favoured by the United States in Afghanistan and elsewhere is more likely to address the consequences of drugs and terrorism than their causes, in spite of tactical and potentially strategic failures.

Narco-terrorism in Afghanistan?

In Afghanistan, and also in Burma, drug production is closely linked to territorial control and to political (il)legitimacy, as are guerrilla warfare and terrorism. In such a conflictual context, the value of a given territory increases along with the value of the opium crops it can bear for the benefit of whoever controls it. Thus, such a war economy/illicit economy nexus is likely to benefit terrorist organizations, who can easily take advantage of the power vacuum created by war.

A number of cases have been related by the media as evidence of al-Qaeda being funded by the opium economy in Afghanistan, all alleging only partial funding of terrorist-related activities/organizations by illicit drug proceeds, thus logically dismissing the existence of any real 'narco-terrorism'. Terrorist outfits are no less likely than others to try to benefit from such a resource, especially in a country like Afghanistan where the opium economy is pervasive and has been estimated to equal up to half the country's legitimate gross domestic product.

In *Time Asia Magazine*, Tim McGirk offered one of the most detailed media reports regarding alleged links between drug traffickers, warlords, militant groups and terrorist outfits in Afghanistan (McGirk, 2004). He referred to 'recent busts' that, according to Western intelligence agencies, 'have revealed evidence of al-Qaeda's ties to the trade'. Such ties were inferred by seizures of narcotics, such as one made by the US Navy in the Arabian Sea, where aboard a small fishing boat 'several al-Qaeda guys sitting on a bale of drugs' were found. In another case, the Kabul house of a drug trafficker was raided and a dozen satellite phones were found, used to call numbers 'linked to suspected terrorists' in Turkey, the Balkans and Western Europe. So far, what seems to be the most serious case of ties between drug traffickers and 'terrorists' has been that involving Haji Juma Khan, an Afghan national. According to McGirk, Western intelligence agencies believed that Khan was the head of a heroin-trafficking organization that is a 'principal source of funding for the Taliban and al-Qaida terrorists'. Khan's boats allegedly shipped Afghan heroin out of the port of Karachi (in Pakistan), and returned from the Middle East loaded with arms for both al-Qaeda and the Taliban. In 2004, Mirwais Yasini, then head of Afghanistan's Counter Narcotics Directorate, estimated that the Taliban and its allies had derived more than US$150 million from opium in 2003 and assumed that there were 'central linkages' between Khan, Mullah Omar and Osama bin Laden.

The National Commission on Terrorist Attacks Upon the United States (also known as the 9–11 Commission), however, an independent, bipartisan commission created by Congressional legislation and the signature of President George W. Bush in late 2002 to investigate the 11 September 2001 attacks, stated that 'the US government still has not determined with any precision how much al Qaeda raises or from whom, or how it spends its money'. According to this report, al-Qaeda is mainly funded by rich individuals from the Persian Gulf and by some Islamic charities. Of greater interest, still, is the commission's assertion that there is 'no substantial evidence that al Qaeda played a major role in the drug trade or relied on it as an important source of revenue either before or after 9/11'.[23]

In any case, should al-Qaeda happen to really be involved in the opium economy in Afghanistan, it would most likely not be at the production level but higher up in the drug chain, probably in the protection of heroin laboratories and trafficking caravans: i.e. where most of the profits are made. Moreover, al-Qaeda consists of a network that, as such, lacks the extensive territorial control that is needed to control production areas. As for where the money generated from drug production and trafficking goes, it has always been divided iniquitously, in Afghanistan and elsewhere, among farmers (who receive the smallest share), warlords, who condone or encourage production in their territory, and local and regional traffickers (who get the biggest share). It seems, then, that if al-Qaeda's alleged involvement in the drug trade is true and is as significant as often claimed, it is something that developed only after the ousting of the Taliban who, until 2001, were levying Islamic taxes on the opium trade. In this connection, it must be stressed that it is the Taliban who benefited from al-Qaeda's funding and not the other way round. Indeed, as stated by the 9–11 Commission, 'prior to 9/11 the largest single al Qaeda expense was support for the Taliban, estimated at about US$20 million per year'.[24] On the other hand, knowledgeable observers such as Pakistani journalist Ahmed Rashid (Rashid, 2000) agreed that the drug trade was then only the Taliban's second source of revenue, estimated at US$80–100 million in 1999. Quite interestingly, the 9–11 Commission declared that:

> intelligence collection efforts have failed to corroborate rumors of current narcotic trafficking. In fact, there is compelling evidence the al Qaeda leadership does not like or trust those who today control the drug trade in Southwest Asia, and has encouraged its members not to get involved.[25]

Narco-terrorism: a convenient 'unknown known'?

Serious evidence is still needed to establish that narco-terrorism does exist in Afghanistan. That some drug money plays a significant role in the ongoing Afghan conflict is manifestly clear and is no novelty in recent Afghan history. Yet, in the absence of evidence of true narco-terrorism in Afghanistan (or elsewhere), reports of such terrorism may well come from 'political intelligence', for which, according to Abram Shulsky and Gary Schmitt, senior associates at the National Strategy Information Center (NSIC) in the 1990s, 'truth is not the goal' of intelligence gathering – it is 'victory'.[26] Hence it may be that the recent efforts to link the narcotics economy/threat to the terrorist economy/threat are in reality designed to link the war on drugs to the war on terrorism. Although it is still to be proved that drugs and terrorism are two faces of the same coin in Afghanistan, the war on drugs and the war on terrorism are likely to serve the same political and financial agendas by conveniently lumping together two 'evils' (Chouvy, 2004d, 2004e; Laniel, 2003).

A good example lies in the recent efforts of the US Southern Command to maintain its enhanced funding and establish renewed relevance by raising the threat of 'narco-terrorism' in Latin America, where 'US military aid and training, which previously were focused on counter-narcotics operations, have now been re-tasked as counter-terrorism responsibilities'.[27] Indeed, 'preying on the terrorist fears that are currently dominating Washington's defense plan, SouthCom claims that it is now pursuing narco-terrorists to justify its expanded congressionally-approved budget'.[28]

Paradoxically, perhaps, the problems posed by the analysis of 'intelligence' and its application to policy have been summed up best by Secretary of Defence Donald Rumsfeld (2001–6) on 6 June 2002 in Brussels:

> The message is that there are no knowns. There are things we know that we know. There are known unknowns. That is to say there are things that we now know we don't know. But there are also unknown unknowns. There are things we don't know we don't know. So when we do the best we can and we pull all this information together, and we then say, well that's basically what we see as the situation ... There is another way to phrase that and that is that the absence of evidence is not evidence of absence.[29]

And so it could be that the analysis of the 'situation' regarding so-called narco-terrorism – whatever its definition – in Afghanistan proceeds more from political propaganda needs than from the teachings of intelligence. In fact, if the line between 'Good' and 'Evil' appears to be rather thin and easily crossed, the line between resistance and terrorism seems to be even thinner and politically, rather than objectively, defined.

To overcome both opium production and terrorism in Afghanistan (where terrorist and suicide attacks have multiplied since 2004), the government and the international community should focus less on waging war on drugs and terrorism and more on implementing the rule of law and promoting the broad economic and political development of the country, although a multi-level strategy involving effective sanctions on illicit and criminal activities is critical.

7. Thai Border Patrol Police watching the border with Burma, Chiang Rai province, Thailand.

7

Opium Poppy Cultivation

THE OPIUM POPPY: ECOLOGY AND BOTANY

The broad adaptability of the poppy enables it to thrive in the most varied climatic conditions and soils and cultivars are successfully grown in Europe, Asia, the Americas, Africa and Australia. There are around 110 species, and many more varieties, in the genus *Papaver* and although some are perennial most are annual (Kapoor, 1995: 19, 24). *Papaver somniferum* itself is an annual herb that thrives differently depending on the poppy variety but also according to latitude, altitude, insolation (location on sunny or shady slopes), wind, temperature, rainfall, seasonal cycle and soil. Cultivated in so many different places and settings, the flowers and fruits (capsules) of the opium poppy vary greatly in colour, form and size.

The opium poppy has a 'relatively broad soil tolerance' (Merlin, 1984: 46). Back in 1939 Tjako Johan Addens noted that varieties of the species have been cultivated in,

> the somewhat humid open forest tracts in Australia, the river clay along the Yellow River in China, the Ganges in India and the rivers in Iran, the 'cotton' soils in Malwa, the loess in Central Asia, the slowly decaying volcanic soils in Asia Minor, the Nile islands in Egypt (consisting almost solely of pure sand), the 'Black earth' in Russia, the sandy soils of the lowlands and the calciferous loamy soils in Germany, the sea-clay soils in the province of Zealand and the gravel (sand and clay) soils in the province of Groningen (situated in the Netherlands) (Addens, 1939: 12).

However, the best soils in which to grow opium poppies are sandy loam or clay loam soils with high organic matter and with a neutral or slightly alkaline pH, as they facilitate 'both water-holding capacity and drainage capacity to avoid water stagnation' (Kapoor, 1995: 65). Soils that are too light or too heavy suffer respectively from too much drainage or too much water retention, which slows down (or accelerates) the flowering and the formation of the capsules (Merlin, 1984: 45–6). Heavier soils will yield decent opium production, however, if they are properly ploughed, drained and/or irrigated.

The wide soil tolerance of the opium poppy is matched by its wide climatic adaptability and it grows as well under temperate climates as under tropical climates, although rather cold temperatures are required for proper seed germination. In fact, sowing must be undertaken at between 5°C and 10°C and seed germination occurs only at a few degrees above zero. This is why, in the tropics, the poppy must be grown in mountainous areas, where temperatures are cooler than in lowlands. In regions of tropical monsoon climate, too much summer rainfall limits opium poppy cultivation to the winter months, for too much water ruins the crop. In recent years, reports from Burma, Laos, and even Thailand, have mentioned increasing occurrences of multiple cropping. Supposedly, some opium farmers 'are changing their cultivation practices, possibly to counter the effects of eradication activities'. Poppies have reportedly been cultivated in the three Southeast Asian countries during the monsoon season – that is, off season – although only at high altitudes and on well-drained slopes protected from water erosion by stone and bush barriers and drainage canals (UNODC, 2007c: 67). In some regions, a number of opium farmers allegedly achieved three opium crops[1] in the same year (UNODC, 2006d: 72–5).

In Asia – from Turkey to Afghanistan, India and Southeast Asia – the opium poppy largely tends to be a winter or a spring crop that is sown from October to February and harvested between 120 days and 250 days later, depending on the variety, date of sowing, latitude, altitude and temperature. Obviously, cultivation calendars differ greatly between Afghanistan's north-eastern mountains, where snow can be abundant, its southern semi-arid provinces; northern India, where heat and monsoon rains prevent the poppy from being cultivated during the summer; and Mainland Southeast Asia, where the poppy is only cultivated above 800 metres and during the dry and cool season (winter) (Chouvy, 2002a: 43–56). Agricultural calendars determine many things, from maturation period to opium yield. In northern Afghanistan, autumn poppies take longer than spring poppies to mature, and in India, autumn poppies yield more opium and morphine than spring poppies.

The goal of opium poppy cultivation – licit as well as illicit – is not just to extract opium, but to produce morphine and, ultimately, heroin. Variations in opium and morphine yield depend to some extent on the sowing period and the harvest period but also on water availability and the weather. As L.D. Kapoor explains: 'it has been observed that irrigated plants contained more alkaloids than unirrigated ones' and 'moisture stress during main growth period and flowering had an adverse effect on morphine accumulation' (Kapoor, 1995: 70). Additionally, warm and desiccative winds may alter morphine production if they occur during the period of capsule formation. Of course, rainfall also affects opium and morphine production, although the impact of rainfall will also be influenced by the type of soil (as water retention and/or drainage may increase or decrease the water available to the poppy).

Irrigation is more common in Afghanistan, where a semi-arid to arid climate prevails and where recently there has been recurrent drought. In Burma and Laos, rain is much more abundant. As a consequence, opium yields vary widely not only between countries but also within each country. Higher morphine content is more likely when harvesting takes place during warm and dry weather; cloudy and rainy weather decreases morphine yield.

OPIUM POPPY CULTIVATION AND OPIUM PRODUCTION: A LABOUR INTENSIVE ACTIVITY

Compared with other crops (both food and cash crops), opium poppy cultivation is labour intensive. It is also risky, not only because it is mostly undertaken in rather difficult environments but also because, as an illicit crop, opium farmers are at risk from forced eradication and violence (Steinberg, Hobbs and Mathewson, 2004). The extent of labour involved depends on the region and the agricultural methods used, since preparation of the land differs greatly between the permanent fields of Afghanistan and India, and the shifting cultivation methods of Mainland Southeast Asia. There is considerably less work involved in ploughing a flat and permanent field than in clearing brush and trees on forested hillsides. And the slash-and-burn process is both time-consuming and physically demanding. After the land has been ploughed, either with a swing plough (Afghanistan,[2] India) or, in a very laborious process with a short-handled hoe (Southeast Asia's upland fields, where steep slopes make animal labour difficult, when available), the poppy fields need to be thinned but also weeded about three times (another laborious and time-consuming task).

Harvesting the opium begins four months after planting, 'when the capsules become swollen and green, but are still immature' (Kapoor, 1995: 71). The opium is harvested from the poppy capsules in an exacting, and highly time-consuming, process. Each poppy capsule is incised (lanced) with a tool made of multiple blades and the opium sap is left to ooze and dry before it is scraped. If the cut is too shallow the yield of latex will be low; if it is too deep, the latex will exude into the interior of the capsule and will be lost (Kapoor, 1995: 73). Yet, 'an experienced skilled worker knows the optimum depth of lancing and 150–200 capsules can be lanced in an hour' (Kapoor, 1995: 74–5). Some days later the capsules are lanced a second time, sometimes a third time and even a fourth time (on average, opium poppies were lanced four times in 2006 in Afghanistan but it could be up to six or seven times). The entire opium harvest usually lasts between 14 and 18 days but may take up to three weeks, since one hectare can bear between 60,000 and 120,000 poppies: i.e. between 120,000 and 275,000 capsules (Drug Enforcement Administration, 1993). Yet the number of poppies and capsules determines less the time taken by the harvest than the available labour force. Once all the capsules have been lanced and the opium gathered, the poppies are left in the fields for a further 20–25 days, until the poppy seeds have fully matured. Then the drying capsules are 'picked, spread in open yards for further drying, and thrashed to obtain the seed crop' (Kapoor, 1995: 75).

Opium production is such a labour intensive activity that labour alone can account for up to 80 per cent of the total production cost (Mansfield, 2002: 5). And despite the significant average size of households[3] involved in opium production in Asia, the labour requirement is too high for most households (whether in Afghanistan, Burma or Laos) to cultivate even a single hectare. Thus the average poppy field surface was 0.17 ha per household in Burma in 2005 (UNODC, 2005b: 16), 0.29 ha in Laos in 2005 (UNODC, 2005d: 8), and 0.37 ha in Afghanistan in 2006 (UNODC, 2006b: 69). In India, where licit opium production is undertaken under licence and where yields are the highest, the largest surface authorized for cultivation was 0.10 hectare in the 2004–5 season (Chouvy, 2006a).

Opium production involves many more person-days of work than cereal production, whether compared with Afghan wheat and maize or upland rice and maize from Southeast Asia. The socio-economist and drugs and development expert David Mansfield notes that in late 1940s Turkey a good male labourer could harvest 1 kg of opium in 72 hours while women and children took three times as long to do the same work. Depending on the composition of the workforce, therefore, between 180 and 540 person-days of work were needed to yield 30 kg of opium per hectare (Mansfield, 2002: 9, note 20). In Afghanistan, estimates indicate that one hectare of opium requires as much as 350 person-days of work compared with only 41 days for wheat (some estimates say 54 person-days) and 135 for black cumin (UNDCP, 1999). In Southeast Asia, according to Mansfield's review of the existing literature on the subject, opium production requires between 300 and 486 person-days of work (Mansfield, 2002: 9, note 20).

Cereal production is more labour intensive in the uplands of Southeast Asia than in Afghanistan, however. In a study conducted in the late 1990s in the northern part of the Phongsaly district of Laos, agronomist Emmanuel Baudran (Baudran, 2000) compared the technical itineraries of rice, maize and opium production, and found that slash-and-burn cultivation of rain-fed rice required between 160 and 210 person-days of work per hectare, maize cultivation required 155 person-days and opium production required 301.[4] Interestingly, his detailed study shows that clearing trees and brush can take up to 22 per cent of the agricultural workload (in terms of time) invested in rice or maize production but that it is weeding that is the most time-consuming aspect of upland agricultural production – as much as 44 per cent (80 person-days) during some years of upland rain-fed rice cultivation and as much as 50 per cent (150 person-days) for poppy cultivation.

Harvesting opium harvest is also highly labour intensive because of the need to lance the poppies. It takes about 70 person-days per hectare (24 per cent of total work) to do so and to gather the coagulated opium. Harvesting and threshing rice crops, by comparison, requires 40 person-days only (from 20 to 25 per cent of total work). Harvesting maize is more complicated since two types are produced and harvested simultaneously, each requiring 15 person-days. (Baudran, 2000: 33–65). As Olivier Ducourtieux, another agronomist, stresses, what constrains the slash-and-burn crop system is weeding and low population density. The workforce required by this labour intensive activity is too often insufficient to expand farmed land, given that 'the maximum surface area farmable per active worker is approximately 0.8 hectare' (Ducourtieux, 2004: 75–6).

Confronted with such highly labour intensive agriculture, opium farmers, whether in Afghanistan, India or Southeast Asia, have come up with elaborate strategies for reducing the cost of labour for their households. These include 'staggered planting, the cultivation of a combination of both short and long maturing varieties of opium poppy,[5] and maximising the use of family and reciprocal labour' (Mansfield, 2002: 9). The Mien of northern Thailand used to stagger their planting of poppy seeds, while the Hmong tended to sow an entire field at the same time in order to shorten the harvest period. As botanist, Edward Anderson, explains, the Hmong claimed that 'although the work load is intense, it is easier to simply move through the field tapping all the plants rather than having to select only the mature ones in several sweeps of the field' (Anderson, 1993: 120). Staggered planting can also be a good strategy for reducing the risk and impact of crop damage caused by rain, wind, or even hail. Clearly, choosing one strategy or the other largely depends on the size of the opium-producing household, but also on the availability and cost of seasonal workers.

Botanical knowledge is also likely to play a significant role in the choice of strategy. In northern Thailand, in the late 1970s, anthropologist Anthony Walker compared a Hmong village with a Lahu[6] village and observed that the Hmong seemed to have a 'more sophisticated knowledge of poppy varieties and of the value of seed selection' than the Lahu. The Hmong knew of 'five named varieties of poppy, with distinctive physical characteristics, maturation periods, yielding properties and usefulness'. By contrast, the Lahu planted only two varieties of poppy, and the seeds were generally mixed. Yet, 'by planting seed varieties with different maturation periods', as the Hmong did, 'or by staggering the planting times for the same seed stock' as did the Lahu, 'both communities were able to harvest over a fairly lengthy period' (Walker, 1980: 143–4).

In the 2000s, UNODC observed a variety of practices aimed at reducing the cost of labour and/or protecting the crops from weather damage or complete eradication. In the southern Shan State of Burma, surveys have documented off-season planting, multi-stage cropping (two seed broadcasts in the same field with an interval of 1–2 months), and staggered cropping (seed broadcasts on different fields at different times) (UNODC, 2007c: 66–70). Opium production is therefore not only a labour intensive activity but also a time-sensitive one. As David Mansfield explains about opium production in Afghanistan, 'it is not only that the crop requires a large amount of labour but also the timing of labour inputs is critical, especially during the harvest period when a delay in lancing can have a significant impact in the final yield of the crop' (Mansfield, 2004a: 6).

Yet, the opium poppy is rarely the only crop grown by farmers, whether in Afghanistan, India or Southeast Asia. In Afghanistan, wheat – the main staple crop – is predominantly a winter crop and is grown during the same period as the opium poppy. Most opium farmers reserve part of their land for food crops (wheat included) and very few of them rely on poppy cultivation alone. In fact, cereal crops still make up the majority of the land cultivated by most farmers. Summer crops are numerous and include maize, pulses, vegetables, sesame, mustard, sunflowers, cumin, and saffron. Fruit and nut orchards were the main cash crops before the war, and before opium production developed. In India, poppies often follow a crop of maize, capsicum or ground-nut. In the highlands of Southeast Asia, where generalized ecosystems prevail, the poppy also often follows a crop of upland rice or of maize (harvested in September and October), whose stubble provides some protection to the young poppy seedlings. Mixed crops are characteristic of Southeast Asia:

Often growing with the distinctive bluish green, waist-high poppies and maize stubble are many other plants, such as peaches, Chinese pears, wild beans, taro, sorghum, green peas and a variety of herbs and spices such as ginger, coriander, lemon grass, mustard, fennel and mint.

Also, 'marijuana is often grown as a border plant in Hmong poppy fields', yet mostly for its strong fibres (Anderson, 1993: 119, plate 155).

THE DRIVERS OF OPIUM PRODUCTION: DIVERSITY WITHIN UNITY

Whatever their environment or their agricultural techniques, most Asian opium farmers seem driven to opium production for the same reason: to cope with food insufficiency and food insecurity. Reasons for food insufficiency and food insecurity differ in Southeast Asia and Southwest Asia. In Southeast Asia, the highly labour intensive upland rice production is limited less by land scarcity than by available workforce (limiting maximum cultivated areas per household). And lack of irrigation techniques and severely limited availability of wet lands (valley bottoms) also contribute. In Afghanistan, when wheat self-sufficiency is not achieved it is mostly because of land scarcity together with the very large size of households. It is in these circumstances that farmers turn to the production of opium, which provides them with the means to buy wheat to feed their large but resource-poor families.

Burma and Laos: labour intensive rice production and insufficient workforce lead to food insecurity

In Burma and Laos, the hill tribes rely on slash-and-burn cultivation and have very little access to irrigation techniques and irrigable land, as the lowlands and valley bottoms are already densely occupied, often by ethnic Burmese, Tai, and Lao paddy growers. Even when forested land is available for slash-and-burn agriculture, it is only for a limited time since this method of cultivation involves shifting fields every two years or so in order to respect fallow periods (10 years) and allow forest re-growth. Moreover, forest cover has dramatically fallen in Burma and Laos and forest clearings may even be prohibited by government bans on slash-and-burn agriculture – as in Laos where 250,000 people from amongst the poorest families (mostly hill tribes) employ slash-and-burn methods but face the suppression of this type of cultivation by 2010 (Ducourtieux, 2005: 193).

The ecological constraints on the poppy mean that opium production takes place almost exclusively at altitude: 93 per cent of poppy fields surveyed by the United Nations in 2002 in Burma's Wa region were above 800 metres and, in Laos, in 2001, 80 per cent of the opium-producing villages were located above 700 metres (UNDCP, 2002a: 21; UNDCP, 2001c: 16). Specifically, their location in mountainous regions, the scarce availability of arable land, and the priority given to paddy on irrigable land when it exists (mostly in valley bottoms), means that most poppy fields are located on steep slopes. In the Wa region in 2002, 65 per cent of poppy fields were located on slopes while only 24 per cent were on flat lands and 8 per cent were on terraces (UNDCP, 2002a: 21). As a consequence, but also because irrigation techniques have never been mastered in the region, for the year 2002 almost 99 per cent of poppy fields of the Wa region were rain-fed (UNDCP, 2002a: 22).

Socio-economic surveys by UNODC have shown, in fact, that in Southeast Asia the extent of opium poppy cultivation depends largely on the availability of paddy land, which in turn means upon the degree of food security achieved by households. Yet evaluating food security only on the basis of rice yields would be somewhat misleading 'as it does not take into account the other crops associated with the swidden crops' (Ducourtieux, 2004: 76). In any case, yields are much higher for irrigated rice (predominantly in lowlands) than for rain-fed rice (exclusively in uplands). In fact, in Burma, 'opium poppy growing households rely much more on shifting cultivation than non-growing households' mainly because in poppy growing villages, fewer households own or have access to paddy land (UNODC, 2006d: 91–2). In northern Laos and in Burma, the area that a household can cultivate, whether in rice, maize or poppies, is limited to an average of 0.8 ha because the substantial manpower that weeding requires (75 person-days per year) is limited by low population densities. In fact, soil fertility and land scarcity are not the limiting factors, as 'there are more potentially farmable areas than are as actually farmed' (Ducourtieux, 2004: 75–6).

Food security and poverty may explain, more than any other factors, why opium production is more important in some regions of Burma and Laos than in others. According to UNODC, in 2005 some 57 per cent of villages of northern Laos and 90 per cent of villages in Burma's Wa region experienced rice deficit. The situation was particularly difficult in the Wa region, where average households only produced enough rice for 4–6 months of consumption and where the poorest families often had only 1–3 months worth of rice. Thus, while on average opium production contributed to 10 per cent of total household income in 2005 in northern Laos (but 42 per cent in 2003, when poppy cultivation was much more important), it was as high as 73 per cent in Burma's Wa region before the 2005 opium ban. In the Wa region 82 per cent of the people cultivated opium poppies in an attempt to achieve food security (UNODC, 2006d: 26–7). In the previous year, the contribution of opium income to overall income was particularly high in the Wa region (almost 90 per cent), medium in South Shan State (50 per cent), and low in North Shan state (5 per cent) (UNODC, 2004b: 22).

The income of swiddening households can vary greatly, which in turn influences the extent to which they need to resort to opium production. In Phongsaly province in northern Laos, for example, some rely largely on the diverse and abundant non-timber forest products (NTFP), available from the rich surrounding tropical rain forests. They have no need to resort to opium production. In these villages, NTFPs contributed as much as 40 per cent of household income in the early 2000s (before income from cereal production) (Ducourtieux, 2004: 80). On the other hand, UNODC socio-economic surveys also conducted in northern Laos determined that, on average, opium producing households relied more on cereal production (31 per cent) than on forest products (7 per cent). Interestingly, these surveys also showed that the overall household income of opium producing villages was 6 per cent lower than that of non-opium producing villages and that opium producing villages had almost always a less diversified economy than non-opium producing villages, with a higher reliance on cereals and on livestock and a much lower reliance on forest products, fruit, vegetables and non-farm employment (UNODC, 2004d: 14). Therefore, when food security is fragile or is not achieved, and when licit cash crops are not available or marketable, opium production is often the only solution remaining. Yet, as the Burmese case showed, the levels of dependency on the opium economy vary greatly from one country to another and even within the same country.

Afghanistan: limited land availability and large households lead to food insecurity

Afghan farmers are in a very similar yet very different situation, as many of them belong to large households who must cope with land scarcity and food insecurity. In this semi-arid to arid country, where irrigation is often crucial for agricultural production, decades of war have contributed to the prolonged lack of water for agriculture, destroying traditional irrigation channels and displacing significant segments of the population. In addition, successive years of drought have made matters worse. After the fall of the

Taliban, the Food and Agriculture Organization (FAO) maintained that irrigated surfaces had declined by about 60 per cent since 1978 (in a country where only 15 per cent of agriculture used to be rain-fed), the last year of comparative peace in the country and when it was on the verge of attaining food self-sufficiency. Arable land, which before the war stood at only 12 per cent of the country's total area, fell by 37 per cent during the 1990s. It was estimated that 7 million people – a third of the total population – suffered from hunger in 2001, partly because of the drought that prevailed in 2000/2001. Yet, in 2002, owing to less problematic weather conditions, Afghanistan produced some 2.7 million tonnes of wheat, i.e. 82 per cent more than in 2001. Wheat production increased again in 2003, by 58 per cent, producing the largest wheat harvest in twenty-five years. However, in 2006, after another record harvest in 2005 (5.3 million tonnes), further drought again reduced wheat production, by 13 per cent: the 4.8 million tonnes of cereal (of which 3.9 millions tonnes was wheat) produced by Afghanistan in 2006 was far below their total cereal needs, estimated at 6 million tonnes. The 2006 drought directly affected some 2.5 million more people, living mostly in rain-fed zones, in a country where 6.5 million people are seasonally or chronically food insecure.[7] In the meantime, between 2005 and 2006, opium production increased by 49 per cent, then yielding the country's highest ever opium crop. In 2007 wheat production increased again, surpassing the 2006 figure by 700,000 tonnes but remaining short of the 2005 record. Opium production also reached unprecedented levels in the country (8,200 tonnes from 193,000 hectares in 2007), most likely because levels of opium production are determined less by food sufficiency than by food insecurity: i.e. by the risk of not being food self-sufficient. The fact that wheat production has proved unreliable in recent years, notably due to recurring drought, has probably persuaded some farmers to opt for poppy cultivation as a means of securing a minimum income with which to purchase wheat. This is all the more likely since wheat prices have fallen in the country in recent years (at least until 2005) and because wheat (whether locally produced, imported, or obtained through international aid) has been widely available in the markets.

Whilst environmental conditions and growing methods are very different in Afghanistan and in Burma and Laos, the drivers of opium production are very similar. In Afghanistan – as opposed to Burma and Laos – altitude is not a determining factor, as poppies can be grown both in the lowlands and uplands. Almost all opium poppy cultivation occurs on irrigated flat or terraced land. In fact, in 2004, 92 per cent of opium poppy cultivation took place on irrigated land. Yet only 7 per cent of total irrigated land was devoted to poppy cultivation (UNODC, 2004a: 4), as opium farmers very rarely devote all their land to opium production. As with Burma and Laos, food insecurity is one of the main reasons why Afghan households resort to opium production. As David Mansfield explains: 'in Afghanistan the majority of households do not produce sufficient wheat flour to meet their basic food requirements even if they cultivated wheat on all their land' since 'land holdings are typically too small, household members too numerous and wheat yields too low' (Mansfield, 2007a: 19–20). As the author showed in a 2004 case study in Nangarhar, self-sufficiency in wheat is therefore 'closely tied with the incidence of opium poppy cultivation' as, on average, households that were self-sufficient in wheat allocated only 25 per cent of their winter land to opium poppies while those experiencing a deficit in wheat devoted 55 per cent of their winter land to this illicit cash crop (Mansfield, 2004a: 23). In Afghanistan, self-sufficiency in wheat depends to a large extent on land tenure, and landowners make up a socio-economic group with a much higher rate of self-sufficiency than sharecroppers. Yet, due to years of fragmentation of landholdings, caused by family growth and the return of refugees, but also due to recurrent drought and falling wheat prices, in the Nangarhar and Laghman provinces only 5 per cent of a household sample were self-sufficient in wheat in 2004: a profound change, since 56 per cent of them once produced enough wheat to feed their families all year long (Mansfield, 2004a: 22).

David Mansfield has shown how resource-poor Afghan households who do not have access to enough land and who do not benefit from decent irrigation resort to opium production. When lack of land and water permits only one annual wheat crop instead of two, and when the drought affects wheat yields, many Afghan farmers tend to devote some of their winter land – if not most of it – to poppy cultivation (Mansfield, 2004a: 67).

Of course, Afghan farmers do not benefit from forest resources in the way that most upland Southeast Asian rice farmers do. Instead, they usually rely largely on animal rearing. However, drought has also affected this activity, especially in 2000/2001, when cereal production declined by 50 per cent and cattle numbers were reduced by almost 60 per cent (Chouvy, 2003c). Years of drought have also reduced 'the amount of water available for animals, prompting sales, lowering the demand for wheat straw, and consequently creating greater space for increased opium poppy cultivation in subsequent seasons' (Mansfield, 2004a: 67). The complex dynamics prompting Afghan farmers to turn to opium production is compounded by, and cannot be understood outside, the global Afghan economic context. Again, David Mansfield explains how opium production is linked to the ups and downs of wheat production and therefore to wheat availability, prices and market:

Whilst in the past concerns over the availability (and affordability) of wheat in the local bazaar prompted households to allocate a minimum amount of land to the [wheat] crop, until recently falling prices and a growing confidence that households can meet any shortfall in production through purchases on the local market have only added to the conditions for increased opium poppy cultivation (Mansfield, 2004a: 68).

Hence the concurrent increase in wheat production and opium production in recent years, since wheat production has increased but is still perceived as unreliable, and because wheat prices have fallen (or only remained stable) as opium prices have risen.

THE RELATIVE ECONOMIC SUPERIORITY OF OPIUM PRODUCTION

It is often explained, in a rather simplistic way, that people resort to illicit agricultural production because of its unbeatable superior economic profitability and that, therefore, it is near impossible for licit agricultural production to compete with opium (or cannabis in Morocco and coca in Colombia). Of course, illicit crops often yield gross revenues that are much higher than those allowed by licit crops. In Afghanistan in 2006, for example, opium production brought a much higher gross income per hectare than wheat: US$5,400 versus US$550 (UNODC, 2006b: 1). In Burma's Wa region, farmers reported that, prior to the 2005 ban, opium production brought 'four to five times more income than rice'.[8] Understandably, such price differentials leave little apparent hope of success for alternative development and therefore provide a convincing argument for the proponents of crop eradication. There are, however, a number of flaws in this explanation: comparing a cash crop to staple crops; neglecting to consider price fluctuations (wheat/rice and especially opium); and, last but not least, comparing gross incomes (value of the crop) rather than net incomes (profits). The Afghan case is especially meaningful since poppies have been cultivated in every single province of the country. (In Burma and in Laos, on the other hand, opium production is limited to hilly and mountainous areas due to ecological and climatic constraints.[9]) David Mansfield's extensive studies of opium production in Afghanistan have shown that despite the much higher gross revenues of opium over wheat there is no direct competition between wheat and poppy cultivation. In fact, despite its alleged high profitability, Afghan opium production has far from replaced wheat production. The opium poppy is rarely mono-cropped and 'despite suitable agricultural conditions across much of the country, only a fraction of the total cultivated land was planted with opium poppy, even when cultivation was at its height in 1999', (Mansfield, 2002: 1). In 2006, the 165,000 hectares of poppies – then a record high – accounted only for 3.65 per cent of Afghanistan's arable land. In truth, opium is produced less because of its price differential with wheat than because of food insecurity, lack of land availability, large workforce, and lack of off-farm employment. Of course, the price differential is important since opium sales must enable households to make up for wheat shortages or, in Southeast Asia, for rice shortages.

Yet, lucrative cash crops other than opium can be grown in Afghanistan, Burma and in Laos. Afghanistan has a long pre-war history of international trading in cash crops, and the country's opium production is largely the result of the destruction of its pre-war economy. In Southeast Asia, where the exports of swiddeners from Burma and Laos have been very much limited to opium, it is opium production that has brought the region's highlands into national, regional and global economies. Afghanistan once had valuable and even renowned cash crops that were export commodities, while the hill tribes of Burma and Laos never produced and traded cash crops before opium, at least before the Second World War that is, when poppy cultivation changed the 'hill tribe economy from subsistence agriculture to cash-crop opium farming' (McCoy, 1991: 119).

In Afghanistan, 'horticultural crops like pistachios, citrus fruit, figs, dates and almonds once accounted for 30 to 50 percent of Afghanistan's export earnings'[10] but these crops have suffered from decades of war and recurring drought, and time is needed to restore pre-war levels of production. However, in Afghanistan it makes more sense to compare opium production to horticulture than to wheat production, as the gross incomes per unit area for fruits and nuts are 3 to 7 times that of wheat.[11] In 2000, the gross income of wheat per hectare was half that of tomatoes and onions, a quarter that of apples and potatoes, a seventh that for almonds and an eighth that for opium (World Bank, 2004: 69). The gross revenues of almonds and of some other nuts such as pistachios were, then, comparable with those from opium but this changed after 2000.

In 2000, after the record crop of 1999 (4,600 tonnes), the average farm-gate price of fresh opium was still low: only US$30 per kilogramme, or about what prices had been during the 1990s. But in 2001, after the opium ban of the Taliban almost suppressed opium production in the country (185 tonnes), prices increased to US$700 per kilogramme. In 2002, after the fall of the Taliban, opium production resumed, though with much higher prices than before the ban (US$350/kg) (UNDCP, 2002b: 36). Although average farm-gate prices of fresh opium at harvest time went down after 2003 (US$283/kg in 2003; US$102 in 2005; US$94 in 2006; US$86 in 2007), mostly due to rapidly increasing production, they nevertheless remained much higher than in the 1990s and in 2000, when the gross income from almonds was almost the same as the gross income from opium.

In Southeast Asia, opium prices have also been inversely proportional to supply trends. Yet, as Southeast Asian production has been rapidly decreasing in recent years, opium prices have risen without ever decreasing. In Burma and in Laos, 'bumper crops of opium in the early 1990s caused the farm-gate price for raw opium to drop significantly', although 'prices rebounded somewhat in the mid-1990s' when recurring drought and 'uncharacteristically cold weather damaged poppy crops in Burma and Laos' (DEA, 2001). But, most recently, opium prices in Burma and in Laos have also increased as a direct consequence of forced opium suppression and eradication. In Burma, the average farm-gate price of opium increased from US$151 per kilogramme in 2002, when the country produced 808 tonnes of opium, to US$187 per kilogramme in 2005, when production was estimated at 312 tonnes, to US$230 per kilogramme in 2006, when production was estimated at 315 tonnes, and to US$265 per kilogramme in 2007, when UNODC reported a 460-tonne opium crop: prices therefore rose by 75 per cent as production decreased by 43 per cent in five years (UNDCP, 2002a: 4; UNODC, 2006d: 5; UNODC, 2007c: 50). In Laos, where local opium consumption has been directly affected by a 94 per cent decline in production between 2001 (167 tonnes) and 2007 (9.2 tonnes), prices rose by 500 per cent to reach US$974 per kilogramme (US$550 in 2006) (UNDCP, 2001c: 3; UNODC, 2006d: 5). It is in Thailand, where opium production has stabilized at a very low level (around two tonnes) and where most of the crop is consumed by local users, that average opium farm-gate prices are the highest: US$1,071 per kilogramme in 2007 (UNODC, 2007c: 122).

Thus, the profitability of opium production has increased largely in Afghanistan during the 2000s, and rapidly increasing farm-gate prices have made poppy cultivation much more lucrative than other (licit) crops. But the economic superiority of opium over wheat and other food crops (staple and/or cash crops) must be evaluated according to market prices, as fluctuating prices of staple/cash crops and of opium obviously affect price differentials and make legal alternatives more – or less – interesting. From a strict economic point of view, and regardless of the conflictual and political environment at the time, finding and promoting such alternatives would have been much easier in Afghanistan in the late 1990s or in 2000, when the average farm-gate price of opium was US$30 per kilogramme, than in 2003, when the gross value of opium was no longer eight but 28 times that of wheat (wheat prices had also been falling for a few years) (World Bank, 2004: 69). This is even more the case in Burma and in Laos, where the price rise provoked by forced suppression and eradication has persisted and compromised licit alternative crops.

Claiming economic superiority of opium over wheat (in Afghanistan) and/or rice (in Burma and in Laos) on the basis of comparing their respective gross incomes per unit area is misleading, for opium production is extremely labour intensive and accordingly suffers from much higher production costs than wheat and even upland rice production. One should therefore compare net returns rather than gross incomes per unit area in order properly to evaluate both the alleged economic superiority of opium over licit agricultural products and the economic viability of legal alternatives to opium production.

Once again the Afghan case is especially meaningful, as in Afghanistan the 'opium poppy is not necessarily a profitable crop in all circumstances' (Mansfield, 2002: 3). In the context of food insecurity, where resource-poor households have no or insufficient land to feed their members with self-produced wheat, opium production of necessity tends to concentrate in areas 'where land holdings are small and access to both irrigation water and markets is more problematic' (Mansfield, 2002: 3). In fact, 'sharecropping is a common practice in the opium poppy producing regions of Afghanistan, particularly in the southern region where access to land is particularly inequitable' (Mansfield, 2002: 5): the resource-poor have few other options than to become sharecroppers when their households lack land, for they only have their labour to sell. Opium production is such a labour intensive activity that sharecroppers can receive up to one-third of the crop instead of the fifth they are usually entitled to. Yet, being among the poorest of Afghan farmers and faced with food insecurity, sharecroppers (who cannot afford to be tenants) often have no other option than to turn to credit to make ends meet during the long and harsh Afghan winter months. In becoming more lucrative, opium production has increasingly become a means of access not only to land[12] but also to credit through the *salaam* system. In this system, credit is obtained as an advance payment against a fixed amount of most crops but recently lenders have naturally favoured the most lucrative crop, opium: 'the salaam system provides the poor with the means of survival; and in many districts opium poppy is the only crop on which an advance can be obtained' (Mansfield, 2002: 6). Under the *salaam* system, necessitous Afghan opium farmers borrow significant sums or benefit from advances against takings: their opium crops are thus sold one or two years in advance at half the price of their value at harvest time.

Profiting from opium production is very difficult, therefore, for an Afghan sharecropper. As David Mansfield has shown in 2002, on the basis of 'normal' opium prices with a yield of 46 kilogrammes of opium per hectare and an

average price of US$37 per kilogramme, the annual gross income from opium
production would be US$1,702 at harvest time (Mansfield, 2002: 8).
Notwithstanding the fact that, due to the intense labour requirements, a
sharecropper cannot cultivate one entire hectare of poppies, the net return
from one hectare of opium production is much lower than the gross return.
Sharecroppers keep only one-third of the opium crop after deduction of
ushr – the agricultural tithe – and deduction of the cost of hired harvesters.
Itinerant harvesters receive one-sixth (or, when labour is short, one-quarter)
of the total crop. Yet sharecroppers often sell their harvest in advance at
around half its price. Therefore, in Mansfield's example, the sharecropper
receives between US$382 and US$ 425 at harvest time and half that (US$191
/ US$ 212) if he is part of the *salaam* system, which is likely. On the other
hand, the landowner receives US$851 for the crop produced on his land and
even more if he can afford to retain his opium and sell it later at inflated
prices. If the landowner has the means to buy the opium crop of his
sharecropper in advance at half its price and is able to sell it at the highest
price during later winter months, he can achieve a net return of US$1,957,
nearly ten times as much as the US$212 of the sharecropper (Mansfield,
2002: 8). Mansfield also explains that, given these figures, 'were the cost of
family labour to be factored in, the sharecropping household could actually
make a loss from opium poppy cultivation' (Mansfield, 2002: 9). In reality,
drought and/or forced eradication of their crops, means that many Afghan
opium farmers do not even manage to pay the debts they have accumulated
over the years.

The economic superiority of opium is thus more complex than might
first be thought. Many factors make opium production more – or less –
lucrative and advantageous. It is a labour intensive activity that requires a
large and cheap workforce in order to keep its rather high production costs
manageable. Clearly it is most lucrative when opium prices and opium yields
are high: but if opium prices can vary a lot between countries, and even
within the same country (depending on location but especially on years),
so, too, can opium yields. In 2006, according to UNODC surveys, the average
opium yield in Afghanistan was 37 kilogrammes per hectare, much higher
than in Burma (14.6) and Laos (eight). Average farm-gate prices of opium
in Burma differed greatly between South Shan State (US$214), where yields
were high and where no eradication or suppression was taking place, and
North Shan State (US$436), where yields were lower and where opium bans
and suppression programmes drove prices up (UNODC, 2006d: 80). Land
tenure and the availability or scarcity of arable land also determine the extent
of opium's profitability, as the proceeds from poppy cultivation differ greatly
for Afghan landowners and sharecroppers. In Southeast Asia, opium

production occurs mostly where availability of paddy land is limited. Off-farm employment also determines how attractive and profitable opium production can be, as lack of off-farm employment in a given region implies low wages and low costs of opium production. In Burma's Shan State, in 2003, higher wages in poppy fields (600 to 800 kyat per day) than in bean, onion and tea plantations (300 to 400 kyat per day) drove many Palaung people to work as opium harvesters.[13] Finally, the profitability of opium production must also be compared with that of licit crops (staple and cash crops) since crops such as fruits, nuts, and even tea, can bring net returns similar to opium. David Mansfield stresses the fact that alternatives exist and have proven to be viable:

> Experience has shown that there are crops that are more profitable than opium poppy. For instance, in Thailand, the substitution of opium poppy for flowers has led to profits per square metre being increased by over 50 times. In Pakistan, onion has proven to be a more profitable crop than opium poppy, whilst in Lebanon, garlic has been the more profitable alternative. In Laos, the income from kissina [agarwood or aquilaria tree[14]] exceeds that of opium. The list goes on (Mansfield, 2002: 11).

Of course, for legal alternatives to compete with poppy cultivation, opium prices must be low and local and regional markets for licit crops must be easily and quickly accessible.

The economic superiority of opium, therefore, is real but it is highly contextual and relative. Opium production is a consequence of poverty and food insecurity but rarely constitutes a way out of poverty. Opium farmers clearly have very little choice but to engage in a production process that is labour intensive and attracts high production costs. Opium production clearly depends upon local and regional contexts, and must be addressed according to its diversity and complexity. Opium production is a consequence rather than a cause and must be addressed through its causes: it is the drivers of opium production that matter. Eradication or simple crop substitution falls short of addressing the causes of opium production. Finding and encouraging licit crops is only one of the ways of making opium production less profitable, for 'opium poppy cultivation is not purely a function of the income that it generates' (Mansfield, 2002: 12). Development programmes must not only propose alternative developments to opium farmers, therefore: they must also address the socio-economic and political drivers of opium production if illegal poppy cultivation is to stopped, or at least considerably reduced, in a humane and sustainable way.

8. Opium poppy lancing, Special Region n° 2 (UWSA), Shan State, Burma.

8

Successes and Failures

DRUG SUPPLY REDUCTION: THE CORNERSTONE OF ANTI-DRUG POLICIES

For decades now, especially since the launch of Richard Nixon's war on drugs, drug supply reduction has been the main goal of anti-drug policies. By reducing or suppressing the supply of drugs in foreign countries it was thought that drug prices would rise on the US retail market, thereby deterring Americans from consuming drugs and forcing them to quit or seek medical treatment. Attempts failed, however: production continued to increase, notably from the development of new areas. In fact, drugs actually became more easily available, cheaper and purer: in March 1995, after three decades of a US-led war on drugs, Thomas Constantine, administrator of the Drug Enforcement Administration (DEA), admitted to Congress that 'availability and purity of cocaine and heroin are at an all-time high'.[1]

An increasing number of analysts, social scientists, politicians, and journalists now claim that the war on drugs is lost. After billions of US dollars spent fighting a global war on drugs, cocaine – but also heroin and cannabis – have never been so easily and cheaply available. Part of the problem, many argue, lies with prohibition. Prohibition is deemed counterproductive because it creates illicitness, which in turn renders drug production and trafficking more profitable. According to Charles-Henri de Choiseul-Praslin, co-founder of the former Geopolitical Drug Watch (OGD – Observatoire géopolitique des drogues), the illicit drug economy is stimulated not only by prohibition but also by law enforcement (Choiseul-Praslin, 1991). Prohibition gives 'narcotics huge added value as a commodity' but falls far from deterring producers, traffickers and consumers. In fact, now, supply is so plentiful that the price of a gram of heroin is plummeting in Europe, especially in the United

Kingdom. As for cocaine, according to the UNODC, the street price of a gram in the United States is now less than $70, compared with $184 in 1990. Adjusted for inflation, that's a threefold drop.[2]

Yet, between 2001 and 2006, 'overall, American spending on drug control has increased 34.4 percent' and 'there has been a 136.7 percent increase in US spending abroad and a 20.9 percent decrease in spending on domestic prevention programs, due to budgetary constraints forced by profligacy overseas'.[3] In 2007, the US National Drug Control Budget was US$13.84 billion of which 35 per cent went to demand reduction activities and 65 per cent to supply reduction activities.[4]

Past decades have shown that reducing drug supply alone will not work. Many argue, therefore, that since the global drug market is defined by the mechanisms of supply and demand, a 'balanced approach' needs to be adopted in order to reduce production and consumption. Indeed,

> a landmark study of cocaine markets by the RAND Corporation for the US Army and the Drug Czar's office found that, dollar for dollar, providing treatment to cocaine users is 10 times more effective at reducing drug abuse than drug interdiction schemes and 23 times more effective than trying to eradicate coca at its source.[5]

This is also true of opium production and heroin consumption.

Despite its past failures and its lack of cost-effectiveness, and despite the stimuli of prohibition, drug supply reduction is not impossible, however. One of the main reasons why drug supply reduction has so far failed is that it has been predominantly conducted through the US-led global war on drugs with its mostly repressive methods: i.e. through forced eradication of illicit crops. While development-based approaches – such as crop substitution – have long existed, it is only during recent years that international drug policy discourses have revealed 'an increasing acceptance of the alleged need to integrate AD [alternative development] concepts into a so-called comprehensive "three-pronged strategy of eradication, interdiction and alternative development"' (TNI, 2002). The UNGASS Action Plan on International Cooperation on Eradication of Illicit Drug Crops and on Alternative Development (1998) stressed that alternative development alone was not enough: 'National drug crop reduction and elimination strategies should include comprehensive measures such as programmes in alternative development, law enforcement and eradication'.[6] In 2002 the Transnational Institute deplored the fact that the terms 'balanced approach' and 'comprehensive measures' were employed in the UNGASS text as 'euphemisms used for what is commonly referred to as the 'carrot and stick' approach' (TNI, 2002). In fact, during an international conference on the 'Role of Alternative Development in Drug Control and Development Cooperation', held in Feldafing, Germany, in January 2002, Doris Buddenberg, former head of UNODC's alternative development section and then UNODC representative in Vietnam, declared:

> the balanced approach, originally a term developed to denote a balance between supply and demand reduction measures, has been used here to denote a balance between repressive law enforcement approaches and more liberal development oriented approaches (Feldafing Declaration: 12).

The Drugs Strategy designed by the European Union for the period 2005–12 is also based on a balanced approach, since it concentrates on two policy fields: demand reduction and supply reduction. The law enforcement part of the EU focus on supply reduction is mostly directed at drug trafficking, not at forced eradication. Alternative development in producing countries is favoured by the European Union, and the EU Drugs Strategy is about 'mainstreaming drugs issues into the general common foreign and security policy dialogue and development cooperation' between key drug producing and transit countries.[7]

The Feldafing Declaration stressed the fact that for reduction of drug supply to be effective and sustainable, 'alternative development should neither be made conditional on a prior elimination of drug crop cultivation nor should a reduction be enforced until licit components of livelihood strategies have been sufficiently strengthened' (Point 4 of the Feldafing Declaration: 5). Therefore, in recent years, the 'carrot and stick' approach has been increasingly criticized. In 2005, a global thematic evaluation of alternative development, conducted during the forty-eighth session of the UN Commission on Narcotic Drugs, stated that law enforcement was vital to successful alternative development but that 'to be effective it must use strategies to reduce demand at the farm gate rather than directly target peasant farmers' (Commission on Narcotic Drugs, 2005: 3). The global thematic evaluation went further still by stressing the role and importance of correctly sequencing counter-narcotics steps in order to avoid counterproductivity and unintended effects. Indeed, one of the few 'basic recommendations' of the final report consisted in making the 'elimination of illicit crops conditional on improvements in the lives and livelihoods of households' rather than making it 'a prerequisite for development assistance' (Commission on Narcotic Drugs, 2005: 3).

This is what was stressed in a 2006 document issued by the Council of the European Union, according to which there is 'a strong European reluctance to making coca, poppy and cannabis growers the culprits in the drug chain'. The report stated that 'the EU concerns against forced eradication are not ideological, but rather pragmatic and evidence-based' and that 'explicit conditionality as a means of facilitating eradication can appear as a disguised form of forced eradication'. The EU document, therefore recommended that 'forced eradication should remain an option but should only be pursued when ground conditions ensure that small-scale farmers have had access to alternative livelihoods for a sufficient time period' (Council of the European Union, 2006: 3–5). In fact, as political scientist and TNI fellow, Martin Jelsma, remarked at Feldafing:

> Assistance has been made far too conditional on hectare reductions and, moreover, the discourse has gained ground that 'if the carrot does not work, we'll show them the stick.' In a sense, de-linking AD from this 'comprehensive policy framework' means turning the burden of proof around. Communities would no longer have to 'prove their willingness to substitute' but the government and the international community would have to 'prove the viability of alternatives' before they could demand from peasant and indigenous communities to place at risk the fragile foundations of their survival economy' (Jelsma, 2002).

Yet, despite more than three decades of documented failure, despite their counterproductivity, side-effects and heavy human cost, at the beginning of the twenty-first century opium bans and forced eradication are still largely imposed upon the opium farmers of Afghanistan, Burma and Laos.

SIXTY YEARS OF OPIUM BANS IN ASIA, FROM CHINA TO LAOS

The global prohibition of opium production means that opium poppy cultivation is forbidden except for pharmaceutical purposes. However, prohibition is not systematically or properly enforced everywhere: some countries lack the means (financial, material, technical) to enforce anti-drug laws within their territory; others suffer from having their writ challenged by anti-government forces and do not completely control their territory; and yet again others tolerate illicit crops in some sensitive areas of their territory, often out of (geo)political realism. When governments or local authorities are able to enforce their wishes, most often they do it first and foremost by banning opium production.

An opium ban differs from eradication for it amounts to the prohibition of cultivation, not to the forced destruction of standing crops. Success depends upon authority and power: a degree of political legitimacy is needed if a ban is to be effective. Political legitimacy may be defined as 'the rightfulness of a state, in its authority to issue commands, so that commands are obeyed not simply out of fear or self-interest, but because they are believed to have moral authority, because subjects believe they ought to obey' (Barker, 1990: 11). History shows us that political or religious ideologies have often conferred a degree of legitimacy on some Asian opium bans, whether in China (1949–60) or in Afghanistan (2000–1). Of course, a ban may also be obeyed out of fear – as in Burma, where the Wa opium ban was also heeded out of fear of retaliation by the authoritarian UWSA. In fact,

> the legitimation of power relies on the conviction of the governed that their government (whether democratic, monarchic, Communist, theocratic, or authoritarian) is morally right and they are duty-bound to obey it. In the absence of such conviction there can only be relations of power, not authority, and political legitimacy will be contested, (Alagappa, 1995: 2).

It is very unlikely that the opium ban eventually (2000) imposed by the Taliban – whose legitimacy was at best extremely tenuous and who could ill afford to deprive part of their mostly rural population from a much-needed cash crop – could have been prolonged, even with international aid. History teaches us that the Taliban's opium ban was most likely set to fail. But just as history largely repeats itself, so other opium bans have since been issued in Asia and have yet to be proven sustainable.

The first opium bans: China, Iran, Turkey, and Pakistan

In Asia, only a few of the major illicit opium producing countries issued total opium bans that led to the effective – albeit mainly temporary – suppression of poppy cultivation without the need to resort to forced eradication. Most did so from a position of authority because they were in the main authoritarian regimes (military, Communist, theocratic regimes).

CHINA: The first successful opium ban in history was in China between 1949 and 1960. The largest ban ever, it is also the most successful, for it eventually proved both efficient and sustainable. The ban was issued in a newly Communist China and its success owes much to the fact that it was part of a larger anti-drug campaign that rested upon the ideological articulation of socialism and nationalism[8] (Zhou, 1999: 172). Yet, as Zhou Yongming explains, the Chinese Communist authorities adopted different measures against opium production and trafficking according to whether such activities were carried out by Han people (ethnic Chinese) or by ethnic minorities (Yi people of Liangshan Prefecture (Sichuan) in his example): 'Since opium played such an important role in Yi life, the Communists were very cautious initially in dealing with the Yi', even proclaiming that 'anti-drug campaigns would not be carried out in ethnic minorities areas' (Zhou, 1999: 154).

The Yi case shows how an opium ban allied to compensation and economic aid can work well, and how forced eradication resulted in major riots that led the authorities to promptly remove eradication teams: 'Without resorting to any form of coercion, the propaganda and persuasion seemed to work quite well in several Yi areas', while 'in contrast, the authorities met with strong resistance when they used force to uproot poppy fields in the Yi area' (Zhou, 1999: 155). It was only after fundamental changes occurred in Yi society that the final phase of opium suppression took place. (The fundamental changes included the abolition of slavery and the launch of a land reform that deprived Yi slave owners from their land and workforce – poppies were cultivated by slaves for the benefit of their owners.) The Yi area was declared poppy free only in 1959 (Zhou, 1999: 156–7).

By the early 1960s, China had suppressed both opium production and opium consumption. It did so by taking advantage of the strong Chinese nationalist feelings and of the motivation and new legitimacy offered by the Communist victory and also through the 'ability of the state to conduct a revolution in social organization, which enabled the state and the party to penetrate and control all aspects of people's everyday lives' (Zhou, 1999: 172). This success spared China from drug-related problems until the late 1970s, when illicit drug consumption was fuelled again by trafficking, firstly trafficking in Burmese heroin and amphetamines (in itself a consequence of Chinese anti-drug measures as the rapid Chinese opium suppression largely favoured the emergence of the Golden Triangle) and then, more recently, by local production (amphetamines and most likely opium).

IRAN: The next Asian ban was in Iran, where 40 per cent of the world's medical morphine came from in 1936 (McCoy, 2004: 468). But banning opium in Iran proved difficult and, at first, unsuccessful, at least until the 1979 Islamic revolution. A large opium consuming population – maybe the world's largest – combined with corruption, made opium prohibition and its enforcement problematic. In the early 1950s, the head of the opium monopoly in Isfahan told the first resident agent of the US Bureau of Narcotics: 'We have been accepting bribes for so many years that it would be impossible for us to enforce a law like that' (McCoy, 2004: 468). Yet, under pressure from its close ally the United States, the Shah issued a total ban on opium in 1955. As poppy fields were eradicated and the number of opium users was cut five-fold, illegal imports from Afghanistan and Turkey quickly developed to cater for the remaining 350,000 Iranian opium users. Payment for large quantities of contraband opium using gold ingots severely depleted the Iranian gold reserves and the Shah decided to back peddle on his prohibitionist policy (June 1969) and launched a program of licensed poppy cultivation, to the great disappointment of the United States. Thus, neither the Shah nor the United States succeeded in enforcing a total and sustainable opium ban in Iran. It was, in fact, the Islamic regime of the Grand Ayatollah Ruhollah Khomeini that eventually succeeded in completely suppressing the country's opium production in the early 1980s. The two bans eventually succeeded in suppressing production in the country but in doing so also favoured the development of Afghan and Pakistani opium production: Iran is still one of the world's largest consuming countries of illicit opiates and has been fighting a long and costly battle against drug traffickers on its Afghan and Pakistani borders (Chouvy, 2003a).

TURKEY: A third opium ban took place in Turkey, where opium production had long existed but had increased following the 1955 Iranian ban. This new ban did not prove successful either, at least not completely. Under considerable pressure from the United States, Turkey first issued a partial opium ban in 1967 and, 'after the Nixon administration used a mixture of diplomatic pressure and promises of $35 million in aid, the Turkish government imposed a total opium ban after the 1972 harvest' (McCoy, 2004: 72–3). The Turkish government banned all poppy cultivation, including that destined for the pharmaceutical industry: by doing so, it deprived more than 100,000 farmers of their cash crop and deeply affected the already limited world supply of legal opiates (McCoy, 2004: 393; Dudouet, 2002: 211). The Soviet Union also banned opium production in 1973: until then, Kyrgyzstan produced up to 16 per cent of the world's legal opium. While the Soviet Union never reconsidered its decision, Turkey resumed poppy cultivation as early as 1974, arguing that substitution crops had not acclimatised, that former poppy farmers resented the government, and that other countries had increased (India) or initiated (France) legal opiates production following the Turkish ban (Dudouet, 2002: 211, 238). From that time on, Turkey has been a licit cultivator of opium poppy. However, it no longer produces opium (as in India), but rather concentrate of poppy straw (of which it was already the world's main producer before the 1967–74 ban), as does France and other licit producer countries (Mansfield, 2001: 3; Dudouet, 2002: 238).

PAKISTAN: A fourth Asian opium ban took place in Pakistan in 1979. In pre-partitioned British India, all legal poppy fields were located in what became independent India in 1947. When Pakistan was formed, in 1947, very little opium poppy cultivation was undertaken in the country and all of it was illegal. Attempts at legal cultivation of poppies failed in the Pakistan part of the Punjab in the early 1950s and legal opium production was therefore concentrated, between 1953 and 1979, in the Settled Districts of the North-West Frontier Province, where government control (covered under the Opium Act of 1857) was effective, 'Annually about 1,000 hectares of poppies were thus cultivated in the NWFP' (GTZ, 1998: 26). However, in addition, in the 1970s between 10,000 and 30,000 hectares (GTZ, 1998: 26) of poppies were also cultivated illegally, outside the Settled Districts, in the Merged Districts (where Pakistan's narcotic laws extended but were not easily enforced) and the Tribal Areas (also known as the Federally Administered Tribal Areas and where none of the ordinary laws of the country, including the narcotic laws, were applicable) (Khan, Wadud, 1977). Strictly speaking, opium poppies cultivated in the Tribal Areas were not illegal:

> In Pakistan opium production is covered under a dual system. In the settled districts, control is made effective by application of narcotic laws, while in the tribal territory these laws are not applicable, and thus opium production is practically not banned by existing laws (Khan, Wadud, 1977).

However, the 1979 Prohibition Order, or Enforcement of Hadd, made all opium poppy cultivation illegal in Pakistan after 1979. That the 1979 illicit crop became the largest in Pakistani history (800 tonnes) is perhaps not surprising, for the population had been warned of the prohibition order in 1978. The opium ban later led to a brutal decrease in production (125 tonnes in 1980) and it took the Pakistani authorities fifteen years of eradication and alternative development efforts to bring illicit opium crops below the 100-tonne level. Production dropped from 112 tonnes in 1995 to 24 tonnes in 1996 and eventually reached an all-time low of five tonnes in 2002. However, the Pakistani opium ban cannot be deemed successful as it is now common knowledge that most of Pakistan's opium production has simply moved across the border to Afghanistan, in a so-called balloon effect. Yet, in the context of the US-led war on terrorism waged in Afghanistan and in Pakistan's tribal areas, illicit opium production resumed in and after 2003: from five tonnes in 2002 to 52 tonnes in 2003 and 39 tonnes in 2006 (UNODC, 2007a: 40[9]).

The latest opium bans: Afghanistan, Burma and Laos

AFGHANISTAN: The next opium ban – in Afghanistan, – occurred at a much later date: in 2000. Opium production had increased from 130 tonnes in 1970 to 4,600 tonnes in 1999, partly as a consequence of the Iranian and

Turkish bans. The largest growth in Afghan opium production occurred in the 1990s, after the war against the Soviet Union and during the internecine conflicts that ensued. No ban was issued before 2000, however, since, prior to the Taliban, no Afghan faction had ever controlled sufficient territory for long enough to enforce any prohibition they might declare (if opium suppression was ever any faction's priority). Only in 2000, when they controlled about 85 per cent of Afghanistan and believed themselves powerful enough, did the Taliban (1994/1996–2001) choose to ban opium production. Up to that point, the Taliban leader and *Amir-ul Momineen* (Commander of the Faithful), Mullah Mohammed Omar, had emphasized on a number of occasions his willingness to suppress opium production, but he had most likely refrained from actually doing so because of the Afghan peasantry's heavy dependence upon opium production (the Taliban had first tried to ban opium production in 1997 and had again called for a reduction in production in 1999). 'It is simply not possible to eradicate the poppy without alienating the farmers', explained Abdul Rashid, director of drug control for Kandahar province in 1997 (Chouvy, 1999). Yet, in July 2000, Mullah Omar did proclaim a total ban on opium production, officially in a bid to obtain international recognition and financial aid. Leaving aside the controversy over the reasons for the ban, it is beyond doubt that 'the total ban of 2000 was initiated by the Taliban in the knowledge, at least by some ranking Talibs, that it could be no more than a temporary, and unsustainable, measure' (Macdonald, 2007: 84). The ban was to prove successful but was indeed short-lived: the United Nations reported that Afghan opium production fell from 3,300 tonnes in 2000 to 185 tonnes in 2001 but the ban was not renewed as the Taliban were overthrown by the United States in late 2001. The main consequence of the ban, apart from allegedly producing large profits for the Taliban, for the value of opium largely increased, was to augment the debt burden of many Afghan farmers who had been permitted to produce opium unimpeded over the previous years. Were the ban to have been renewed the Taliban would have undoubtedly faced a serious 'risk of a revolt from many of the farming communities left debt-ridden because of the ban' (Macdonald, 2007: 84).

A direct consequence of the ban was the steep rise in opium prices in the country: the farm-gate price of Afghan opium was on average US$30/kg before the proclamation of the religious edict but US$700/kg by March 2001 (harvest time) (Chouvy, 2002e: 28). The other direct consequence of the ban was that poppy cultivation resumed with renewed vigour as early as 2002 (3,400 tonnes of opium were produced because of increased yields) as the many opium farmers had to quickly repay their debts (aggravated by the ban) and took advantage of inflated opium prices. These two factors continued to drive Afghan opium production up in succeeding years, despite repeated opium bans by the US-supported Karzai administration.

Though it lasted only a year, the opium ban of the Taliban proved highly successful – so much so, that ultimately it was extremely counterproductive, driving up opium prices and production for years and making any legal economic alternative to opium production all the more difficult: six years after the ban, opium prices were still too high for most legal crops to compete. The opium ban of the Taliban had long-term consequences which should be acknowledged and remembered before any other similar ban – i.e. one that is hastily enforced and carries no compensation for the resource-poor – is enforced or even considered. Clearly, however, the lesson was lost, for the sharp decrease in opium poppy cultivation that took place in 2005 in Nangarhar was quickly branded a 'success story' by many, including UNODC, even though it eventually proved unsustainable (if not totally counterproductive). Content with the 96 per cent decrease in cultivation in Nangarhar province, UNODC then claimed to have 'learned a valuable lesson in 2005' as it was also in Nangarhar province that the largest contribution to alternative development had been made (US$70.1 million) (2005a: iii–iv). Yet what was the largest contribution for alternative development in the country was maybe not large enough and had evidently been made available too late. But the production decrease could also be partially attributed to forced eradication, as almost three-quarters (72 per cent) of the eradication carried out in 2004–5 had also taken place in Nangarhar and Helmand provinces. In early 2007, David Mansfield reported a resurgence of poppy cultivation in Nangarhar province 'in areas that have experienced two years of very low levels of opium poppy cultivation and where many households have had to sell off long-term productive assets, migrate and borrow to sustain themselves' (Mansfield, 2007: iii). Indeed, between 2004 and 2007, opium poppy cultivation in Nangarhar province decreased, from 28,213 to 1,093 hectares, then rose to 4,872 hectares, and eventually rose further to a staggering 18,739 hectares (a 285 per cent increase between 2006 and 2007) (UNODC, 2007b: 5).

BURMA Opium bans called for in the mid-1990s in Burma were implemented in the mid-2000s, irrespective of how counterproductive the Taliban opium ban had proven to be. The Kachin Independence Organization (KIO) pledged to ban opium production after its 1994 ceasefire agreement with the junta. This was followed by pledges by the United Wa State Army (UWSA) in 1995, and by the Myanmar National Democratic Alliance Army (MNDAA) in 1997. In a matter of a few years only, the Kokang region (2003) and the Wa region (2006), both in Shan State, were declared opium free. These three bans actually proved successful in bringing about a reduction in Burma's overall opium production, since Shan State was producing up to 90 per cent of Burmese opium in the early 2000s. In the mid-2000s, opium production was clearly on its way down in northern Shan State, but also in Kachin State. However, opium is still produced in Burma: in southern Shan State, where poppy acreage increased in 2005 and 2006, in parts of Kachin State and most likely in Chin State and Kayah State (UNODC, 2006d: 64).

Despite being very recent, the Kokang and Wa opium bans were quickly deemed successful by UNODC and, in 2006, its executive director, Antonio Maria Costa, bolstered by the rapid decline in opium production in Laos, did not hesitate to claim that the days of the Golden Triangle might 'soon be over'. Oddly forgetting about Colombian, Mexican, Pakistani and Indian (both illicit and diverted) opium production, he anticipated that 'if the current trend continues', there would 'soon be only one heroin producing country left in the world – Afghanistan' (UNODC, 2006d: Preface). Nevertheless, Costa also questioned the sustainability of the Burmese bans: 'Farmers need to feel confident that alternative livelihoods are sustainable. Otherwise the temptation to return to opium poppy farming will be too great' (UNODC, 2006d: Preface). Considering what little international aid is made available to either the Kokang or Wa areas, the sustainability of the Burmese bans will only be possible at a high human cost: a large, rapid reduction in the main, and sometimes only, cash crop (opium), will have dire consequences for the local population. In the Kokang area, where most farmers can grow only enough rice to feed their families for six to eight months of the year, and where 80 per cent of the people produce opium mainly to bridge these rice shortages, the World Food Programme had to rush in emergency assistance after the opium ban forced one-quarter of the population to leave the area (Chouvy, 2004b, 2004c; TNI, 2005: 3). In 2003, opium production increased by 21 per cent in the Wa area, where UNODC had set up its Wa Alternative Development Project (WADP) in 1998. UNODC officials declared that the production increase in the Wa area was due in part to the 50 per cent drop that had occurred up north, in the Kokang area – a not unusual or perhaps unexpected consequence, given the history of opium bans and eradication. Various NGOs and United Nations agencies, supposedly including UNODC, tried unsuccessfully to advise the Wa authorities against implementing a ban too rapidly but to no avail. Here, as everywhere else, 'the reversed sequencing of first forcing farmers out of poppy cultivation before ensuring other income opportunities is a grave mistake', noted Martin Jelsma and Tom Kramer (TNI, 2005: 3). Once again, the poorest people – the farmers – had to bear the brunt: in 2005, when the ban was issued by the UWSA, assistance was 'insufficient to offset the impact of the opium bans, and to cover basic needs of ex-opium farmers' (TNI, 2005: 16). In fact, according to UNODC, 'in Special Region 2 (Wa) [. . .] where local authorities enforced an opium ban in 2005, farmers have lost up to 70 per cent of their cash income' (UNODC, 2006d: 15). The geographical and political isolation of the Kokang and the Wa regions, worsened by Burma's international pariah status, has led to there being very little early international intervention to offset the dual deficit now bound to occur: structural deficit in rice and lack of money to buy rice, with no obvious way out.

LAOS: The last opium ban in Asia was in Laos in 2005. There also, as the then European Union's chief of mission in Vientiane, Sandro Serrato, stated, the implementation of the opium ban had 'probably been too rapid and lacked resources'.[10] Yet again, a ban was brought in before alternative livelihoods were made available to opium farmers.

Prior to 1996, opium production was not illegal in Laos and the timescale for the changes proved very fast. In 1994, Laos launched its National Drug Control Programme and stressed that opium poppy cultivation was to be eliminated in a gradual and balanced way through alternative development: what now seems to be recognized as a successful alternative development project had been undertaken in Palavek, central Laos, between 1989 and 1996, and had 'demonstrated that strong supportive clan leadership and successful community participation in AD interventions' could 'reduce opium without need for punitive measures or forced eradication' (Boonwaat, 2004: 96). In 1999, Pino Arlacchi, the UNDCP Executive Director (1997–2001), had promised about US$80 million in aid if Vientiane suppressed opium production.[11] The same year, a strategy described as 'The balanced approach to opium elimination in the Lao PDR' was devised, with the aim of suppressing opium production by 2006. However, the 2001 'Lao Revolutionary Party's Socioeconomic Strategy for Poverty Reduction' brought the deadline forward to 2005 and also decided to suppress slash-and-burn cultivation by 2010 (with a decrease of 50 per cent by 2005). The overall goal was to reduce poverty by 2010 (with a decrease of 50 per cent by 2005) and to provide education for everyone by 2015 (Romagny, 2004: 118). As the funds promised by Arlacchi were to be used to 'assist in the rapid and complete elimination of opium production and opium addiction in Lao PDR within six years' and as 'some 60 per cent of the money was to be used for numerous poverty alleviation projects in the poppy growing regions of Northern Lao PDR', the Lao government, 'quite understandably, embraced this plan and began diverting funds from other uses into the anti-drug campaign' (UNODC, 2005e: 15–16).

The money that Arlacchi promised had never been officially pledged by UNDCP, however, and very little of it was eventually effectively disbursed, as securing funding proved either difficult or impossible. As a consequence, 'the UNODC projects in Lao PDR and across Asia that were developed around that time were designed at vastly higher funding levels than actually pledged or promised, and the resulting funding squeeze has had unfortunate effects on project implementation and on UNODC credibility with implementing partners' (UNODC, 2005e: 16). In a December 2000 confidential resignation letter[12] addressed to Arlacchi, the seventh high-ranking (D-2) UNDCP officer to quit the organization in a three-year period, detailed many of 'the internal management problems' that, in his opinion, were likely to 'undermine the long-term credibility of UNDCP', including the credibility of the many promises made on behalf of UNDCP. Although the Lao government accepted it unquestioningly, the US$80 million pledge made by Arlacchi was actually far from credible if one noted that the UNDCP global expenditure budget for 1999 was US$58 million. Out of what was then an unusually high annual budget, only US$38 million was left available for UNDCP's diverse field activities worldwide. In such a context, the resignation letter denounced how 'promises for new and at times huge new programmes have rarely been made with the concurrence, or even knowledge, of those who have to pay the bill – donors'. Its author also regretted that 'programmes that had once been announced with much fanfare quietly slip into oblivion' while 'other promised programmes simply never reach the stage of implementation'. This had clearly been the case in Laos where, once again, and despite the many lessons available from recent Asian history, the carrot-and-stick approach basically meant that the cart was put before the horse. Worse, in Laos there ended up being no horse to be put before the cart. In December 2001 Pino Arlacchi resigned from UNDCP after a United Nations internal investigation 'confirmed reports of mismanagement, a series of aborted programs and corruption in the Vienna-based UN drug agency'.[13]

The Lao opium ban was nevertheless underway, and opium poppy cultivation was reduced from 26,837 hectares in 1998 to 14,000 in 2002, 6,600 hectares in 2004 and 1,800 hectares in 2005, almost exclusively at the expense of the farmers. The rapid decline in opium production and slash-an-burn cultivation resulted in many upland villages being moved to lowland areas: as Laurent Romagny, from Action contre la faim (ACF) put it: 'If development cannot be brought to people, bring people to development' (Romagny, 2004: 117). A 'noticeable lack of means' with which to achieve the goals of the poverty reduction strategy meant that, next to some positive aspects of village resettlement (education, health, economy), many resettled villages experienced economic hardship, food insecurity and increased mortality rates (70 per cent increase during the first five years, due to a variety of epidemics) (Romagny, 2004: 120, 121, 126). In his preface to the

2006 survey, the Executive Director of UNODC, Antonio Maria Costa, stressed that the Lao government was to be 'praised for its efforts' but that it also needed 'much in terms of sustained support and help', as socio-economic studies indicated that 'about 50 per cent of the 2,056 villages that used to grow opium poppy' still required 'development assistance and could revert back to opium for lack of alternatives'. In 2007, 'many former opium poppy farmers are still coping' (UNODC, 2006d: 37).

About sixty years of Asian opium bans have demonstrated that drug supply reduction is very rarely effective and, in fact, is most often counterproductive. The Chinese 'success story' is in fact unique, for it took a full decade (1950s) to achieve and because it was made possible by the very specific nationalistic and ideological context of the Chinese Communist revolution. All other Asian opium bans were brought in too hastily and with no regard for suitable economic alternatives. In Iran and Turkey, the first opium bans failed, and the governments in each case relaxed the bans and allowed a resumption in production. It took a theocracy to suppress opium production in Iran, most likely at high human cost. Turkey eventually opted for licit opium poppy cultivation and is still a producer of concentrate of poppy straw for the pharmaceutical industry. In Afghanistan, the opium ban introduced by the Taliban in 2000 ultimately failed because it fell victim to its own success: the economic shock caused to the country and to the poorest of its farmers rendered the ban clearly counterproductive. In Afghanistan, opium poppy cultivation has expanded from 82,000 hectares in 2000 to 193,000 hectares in 2007, when the country's 8,200 tonnes of opium represented 93 per cent of global illicit opium production. According to UNODC, in the late 2000s Southeast Asia's Golden Triangle would be close to disappearing, Thailand having almost suppressed cultivation and Burma and Laos having largely diminished their respective output. Yet, even UNODC frequently questions the sustainability of these 'successful' opium bans as alternative development is either absent or at least largely insufficient to make up for the loss of income for the poorest of Asian farmers.

If the sustainability of these recent opium bans is to be questioned, the human cost involved is clearly undeniable and raises fundamental questions. When bans are brought in before suitable alternative livelihoods have been devised and introduced the very survival of millions of poor farming people is threatened: in the Wa region, for example, UNODC explains that 'opium reduction has resulted in a serious lack of cash, lack of food, and increased debt for many households' who 'are now unable to purchase not only rice, but also basic household necessities such as cooking oil, salt and clothing' (UNODC, 2006d: 25). Most often, opium bans not only fail, prove counterproductive and put countless lives at risk, they also go against basic human rights and the democratic values that the very proponents of global prohibition and of the war on drugs claim as amongst their foremost objectives. Increasing poverty and threatening livelihoods is indeed clearly contrary to basic human rights. According to the Office of the United Nations High Commissioner for Human Rights (UNHCHR): 'Economic deprivation – lack of income – is a standard feature of poverty'. Yet, 'poverty is not only deprivation of economic material resources but a violation of human dignity too'.[14] Most Asian opium bans have been – and continue to be – issued by authoritarian regimes in countries where human rights and democratic values are far from respected.

FORCED ERADICATION: A FAILED AND COUNTERPRODUCTIVE APPROACH

Eradication is the forced destruction of standing crops, whether manually (thrashing of poppy fields by hand), mechanically (by tractor, helicopter, planes), chemically (use of herbicides such as glyphosate, paraquat, or Agent Orange), or even biologically (use of fungi or mycoherbicides, also known as 'Agent Green', such as *Pleospora papaveracea* against opium poppies or *Fusarium oxysporum* against coca bushes). Eradication relies on force and power, not on authority, and therefore easily leads to violence. The consequences of eradication also often leave farmers worse off. A farmer who complies with a ban often loses revenue but not an entire crop: he can maybe grow another crop. A farmer whose fields are eradicated loses an entire crop and can often find himself with no income at all. Worse still, farmers whose fields are eradicated at a late stage – not long before harvest time – not only lose their costs to date (labour, seeds, water, fertilisers, etc.) but find themselves unable to repay their debts when they have sold their crops in advance or have borrowed against takings, as is often the case for the poorest opium farmers from Afghanistan to Burma and Laos. Eradication is therefore even more destructive than it first appears as it basically targets the crops and the livelihoods of the most vulnerable segment of the drug industry: the farmers themselves and, among them, especially the resource-poor farmers.

Opium production is a means of coping with poverty and food insecurity (whether poverty is war-related or not), and eradication is more often than not counterproductive, threatening as it does precarious livelihoods, increasing poverty and raising opium prices (Chouvy, 2005a). Yet, eradication as a course of action is often encouraged on the premise that opium farmers are breaking the law, thus giving legitimacy to this course of action. A socio-economic issue is addressed from a legal standpoint: as a consequence opium production is targeted as a cause of further problems – illegality, corruption, addiction, etc. – rather than seen as a consequence of poverty related problems such as food insecurity, land scarcity and labour shortages. The causes of opium poppy cultivation are therefore ignored and even exacerbated.

Eradication is also promoted on the grounds that many opium farmers, whether in Afghanistan, Burma or Laos, resort to opium production out of choice (some say greed), and not out of need. In January 2007, for example, the first secretary for counter-narcotics at the British Embassy in Afghanistan stated in an interview about opium production in Helmand province:

> My feeling is that a lot of the poppy is grown here by people who are greedy, not needy, not by people who have to grow poppy. They're growing it for a profit. They're not being forced to grow it, they choose to grow it, and they do it because they can get away with it.[15]

While some deny that opium production is linked to poverty, others (some high-ranking Lao officials, for instance) contend that it is a cause rather than a consequence of poverty. In Afghanistan, as elsewhere, there are those who argue that farmers, whether opium farmers or not, 'are rational economic actors with free choice over what crops they cultivate and who derive considerable riches from that choice'. According to such views the opium poppy is therefore 'a legitimate target for eradication – in fact it is the only action that will deter farmers from the blind pursuit of profit'. To the proponents of eradication, 'the underlying assumption is that there are sufficient livelihoods available to farmers or that development agencies can "create" them quickly, providing "the carrot" to make "the stick" of eradication more politically acceptable' (Mansfield, 2007b: 15).

Poverty, opium production, and eradication

UNODC's Executive Director, Antonio Maria Costa, wrote in the preface of the 2005 Afghanistan Opium Survey:

> History demonstrates that, anywhere in the world, farmers who are given the option to choose between legality and illegality choose legality, even when the money earned is less. When the choice is between hunger and illegality, again, history tells us that farmers choose illicit pursuits, even when they may face serious retribution (UNODC, 2005a: iv).

Yet, one year later, UNODC was claiming in a strategic planning framework for Afghanistan that 'while poverty remains a factor for poppy cultivation at the farm level, there is no causal relationship between poverty and cultivation' (TNI, 2006: 8). Then, in the 2006 Afghanistan Opium Survey UNODC stated: 'the largest opium poppy cultivation provinces are not the poorest' (UNODC, 2006b: 28). Eventually, in 2007, Antonio Maria Costa, explained that 'in centre-north Afghanistan, despite massive poverty, opium cultivation has diminished' while 'in south-west Afghanistan, despite relative higher levels of income, opium cultivation has exploded to unprecedented levels' (2007b: iv). In the same document Costa concluded that opium cultivation in Afghanistan was 'no longer associated with poverty – quite the opposite' (UNODC, 2007b: iv).

In fact, UNODC argues that poverty and opium production are not linked in Afghanistan. It takes a very simplistic and outdated view, seeing poverty simply as a function of income. Such a narrow view of poverty overlooks the basic fact that farmers who resort to opium production are not poor simply because their revenues are low (or rich because their revenues are high) but also because they have meagre or non-existent resources and assets (resource-poor farmers) and must cope with food shortages and insecurity. Defining poverty in terms of provincial income, as UNODC does, is misleading, since the gross and net incomes derived from opium production vary widely both between provinces and between different socio-economic groups: access to land (land tenure arrangements), cash and credit (availability of surplus financial assets or need to access credit); the availability and costs of workforce (labour intensiveness impacts on costs of opium production), are all factors.

According to David Mansfield and Adam Pain, 'the claim of the relative wealth of farmers in the south is not supported by the available data' produced by the Central Statistics Office of Afghanistan. They explain how the divide between the poor (low opium-producing) north and the rich (high opium-producing) south professed by UNODC is based on average income figures at provincial levels, while the average per capita income shows less difference. According to the authors,

> leaving aside the issues of income inequalities within provinces and the well known methodological difficulties associated with collecting data on household income and its reliability in developing countries, the focus on income as a measure of poverty represents a severely limited understanding of the nature and measurement of poverty, particularly under conditions of chronic insecurity (Mansfield and Pain, 2007:14).

By continually challenging the connection between opium production and poverty, UNODC overlooks the conclusions of many recent studies. It has been clearly demonstrated how the returns on opium differ considerably by socio-economic group, mainly because inequitable land tenure arrangements (such as sharecropping) mean that those who have both land and capital (which tends to be the way in Afghanistan) are able to claim most of the profit generated, leaving those who actually do the work – the resource-poor – with as little as one-tenth of the net returns of landowners (Mansfield, 2004c: 85). In Afghanistan, opium production arises mainly from need not from greed: for the land-poor, 'opium is not just a source of income: it provides opportunities to access land on a sharecropping or tenancy basis as well as drawing on the labour supply of the household' (Mansfield and Pain, 2005: 3). Of course, some – such as rich landlords and traffickers – profit from opium production in disproportionate ways. Yet, eradicating poppy fields in Afghanistan effectively amounts to targeting the poorest and the most vulnerable in the Afghan opium industry, since rich landlords have enough land to grow both wheat for their own consumption and poppies for cash. As far as traffickers are concerned, they are the first to benefit from eradication since it raises opium prices and their profit margins. As the Transnational Institute explains, 'there are doubts about the effectiveness of interdiction as a policy instrument' because 'even chemical precursor control, often seen as the most effective kind of interdiction' may increase the price of precursors and thereby augment the earnings of trafficking networks (TNI, 2007: 3).

Opium bans and eradication campaigns can prove even more complex when opium farmers are also opium consumers: unlike Afghanistan and Burma, where local consumption is still very limited, in Laos most of the national opium production is reported to be consumed locally. Opium addiction in the country is frequently denounced for increasing – if not causing – poverty: 'Opium was produced because of poverty', says Leik Boonwaat, UNODC Representative in Laos, 'but its easy availability led to widespread abuse contributing to even greater poverty'.[16] While there is some truth in this statement, high-ranking Lao officials often turn things around by going as far as saying that opium production and consumption are the cause – and not a consequence – of poverty. In the official Lao ideology, suppressing opium production will reduce – if not suppress – poverty: hence the national plan to reduce poverty through the suppression of both opium production and slash-and-burn cultivation (viewed – wrongly, according to most anthropological and agronomic studies – as unecological and economically ineffective). Yet, in Laos, the opium ban may well prove even more harmful to opium farmers than in countries where opium is produced but barely consumed. In Laos, the lack of substitutes to opium consumption adds to the lack of economic alternatives as opium is far from being used simply as a recreational drug: it is also a panacea but especially used as a pain-killer. Of course, opium consumption most frequently leads to addiction and eventually interferes with daily workloads. Yet, as historian Carl Trocki explains about the use of opium by Chinese coolies in nineteenth-century Southeast Asia: 'In contrast to the contemporary anti-opium propaganda, much evidence suggests that opium did not immediately turn its users into soporific vegetables, or sunken chested hulks'. In fact,

> it can be argued, and indeed it was by many defenders of the system, that opium was a necessary work drug for the Chinese laborers. In addition to killing the pain of daily labor, opium was also the coolie's prophylactic against diarrhea caused by dysentery, bad food, and the range of intestinal parasites that plagued one in the jungle.

Of course, 'opium did not cure anything, it simply masked the symptoms' (Trocki, 1999: 144– 5).[17] In the same way that opium made it possible for 'a Chinese coolie 'to ignore the messages of his body, and to go on working for yet another day', it now makes it possible for many Asian opium farmers to cope with poverty and food insecurity without addressing the causes of them. In this context, illness and remedy are largely confused and forced eradication may well be the 'treatment that kills the patient',[18] as eradication clearly increases poverty and threatens fragile livelihoods.

Ultimately (especially when targeted at people without alternatives and when poorly implemented) eradication increases poverty and therefore reinforces the main driver of opium production without addressing its causes, including land scarcity, unequal land tenure arrangements, oversized households (Afghanistan) or inadequate workforce (Burma, Laos), climatic vagaries, political upheaval, armed conflict, etc. The drivers of opium production are many and complex and prevent any 'quick fix solution' from working in a sustainable and humane way. In 2004 the World Bank also stressed how complex a phenomenon poverty was:

> Poverty in Afghanistan is multidimensional, involving a complex interplay between low assets (physical, financial and human), years of insecurity and drought, indebtedness, poor infrastructure and public services, traditional roles and other factors (World Bank, 2004: ii).

In such a context, as Mansfield and Pain explain, 'there are no short cuts [. . .] If the opium poppy is to be eliminated, even over a small geographic area, a broad-based and multisectoral effort is required over a number of years' (Mansfield and Pain, 2005: 3).

Food insecurity and the risk of crop eradication

It is important to understand that opium poppy cultivation is closely connected with poverty because this fact explains why eradication is likely to fail and why it proves counterproductive in most cases. To be more precise, the close links that exist between poverty and opium production need to be acknowledged and understood if eradication is to be used as an effective deterrent, and then only once legal, viable and sustainable livelihoods have been established. In a study in which they ask how it is that eradication can raise the risk (of destruction and thereby economic loss) associated with poppy cultivation when opium farmers have nothing to lose, Mansfield and Pain have shown that:

> Where alternative income sources exist, eradication can push those farmers who persist with drug cultivation. Where alternatives do not exist and in risky contexts, eradication is rarely cost-effective and can create perverse incentives for farmers to grow even more drug crops. It can also fuel violence and insecurity, hostility to national authorities and displace cultivation to less accessible locations. This ultimately undermines long-term efforts to change the conditions that promote drug crop cultivation (Mansfield and Pain, 2006: 15).

In fact, in Afghanistan and elsewhere, poor farmers have no other choice than to risk eradication even if it means the destruction of their entire crop and consequently that their families will be deprived of even the most basic resources: 'simply looking at the risk that destruction of the crop imposes on rural households is insufficient, as a farmer will not associate any real financial costs to the loss of a crop unless there are other legal income opportunities available' (Mansfield and Pain, 2006: 2). The authors explain that even where eradication has been carried out more than once, farmers often continue to grow illicit crops: be they poppies in Afghanistan and Burma, coca in Colombia, or cannabis in Morocco. In fact, as was the case in Afghanistan and Colombia, farmers whose fields have been eradicated often increase the surface areas dedicated to illicit crops and/or scatter them in order to make up for lost income and minimize the threat of eradication.

In any case, 'where there is poor market access or lower resource endowment with limited effective market demand, crop options are very few' and the risk of eradication is not a deterrent because, in Afghanistan 'the opportunity cost of planting opium poppy and having it destroyed is equal to the wheat crop that might have been cultivated in the place of poppy' (Mansfield and Pain, 2006: 7). Since poor farmers have no other choice but to resort to opium production in order to cope with food insecurity and poverty, eradication is a risk worth taking. Once poverty and food insecurity are acknowledged and understood, it is easy to see that resource-poor farmers often have very little choice but to grow illicit crops. In words that echo Antonio Maria Costa in 2005, before he challenged the links between poverty and drug crop cultivation, Mansfield and Pain explain: 'If they [the farmers] refrain from planting opium poppy and plant wheat, their family will go hungry; if they do plant opium poppy and it is destroyed their family will also go hungry. In this context the opportunity cost of opium poppy cultivation is very low even with a risk of eradication' (Mansfield and Pain, 2006: 7).

The failures and counterproductivity of eradication

In its first economic report on Afghanistan in a quarter century (2004), the World Bank warned against the development of the opium economy and described it as 'the lynchpin of a "vicious circle" of insecurity, weak government, powerful warlords, and drug money' (World Bank, 2004: xvi). However, the same report argued that 'limited success in past experience with fighting drugs does not give much ground for optimism, especially in view of the unique aspects of the opium economy in Afghanistan (most notably its sheer size)'. It stressed that 'no single approach is likely to be effective and sustainable', and that, on the contrary, 'a combination of different measures, well-designed and well-sequenced, will be essential to have any hope of success' (World Bank, 2004: 90).

The report also noted:

> Eradication in the absence of alternative livelihoods being available does not work, and eradication followed by assistance does not seem to work well, yet eradication (and its threat) can help reinforce alternative livelihoods development if the former follows the latter (World Bank, 2004: 90).

Drawing on the 'rich international experience with supply-side interventions to reduce drug production, primarily eradication of poppy fields' the World Bank report further asserted:

A key lesson is that eradication alone will not work and is likely to be counterproductive, resulting in perverse incentives for farmers to grow more drugs (e.g. in Colombia), displacement of production to more remote areas, and fuelling of violence and insecurity (Peru, Bolivia, Colombia), which in several cases forced the eradication policy to be reversed and led to adverse political outcomes.

The report then eventually concluded: 'Neither does the approach of making eradication a condition for development assistance work – without alternative livelihoods already in place, premature eradication damages the environment for rural development' (World Bank, 2004: 87).

In a 2004 interview, Doris Buddenberg, then head of UNODC in Afghanistan, shared the same concerns:

> Eradication usually does not bring about a sustainable reduction of poppy crop, it is a one-time short-term effort. Also eradication usually pushes the prices up. As we have seen from the Taliban period, the one-year ban on opium poppy cultivation increased prices enormously the following year and it became extremely attractive for farmers to cultivate poppy.[19]

Yet, as stressed by the World Bank report, eradication may prove useful and even efficient when used against farmers who resort to opium production out of choice and not out of need (those with sufficient assets who could profit from growing legal crops but instead choose to maximize their profits since opium is prohibited but prohibition is not enforced) and/or when used after alternative livelihoods have been promoted and have proven viable and sustainable. In Afghanistan, farmers who enjoy good access to productive assets and produce opium without being dependent on it for their livelihood 'may constitute between 5 and 20 percent of the rural population' (Mansfield, 2007b: 15–16). But as there are many more farmers who are largely, if not completely, dependent on opium production, and as it would obviously prove very difficult to distinguish between resource-poor and resource-rich farmers, eradication should be avoided until alternative livelihoods have been offered to, and adopted by, the poorest farmers: in any case, in Afghanistan, where the British Embassy drug team has used many different criteria to target areas eligible for eradication, such a targeting policy could not be implemented because 'in practice kinship ties and local power relations play a more important role when negotiating targets than these supposedly "objective criteria"' (TNI, 2007: 4) Eradication has already turned out to be unequally enforced in Afghanistan, where widespread corruption often gives the rich and well-connected the opportunity to avoid the destruction of their poppy crop. In fact, 'eradication has often become a new source of income for local officials' (TNI, 2007: 2). In the end, the people 'targeted by eradication are mostly those who have the fewest alternatives available to them' (TNI, 2007: 4). Eradication is therefore largely ineffective and counterproductive, as it worsens poverty and inequality – the main causes of opium production – and does not address the drivers of opium production since it raises opium prices, makes its production more lucrative and attractive, and increases the opportunities for corruption.

Eradication in Asian history

The physical destruction of the cash crops of poor and often marginalized – if not alienated – communities is likely to lead to social and political instability. In Asia, history teaches us that eradication measures have often sparked armed violence and have therefore had to be abandoned by various governments.

THAILAND: In the early 1970s Thailand experienced a brief period of forced eradication until opium-producing communities reinforced the ranks of the Communist Party of Thailand (CPT), at that time in armed conflict with Bangkok. And as early as 1967, the 'Red Meo' revolt in Thailand was sparked after Hmong opium farmers from Chiang Rai province were forced to pay excessive bribes to Thai officials in order to avoid their crops being eradicated and after the Thai police burned one village to the ground. What had started off as a conflict over excessive corruption, ended up reinforcing the role of the KMT in the regional opium trade as the Thai military used the remnants of the Chinese nationalist army to quell what they conveniently denounced as a 'communist uprising' (McCoy, 1991: 362–3). Forced eradication did not resume in Thailand before 1984: i.e. only after the CPT was considerably weakened and 'then only in areas where it was thought the people could make a satisfactory living without relying on opium' (Renard, 2001: 102). Basically, 'although opium production was prohibited as of 1959, up to 1985 the Royal Thai government pursued a "soft" approach, where priority was given to development measures'. Yet, 'from 1985 onwards – complementary to development projects – government agencies began to destroy poppy fields' (GTZ, 1998: 40). Eradication campaigns were carried out annually: in 1997 1,052 hectares out of 1,405 were destroyed compared to 153 hectares out of 157 in 2006 (GTZ, 1998: 40; UNODC, 2006d: 127).

PAKISTAN: In Pakistan things were different, as 'development and enforcement were chosen as a strategy from the start'. Yet, 'generally, government agencies were reluctant to enforce the ban on poppy cultivation' (GTZ, 1998: 52). The death of thirteen people during an eradication campaign in Gadoon Amazai, in the Swat Valley in 1987, 'also resulted in the government adopting a more cautious approach' (Mansfield, Pain, 2006: 4). And in 1989, in Buner, also in the Swat Valley, an eradication campaign angered the Yusufzai tribesmen, who attacked the local police station and fired at the Thrush plane used for aerial spraying of the same Agent Orange defoliant that had already been widely used during the Vietnam War (Labrousse, 1992: 637). As Mansfield and Pain remind us, 'subsequently, in the Dir district of NWFP from the mid 1990s, eradication was pursued in phases, implemented in valleys only after a period of broad development assistance' (Mansfield and Pain, 2006: 4). It was only in 1993 that Pakistani authorities eventually deemed eradication measures less risky, although law enforcement usually meant warning farmers not to plant opium poppies rather than forcefully eradicating their crops. While the reduction in opium production that eventually took place in the Dir district was attributed to 'a combination of alternative development and the risk of enforcement', it can be said that it occurred because the opportunity costs of poppy cultivation were high enough: 'Many farmers reported that they changed their cultivation practices after realising that alternative crops and cropping systems could match or even increase their profits and enable them to avoid problems with the local administration' (NWFP Government quoted in: GTZ, 1998: 53).

Yet, the road to an opium-free Pakistan was to prove longer and more difficult than anticipated as tensions arose in 1998 in the Dir and Mohmand districts, where opium poppies were again increasingly replacing wheat. There, eradication campaigns could only be carried out after negotiation with Pashtun tribes (the Sultankhel and Paindakhel tribes warned of a possible 'blood bath' if eradication was carried out in the Nihag Valley of the Dir district) and after the Frontier Corps were deployed on top of the hills surrounding the Shantimena Valley, in Mohmand district (Chouvy, 2002a: 154–7). Yet, Pakistan only enjoyed its 'opium-free' status for four years – from 1999 to 2002 – as production resumed in 2003: from five tonnes in 2002, production increased to 52 tonnes in 2003 and was still at 39 tonnes in 2006. Pakistan's resurgence not only went largely unnoticed due to neighbouring Afghanistan's massive domination of world opium production; it was also made possible by the impact and consequences of the geopolitical and strategic developments in Afghanistan and within Pakistan's volatile North-West Frontier Province. A 2006 report of Pakistan's Anti Narcotics Force (ANF) explains: 'As far as NWFP is concerned, the geo-political scenario of the province, coupled with its complicity with the ongoing war on terror against those camped along the Pak-Afghan border, has continued to defeat possible gains. Moreover, the shift in world focus from anti-poppy to anti-terror has dried up foreign assistance' (ANF, 2006). In a very significant way, in Pakistan the war on drugs suffered from the strategic imperatives of the war on terrorism and while eradication campaigns were initially intensified to counter the spread of poppy cultivation (1,484 hectares eradicated in 2001, 4,185 in 2003, and 5,200 in 2004), they were eventually downsized (only 391 hectares eradicated in 2005 and 354 in 2006) (UNODC, 2007: 39–40).

BURMA: In the two so-called success stories of Asian opium suppression, forced eradication only played a minor role and was implemented at a late stage: in both Thailand and Pakistan, early eradication campaigns proved strategically counterproductive and had to be called off for years, until a more favourable political and economic context had emerged. Yet, as we have seen with the Pakistani case, new strategic imperatives can eventually compromise the resort to forced eradication. In Burma, forced eradication has proved highly inefficient and ineffective. As Ron Renard explains, when Burma received financial aid from the United States (1974–88) to develop its counter-narcotics programme, 'although much opium poppy was destroyed, destruction never amounted to much over 10 percent of the total area cultivated under the high estimate for opium production in Burma' (Renard, 1996: 67). As we have already seen, aerial spraying of a systemic broadleaf herbicide (2,4-D) took place in the Kokang area in the mid-1980s but quickly proved problematic as Burmese pilots refused to fly over the region for fear of anti-aircraft fire and as chemical contamination of streams and food crops was reported (Renard, 1996: 68). Aerial spraying was quickly called off as the United States cut off its counter-narcotics aid to Burma in 1988, the same year the Burmese authorities claimed to have eradicated about 12,000 hectares of opium poppies (GTZ, 1998: 45).

While forced eradication clearly did not work in Burma – where opium production reached its climax in 1996 – it undoubtedly worsened poverty in targeted areas. A United Nations survey conducted in 1991 in eastern Shan State reported:

> In the visited villages under the poppy eradication programme the mission got the impression that most households were facing extreme poverty and starvation. In the first year of the programme, they were able to survive with the relief grain distribution and by selling their livestock. In the second year they do not know how they will survive. This situation affects all households but especially the lower stratum families.

The report concluded that eradication was 'accelerating the downward spiral of impoverishment' (GTZ, 1998: 45). As for the large decrease in opium production that eventually occurred in Burma (in the 2000s), it did not result from forced eradication but from opium bans imposed not by Burma's central government but by ethnic polities and their armies (Kachin, Kokang and Wa) at high human cost.

AFGHANISTAN: Despite what history teaches us about the failures and counterproductivity of forced eradication, this repressive approach to illicit opium poppy cultivation was still widely used and encouraged in Afghanistan in the 2000s. Eradication campaigns have been carried out repeatedly since the fall of the Taliban, despite their limited scope and results (in terms of destruction of standing crops and in terms of disincentive to further cultivation) and have resulted in violent encounters between opium farmers and eradication teams, whether in northern or in southern Afghanistan. Yet the efficiency and the feasibility of forced eradication have been questioned not only by the huge increases in Afghan opium production that occurred again in 2006 and in 2007 but also by the many reports and surveys that have warned against the unintended and counterproductive effects of eradication. In fact, in Afghanistan, projects for the accelerated suppression of the opium economy (one-third of the overall economy of one of the world's poorest countries) basically risk compromising the food security of producers and destabilizing the difficult transition to a peace economy (Chouvy and Laniel, 2006: 49). After his unheeded January 2002 ban on opium production, the Afghan President, Hamid Karzai, made the provincial governors responsible for reducing and eventually suppressing opium production in their provinces. Yet, as the Transnational Institute reported in 2007, 'provincial governors in Afghanistan face a difficult dilemma' as 'too much pressure may lead to violent resistance, further decline of support for the government, and could upset the delicate tribal balance in the provinces' (TNI, 2007: 2).

As a matter of fact, some Afghan governors have commented on the risks associated with forced eradication. While conducting large-scale eradication in Balkh province, Governor Atta Mohammad Noor warned in 2006 that eradicating poppy fields at harvest time was dangerous and politically counterproductive: 'Farmers could definitely get violent if their year's work is destroyed.' In the meantime, in the neighbouring Samangan province, Governor Abdul Haq Shafaq also warned against eradication: 'When we destroy poppy fields, the farmers are waiting for an alternative. When we don't give them anything, they think we have stolen everything and they grow mistrustful of the government.'[20] While armed resistance of farmers against eradication teams is something that has occurred everywhere in

Afghanistan – and not only in provinces where Taliban resistance is active – the most recent and best documented case was narrated by Jon Lee Anderson in the New Yorker in 2007 after he accompanied a team of the US-supported Afghan Eradication Force in Uruzgan province, much of which was classified by the United Nations as 'Extreme Risk / Hostile Environment'. During its second day in Tirin Kot, the AEF team 'came under fire in an ambush apparently orchestrated by the Taliban' and four Afghan team members were wounded (one of them later died from wounds). Ultimately the Uruzgan eradication campaign fell short of its objectives since the AEF team was not able to operate for more than one of the ten days initially planned (Anderson, 2007).

Yet, at the national level, forced eradication largely increased between 2006 and 2007, despite its known failures, costs and risks, and despite the many warnings issued by international organisations and experts. One of them, Barnett Rubin, stressed: 'Introducing eradication before farmers feel secure in the alternatives has led farmers in some areas to call upon the Taliban to protect them and take up arms to prevent eradication teams from entering their areas.'[21] However, resistance to eradication is not limited to areas where the Taliban are strongest or where the insurgency is most developed, for protests and clashes occurred not only in Kandahar province but also in Nangarhar and in Badakhshan provinces: while the drug economy has had long and obvious links with the war economy – and still had some in 2007 – the fundamental drivers of the opium economy are clearly economic in nature. Therefore, in the fragile and difficult context of a transition from war to peace, from a war economy to a peace economy, forced eradication further increases poverty and violence instead of resolving matters. A December 2006 CARE report on 'Curbing Opium Poppy Cultivation in Afghanistan' warned against what many, among scholars, but also in the development community and in the military, have long been wary of:

> There are many ways in which the opium economy promotes insecurity. Although the majority of Taliban funding is believed to come from international sources, drug revenue is an additional source of funding. Potentially more dangerous, however, is the Taliban's ability to tap into rural communities' growing discontent with the current Afghan administration. If counter-narcotics strategies are not carefully thought out, they could exacerbate this already precarious situation' (CARE, 2006: 7).

Political scientist Vanda Felbab-Brown goes even further by warning that 'in the absence of large-scale rural development, eradication is politically explosive' as 'strong-fisted measures to suppress the peasant resistance [to forced eradication] will further fuel unrest' (Felbab-Brown, 2005: 64).

This was even more relevant in 2007, as opium production and forced eradication increased again between 2006 and 2007, leading, as one might expect, to 'much more severe' resistance to eradication in 2007 than in 2006 (TNI, 2007: 5). Yet the situation in Afghanistan in the 2000s provides a classic example of why drug war politics has been described as a politics of denial: because 'reports of failure only reinforced the resolve of public officials to "try harder" to apply a little more funding, a little more firepower' (Bertram, Blachman, Sharpe and Andreas, 1996: ix-x). This is exactly what has occurred in Afghanistan, where the Afghan government – backed by Britain and the European Union – has long resisted the pressing and repeated calls of the United States to resort to aerial or even ground spraying of herbicides. Afghan authorities feared that the use of herbicides would also destroy the food crops grown by Afghan farmers alongside or interspersed with opium poppies. They also feared that the spraying of herbicides would be denounced by the Taliban as US chemical warfare against Afghan farmers. Thomas A. Schweich, the US assistant secretary of state for international narcotics issues, actually acknowledged that in late 2007 when he declared: 'There has always been a need to balance the obvious greater effectiveness of spray against the potential for losing hearts and minds. The question is whether that's manageable. I think that it is.'[22] Interestingly, 2007 saw the transfer to Afghanistan of the US Ambassador to Colombia – aerial spraying advocate William Wood, nicknamed 'Chemical Bill' among British and other NATO officials in Afghanistan.[23] It also saw the policy u-turn of Colombian President, Alvaro Uribe, who unexpectedly put a stop to the failed and highly controversial aerial spraying over Colombia's coca fields: the largest-ever spraying (2006) could not prevent a new increase and spread in coca cultivation in the country in 2007.[24] The Colombian case clearly demonstrated the failure and counterproductivity of forced eradication, including aerial spraying. In any case, in October 2007 the government of Hamid Karzai once again refused to countenance either aerial or ground spraying of Afghan opium poppies.[25] As a CARE-CIC report warned in 2005 about Afghanistan: 'Short-term reductions in poppy cultivation should not be mistaken for long-term success' as 'without sustained, well-funded alternative livelihoods programs, vigorous law enforcement, anti-corruption efforts and a realistic approach to eradication, any reduction in poppy cultivation in 2005 will prove illusory' (CARE, 2005: 7). The 2005 reduction indeed proved illusory – if not counterproductive – as despite increased eradication in 2006 and in 2007, opium production broke two successive records in 2006 and in 2007.

FROM 'CROP SUBSTITUTION' TO 'ALTERNATIVE DEVELOPMENT' AND 'ALTERNATIVE LIVELIHOODS'

About forty years of development-orientated counter-narcotics

Opium bans and forced eradication have long taken priority over economic development in counter-narcotics policies. In the early 1950s, China suppressed its massive opium production almost exclusively through an imposed ban that led to tens of thousands of arrests, thousands of executions, hundreds of thousands of propaganda and 'education' meetings, and a few eradication campaigns (Zhou, 1999: 95– 108). Yet, as we have seen, in the Yi areas of south-western China, where opium poppies covered as much as 40 per cent of some counties' arable land and where 50–80 per cent of local households (both Yi and Han) engaged in poppy cultivation, the authorities managed to reduce part of the cultivated area by convincing Yi farmers to switch from opium to food crops. While the anti-opium campaign came to an end in 1952 in most of the country, in the Yi areas complete opium suppression was only achieved in 1958, after the authorities imposed crop substitution through land and work reforms (so-called democratic reforms: prohibition of slavery by the Yi, redistribution of arable land belonging to slave owners, launch of agricultural cooperatives) and eventually eradicated all remaining opium poppy fields (Zhou, 1999: 150–7). Opium production was halted in a very similar way in the Aba Tibetan Autonomous Prefecture (Sichuan), where the authorities realized that since 'in some areas, opium was still the main source of income for many ordinary households [. . .] conducting opium suppression would have provoked strong resistance' (Zhou, 1999: 161). There, the suppression of opium production was only achieved in 1959, again after so-called democratic reforms and collectivization programmes were introduced in Tibetan areas. As early as the 1950s, the new Chinese authorities had understood that in minority areas where opium production was by far the most important economic activity, it was too politically explosive and risky to eradicate opium poppies prior to economic and social reform.

Yet, if the Chinese authorities urged some Yi and Tibetan opium farmers to switch from poppies to food crops as early as the 1950s, it was only years later – in 1972 – that the world's first international crop substitution programmes took place, in Turkey and, much more significantly, in Thailand. Although the Single Convention on Narcotics Drugs was adopted in 1961 (ratified by Thailand in 1961 and by Turkey in 1967), the world's first development projects aimed at reducing illicit drug crops were initiated in the early 1970s as a consequence of the strong anti-drug stance and focus of the Nixon administration. At this time, Turkey had already done its best to respond to repeated demands from the United States to strengthen the control of licit opium production or to suppress it altogether. Yet on 29 June 1971, faced with internal political instability, with calls by the United States Congress for economic sanctions, and with alleged direct pressure from Nixon – who had just vowed to wage a 'new, all-out offensive' against drugs, which he denounced as being 'America's public enemy number one',[26] – a new Turkish government announced unexpectedly that the last licit opium harvest was to take place in 1972. Turkey had ceded to United States political and economic pressure and had, in the words of a prominent Turkish senator, Suphi Gursoytrak, abandoned its opium farmers to US charity. In the meantime, some Turkish commentators complained that since Turkish opium was deemed the best in the world (because of its very high morphine content), a better choice would have been to create an opium state monopoly in order to supply the world's pharmaceutical industry (Lamour and Lamberti, 1972: 230–4). In fact, what was to become the world's first international drug crop substitution project got off to a bad start as negotiations with the United States had not been held before the passing of the ban. Therefore, Turkey found itself in a weak position to bargain for economic and development aid from the United States, something that Ismail Cem, then a popular columnist, found somewhat odd in a country where bargaining – before rather than after an agreement – had long been part of local tradition. Indeed, after long and difficult negotiations, conducted with almost no bargaining power, Turkey only managed to receive US$35 million out of the US$432 million it asked for from the United States to compensate for the loss of revenue of its 100,000 opium farmers and to restructure this part of its agriculture (Lamour and Lamberti, 1972: 234–9). The Turkish opium ban had been imposed too quickly and without any real negotiations with the United States, whose economic aid ended up being too small to enable Turkish agriculture to switch from opium poppies to other licit crops. Realizing its mistake, and faced with failing substitution crops and with rural discontent, Turkey resumed licit opium production in 1974, arguing, among other things, that other countries had increased (India) or initiated (France) legal opiates production following the Turkish ban. As would happen over and over again in the short world history of counter-narcotics, an opium ban failed through hastiness, poor sequencing (preceding the implementation of suitable alternative livelihoods), and because of inadequately funded and poorly designed development projects.

As Laos was to painfully realize in the early 2000s when the financial pledge made by Pino Arlacchi never materialized, international financial aid should be obtained before rather than after officially banning opium production. This has been the experience of many opium farmers in Burma, where Wa authorities banned opium production in a bid to obtain international aid (if not diplomatic recognition). One of the main differences between Turkey, Laos and Burma lies in the fact that Turkey was a NATO member and an essential strategic ally of the United States, and was therefore strong enough politically to go back on its ban and to license its opium production for the use of the world's pharmaceutical industry. Also, quite significantly, in the early 1970s Turkey was already a democratic country – even if an unstable one marred by military coups – in which the human cost brought about by a hasty opium ban was politically unsustainable. The situation is obviously very different in Laos and in Burma where the people have very few (or no) opportunities at all to challenge what are essentially authoritarian regimes.

The first international development project that was really designed and implemented in order to reduce or suppress agricultural production of illicit drugs began in 1972 in Thailand. Until then, crop substitution had only been implemented after an opium ban had been imposed: either to make forced eradication possible (as in the Yi and Tibetan areas of China) or as a means of compensating for a brutal loss of income (as in Turkey). That the first real crop substitution project took place in Thailand is easily understandable, as opium production had considerably increased in Southeast Asia following opium suppression in China (spurring the emergence of the Golden Triangle), production had not really started in Pakistan (where prohibition was enforced only in 1980) or in Afghanistan (as Iran had just relaxed its 1955 ban), and Thailand – one of the very rare southern countries never to have been colonized – was a privileged partner in the US anti-Communist effort. Thailand also experimented extensively with crop substitution and alternative development programmes because of the very early personal involvement of its monarch, King Bhumibol Adulyadej (crowned in 1950), who initiated a crop replacement project as early as 1969 in an opium-producing village next to which he had recently built his new Phuping Palace (Doi Pui, in Chiang Mai province):

King Bhumibol Adulyadej contributed to highland development work in other ways. Among the most influential was his guideline that opium poppies not be destroyed until viable alternatives existed. The king realized that the radical removal of the hill people's source of income would imperil them' (UNODC, 2006d: 123; Renard, 2001: 76).

As a consequence, forced eradication was only brought in briefly, in the early 1970s, and would not be used again before 1984, twelve years after the start of the first crop substitution project.

In Thailand, opium was exclusively produced by hill tribe minorities in mountain and hill areas along the Burmese border, but, until the early 1970s, the question of the hill tribes was mostly security-related (out of nationalist and anti-Communist concerns) and was dealt with through the National Tribal Welfare Committee, created in 1959 and chaired by the Minister of Interior (Renard, 2001: 6). In the 1960s the Public Welfare Department unsuccessfully moved hill tribe groups to lowlands settlements called *nikhom* and introduced them to lowland agriculture. Slash-and-burn agriculture was then viewed as unecological and mountain livelihoods as not economically viable: therefore (as is still the case in Laos in the early 2000s) the choice had been to move people down to development rather than move development up to their highlands. Between 1965 and 1967 the Thai Public Welfare Department and the United Nations Commission on Narcotic Drugs surveyed the socio-economic needs of opium producers and the scope of opium poppy cultivation. The socio-economic development of the hill tribes was deemed essential if opium production was to be reduced and eventually suppressed, and the UN/Thai Crop Replacement and Community Development Project was launched in 1972, one year after the creation of the United Nations Fund for Drug Abuse Control (UNFDAC) (Renard, 2001: 7, GTZ, 1998: 10). This was the first time that 'strategies were introduced to use development as an instrument of drug control', and Thailand was to keep experimenting with development-based approaches to drug supply reduction for about thirty years and with resources never matched by any other country since (northern Thailand reportedly received US$2.6 billion worth of economic development projects between 1970 and 2000, plus US$460 million worth of alternative development projects (GTZ, 2006: 14)). Crop substitution meant replacing opium poppies with crops that were legal, at least as lucrative as opium, not already overproduced in the lowlands, easily transportable to the lowlands, and easily marketable. Various crops – peaches, red kidney beans, cabbage, coffee, cut flowers, etc. – were introduced in the highlands of Thailand in the 1970s, more or less successfully and with more or less unintended consequences: market gluts and decreasing prices, soil and stream pollution due to an excess of chemical pesticides and fertilizers, etc. (Renard, 2001: 57–68).

In the mid-1970s, Jean Népote, the Secretary General of Interpol-ICPO between 1963 and 1978, was able to visit the Thai part of the Golden Triangle, where a 'multidisciplinary plan to combat illicit opium' was under way. After his visit to the UN/Thai crop replacement project, Népote wrote, in the UN Bulletin on Narcotics:

The person seated in a soft and comfortable chair in an office or conference room, may tend to believe that 'the easiest way of stopping the illicit drug traffic is to declare cultivation of the opium poppy illegal and, because it is illegal, to destroy the plantations'. Such reasoning, applied to the 'Golden Triangle' is quite utopian. It is impossible to control a territory larger than some European countries, mountainous, inaccessible, without roads or any means of communication. In order to destroy the plantations declared illegal, whole battalions of troops would have to be committed, who would certainly be met with bullets from people who would totally fail to understand why their livelihood should be taken from them when hardly out of the ground. [. . .] In the case of the 'Golden Triangle', the entire political and social context clearly precludes any policy of destruction of plantations, even if they are declared illegal (Népote, 1976).

In the mid-1970s the development-oriented approach to drug supply reduction was a radical change from the strictly repressive solutions that had been almost exclusively promoted until then. Népote, the head of an international organization in charge of fighting international crime, was nevertheless much seduced by the project, for he writes that 'something very worthy is taking place in the Thai jungle'. Yet thirty years later, Népote could issue the same warning about Afghanistan, Burma or Laos, maybe because illicit cultivation is still seen as a criminal activity, as suggested by the transformation of the United Nations International Drug Control Programme (UNDCP) into the United Nations Office on Drugs and Crime (UNODC). Matters do not bode well for development-based approaches to counter-narcotics when development programmes are to be carried out not by the United Nations Development Programme (UNDP) but by a UN agency whose name and mandate associate drugs with crime.

Despite appearing quite promising, crop substitution quickly showed its limitations. Népote had noted in his report that 'one of the remarkable features of the plan' was 'the rural simplicity of its implementation', hinting unknowingly at what would turn out to be a major flaw in crop substitution. Crop substitution indeed proved too simple – some would say simplistic – as development programmes then focused less on the causes of poppy cultivation than on poppy cultivation itself: the main focus was on finding which legal crops could replace opium poppies rather than addressing the causes of opium cultivation in specific areas by specific communities. In Thailand and in the rest of the world[27] the crop substitution approach was replaced in the 1980s by integrated rural development: from then on 'the issue was less to find substitute crops than to introduce alternative sources of income and improve living conditions' (GTZ, 1998: 10). Yet, despite the fact that it proved extremely useful 'IRD [integrated rural development] as a development approach collapsed under its own weight'. As a report on worldwide alternative development practices stated: 'The projects were so complex that they were management nightmares, impossible to evaluate. Their long-term impacts were uneven, with some interventions being more effective than others in particular circumstances' (UNODC, 2005ee: 23). Therefore, the development approach to drug supply reduction was modified again in the 1990s and 'alternative development' programmes replaced 'integrated rural development' programmes. Alternative development programmes differed from integrated rural development programmes by their broader perspective, since 'the overall framework conditions for development' in a given country or area had to be taken into account and because alternative development had to be linked to 'other development issues and activities' (GTZ, 1998: 10). At first altogether neglected in southern producing countries, then addressed as 'a medical problem in isolation from other development or community issues', demand reduction was eventually added as a component of alternative development: in fact, in both Thailand and Pakistan the reduction of opium consumption had sparked an increase in heroin consumption and needed to be addressed in a socio-economic way as well as medically (GTZ, 1998: 10).

Of course, alternative development has been carried out in different ways, at different levels, at different times, and with different means in different countries and by different organizations and agencies. For example, the importance and timing of enforcement (including forced eradication) has varied greatly from country to country (GTZ, 1998: 40). Also, alternative development 'has come to mean different things to different people', in part because 'there is no universally accepted definition of Alternative Development operating around the world across agencies and writers, despite the UNGASS definition of 1998' (Mansfield and Pain, 2005: 5; UNODC, 2005e: ix). The Action Plan on International Cooperation on Eradication of Illicit Drug Crops and on Alternative Development, approved by UNGASS in 1998, defines alternative development as:

> a process to prevent and eliminate the illicit cultivation of plants containing narcotic drugs and psychotropic substances through specifically designed rural development measures in the context of sustained national economic growth and sustainable development efforts in countries taking action against drugs, recognizing the particular socio-cultural characteristics of the target communities and groups, within the framework of a comprehensive and permanent solution to the problem of illicit drugs.

The Action Plan further defines alternative development as:

> a comprehensive approach of economic and social policy in view of
> generating and promoting lawful and sustainable socio-economic options
> for these communities and population groups that have resorted to illicit
> cultivation as their only viable means of obtaining a livelihood, contributing
> in an integrated way to the eradication of poverty.[28]

Yet, in the early 2000s, thirty years after the United Nations and Thailand
started the first international crop substitution project, and despite the current
lack of international consensus on what alternative development is, the surge
in opium production in Afghanistan and the inefficiency of existing alternative
development projects in Burma and Laos brought a new development concept
to the fore. In 2005, David Mansfield and Adam Pain wrote that it was then
'widely recognized by drugs and development specialists that given the scale
and nature of the problem in Afghanistan', illicit drug cultivation could no
longer 'be dealt with in isolation from the wider state-building and
reconstruction process – making it no different from other development
problems' (Mansfield and Pain, 2005: 4). Following on the rich and pioneering
work of David Mansfield who, more than anyone, has revealed the diversity
and complexity of the socio-economic drivers at work behind opium poppy
cultivation in Afghanistan, they stressed that,

> the more localised area-based project approaches of the 'alternative
> development' model implemented in Afghanistan and elsewhere in the
> 1980s and 90s were not able to address the different motivations and
> factors that influence households in their decision to plant opium poppy
> (Mansfield and Pain, 2005: 4).

The great extent of opium poppy cultivation in Afghanistan as well as the
better understanding of the great diversity and complexity of its contexts
and causes led them to assert that 'the model of "alternative development"
based on discrete area-based projects is unlikely to contribute significantly
to counter narcotics objectives' (Mansfield and Pain, 2005: 1). After the crop
substitution projects of the 1970s, the integrated rural development of the
1980s, and the alternative development of the 1990s, the record opium
production in Afghanistan and the growing understanding that opium bans
and forced eradication did not address the causes of opium production –
and often proved counterproductive – led to the emergence of the new
'alternative livelihoods' approach. Faced with renewed and unheeded opium
bans, and with increasing but ineffective eradication campaigns, the

'emergence of an "alternative livelihoods" approach, which seeks to mainstream counter narcotics objectives into national development strategies and programmes, is an attempt to respond to the causes of opium poppy cultivation and to create links with the wider state-building agenda' (Mansfield and Pain, 2005: 1–2).

The mixed results of alternative development

During the 2002 Feldafing conference, Martin Jelsma made a 'critical assessment' of alternative development and drug control, stating that '25 years of attempts to reduce supply have had no measurable impact at the global level' (Jelsma, 2002). Jelsma dismissed the role of development programmes in reducing opium production in Thailand, where the 'most substantial decrease took place without any crop substitution or eradication interventions'. He made the same point about Pakistan, where it was impossible 'to argue that the nation-wide decimation in 1980 had any relationship whatsoever with the development programme' but where it had also 'occurred without any need for eradication' (Jelsma, 2002). Many observers agree that,

> in those places where lasting reductions in production have been seen, other possible influences on farmer decisions not to cultivate drug crops can be put forward as being equally likely causes for change. These include: overall economic growth (Thailand and Viet Nam), political change (Myanmar), increasing government access to formerly remote areas (Pakistan), social pressure (Lao PDR, Bolivia), subsidies (Thailand), and booming prices for alternative crops (coffee and cacao growing areas) (UNODC, 2005e: 9–10).

In fact, what has often been neglected in the analysis of the Thai and Pakistani 'success stories' is that their respective opium output had never been very large (a maximum of 200 tonnes for each country, except for the record-high 800 tonnes of Pakistan in 1979) and had mostly been consumed internally and thus not supported by international demand and criminal trafficking networks. In Thailand, the halving of opium production between 1968 and 1975 was in no way the result of the 1959 opium ban, for it was not actually enforced before the mid-1980s. It could not be attributed to development projects either, as the first crop substitution project started only in 1972. Things were different in Pakistan. The 1980 opium ban played a significant role, for it had been announced the year before it was enforced, and this led to a record-high last harvest that drove opium prices down and provoked a decrease in poppy cultivation in subsequent years to pre-1979 levels. Yet, some of the numerous development programmes that were carried out in Thailand and in Pakistan have proved successful, perhaps not directly in terms of drug supply reduction but at least in terms of development and improvement of livelihoods: the most praised projects are the UNDCP Dir District Development Project in Pakistan (1989–98), the Thai-German Highland Development Program (1981–98) and the Doi Tung Development Project (1988–2018) in Thailand (Jelsma, 2002; GTZ, 1998; CND, 2005).

In fact, in June 1994, UNDCP and the Thai Office of Narcotics Control Board reviewed 'Two Decades of Thai-UN Cooperation in Highland Development and Drug Control' and found that between 1971 and 1992, more than 150,000 people (about 28 per cent of Thailand's ethnic minorities) benefited from highland development programmes aimed at reducing opium production. The overall assessment was that 'through these projects, highland communities moved closer to Thai society, with all the advantages and disadvantages accompanying such a move', that 'alternative development contributed to food security and increased rice production among highland communities', that 'soil and water conservation measures were introduced to improve ecological sustainability in the highlands', that 'cash crops were introduced with mixed success', that the 'improvement of the road network increased income and marketing opportunities but also precipitated social change with adverse effects', and that 'alternative development contributed to an expansion of government's health and education services to highland minorities' (GTZ, 1998: 45). Therefore, it can reasonably be argued that if the alternative development projects undertaken in opium producing areas of Thailand have not directly caused the diminution and suppression of poppy cultivation, they have at least helped make opium bans and annual eradication campaigns politically and economically acceptable in the long term.

In Pakistan also, alternative development has at least played a favourable role in opium supply reduction, especially in Dir district. It is important to understand what David Mansfield has shown in the 1990s and the 2000s in Afghanistan about the effectiveness or not of eradication or of its threat. He explained that eradication, or the threat of it, does not raise the opportunity costs of opium poppy cultivation if no alternative is available. However:

> where there is access to viable legal livelihoods, the threat of eradication may deter farmers from planting in the first place. When faced with the risk of eradication, a household that has access to viable alternatives will likely choose not to plant opium poppy and forgo the potential benefits

they could obtain, by instead investing their assets (i.e. land, water, labour, capital) in legal livelihood opportunities (Mansfield, 2007c: 69).

In Thailand and in Pakistan, development programmes as well as lightly enforced opium bans and very little resort to forced eradication most likely raised the opportunity costs of opium production.

In Laos only a few alternative development projects have been inaugurated before (or even after) the imposition of a ban. As a consequence:

> In Lao PDR poppy cultivation has dropped as rapidly in areas without AD projects as in areas with AD projects. There is little evidence that AD projects have influenced Lao farmers' decisions not to grow drugs, although there is evidence that sites with active or recently active AD projects are better buffered against economic hardship (UNODC, 2005e: 9).

Yet Laos had actually experimented with a very successful alternative development project in Palavek (Xaisonboun,[29] Hom District, Lao PDR) between 1989 and 1996. Funded by the United Nations Fund for Drug Abuse Control (UNFDAC, the predecessor of UNDCP and of UNODC) and implemented by the United Nations Department for Economic and Social Development, the project (Highland Integrated Rural Development Pilot Project, LAO/89/550), which 'was awarded the Expo 2000 award in Hanover by an international jury as one of the 'Worldwide projects exemplifying sustainable development', is frequently cited as one of the most successful alternative development projects in the region. Yet it seems that the project succeeded not because of 'the execution of a well thought out design process and an excellent project work plan' but rather because of 'a series of fortuitous decisions that saved the project from disaster' (UNODC, 2005ee: 45). The so-called Palavek project is known for having enabled local Hmong farmers to overcome their structural rice deficiency and even to produce rice surplus for sale but also for 'showing that strong clan leadership and community involvement can reduce poppy without forced eradication or punishment' (CND, 2005: note 38). Yet, the Palavek project proved more successful as a development project than as an alternative development project, for it has been estimated that 'poppy cultivation in Palavek was most probably eliminated by social pressure from clan leaders' (UNODC, 2005ee: 34).

From 1976 to 1989, the United Nations also funded rural development projects in Burma, but these projects had 'little in common with integrated or alternative development measures' (GTZ, 1998: 41). With the financial and material aid of the United States the Burmese government also resorted to forced eradication, but all international aid for supply reduction stopped in 1989, after the bloody 1988 repression by the military junta of street demonstrations in Rangoon. Yet, between 1993 and 1997, two alternative development projects were implemented under UNDCP guidance in Shan State. Then, in 1998, the Wa Alternative Development Project (WADP) was launched by UNDCP in the Wa Special Region n° 2 of Burma's Shan State, i.e. in a region where the control of the Burmese central government is only nominal and where the local authorities (UWSP/UWSA) absolutely wanted to ban opium production by 2005. The United Nations therefore involved itself in a very remote and extremely underdeveloped area of Burma with too little time and too little funding to be able to implement an alternative development project large enough and broad enough to significantly cushion the economic impact of the 2005 ban. UNODC (UNDCP became UNODC in 2002), whose very presence in the area (working both in dictatorial Burma and with the so-called world's biggest drug-trafficking army) has been strongly criticized by advocates of democracy, tried to guide and advise the Wa leadership toward achieving what was a self-imposed goal. For example, UNODC tried to soften the humanitarian impact of the Wa authorities' policy of forced relocation of opium-poppy growers from the uplands to the lowlands within the WADP area (Chouvy, 2004b, 2004c). Basically, WADP was closer to being a small-scale humanitarian aid project than an alternative development project.

In 2005, before any impact from the opium ban could be assessed, the report of the Commission on Narcotic Drugs on alternative development stated:

> Despite slow progress due to mistrust borne of years of armed conflict, the project made laudable gains on the health front. All children under age three have been vaccinated, thus reducing infant mortality. Leprosy has been eliminated in an area with rates four times those elsewhere in Myanmar. The project electrified one township, built 10 primary and two middle schools (Wa illiteracy rates are high), brought potable water to two townships and 16 hamlets, and built 15 kms of roads (CND, 2005: 7).

Obviously, the rapid and complete suppression of opium poppy cultivation that reportedly took place in the Wa Special Region (from 20,400 hectares in 2003 to 12,960 in 2005 and zero in 2006 and in 2007: UNODC, 2006d: 64; UNODC, 2007c: 51) cannot be attributed to the UN alternative development project, as its goal was too large, its financial and material means too small, and its deadline too short.

Quite significantly, in 2006 and in 2007 the UNODC reports on opium production in Burma did not mention its alternative development project but mentioned that 'the assistance currently provided by UN agencies and NGOs is significant but remains insufficient in the face of the magnitude of the vulnerability of the affected population'. It concluded: 'It can therefore be assumed that the vast majority of families in the region will be affected by food insecurity and debt as no adequate livelihood strategies are yet available' (UNODC, 2006d: 98). In 2007, the UNODC report on Burma mentioned: 'The findings also showed that households in former poppy growing villages could not find adequate ways of substituting their lost income from opium. They simply got poorer, and they will need assistance to cope with this difficult situation' (UNODC, 2007c: 53). Yet it seems that things got even worse, since in addition to the few alternative development programmes run by UNODC and others in the north of Burma's Shan State, a 'military-driven Chinese hybrid rice-for-opium crop-substitution program [. . .] has resulted in four consecutive years of poor harvests and driven many ethnic-minority farmers into heavy debt or out of rice farming altogether'.[30] In fact, journalist Clifford McCoy reported that 'after successive bad harvests and lacking the funds to service their debts, many farmers have been forced to sell their land, in many instances to the same Chinese business people who sold them the seeds, fertilizers and pesticides'.[31] It therefore seems that while an uncompensated opium ban further impoverished the already poor and food-insecure opium farmers of the Wa Special Region n° 2, some obviously ill-intended (rather than ill-designed) crop substitution projects ended up pauperizing them even more.

More than thirty years after the United Nations launched its first crop substitution project in Thailand and despite some recognized and lauded successes across the world, it is obvious that alternative development – along with forced eradication – has failed to significantly decrease the illicit cultivation of plant-based drugs in the world. Yet, Martin Jelsma estimates that 'three decades of experimenting with developmental strategies to shift farmers away from illicit crops have brought many improvements to the underlying concept', something that the evaluation report on UNODC practices echoes when it states that 'UNODC has accumulated a considerable amount of experience after decades of implementing alternative development (AD) projects' and that 'UNODC's AD interventions have played a vital and very positive role in the formulation of drug control policy in many countries' (Jelsma, 2002; UNODC, 2005e: iii, x). Indeed, in a recent (2006) report on alternative development, or rather on what he defines as development in a drug environment, David Mansfield concludes:

> Alternative development projects have achieved both development and
> drug control outcomes in specific geographical areas where more

conventional development agencies are often not even present, despite the prevailing levels of poverty and conflict. For those who have experienced the low levels of literacy, high incidence of food insecurity, infant mortality and malnutrition that typically exist in illicit drug crop producing areas, as well as the lack of governance and prevailing levels of violence and intimidation from both state and non-state actors, arguments about the relatively high income of opium poppy and coca growing households seems rather inappropriate and ill informed. To this group the subsequent improvements in the income and quality of life of communities that often accompany alternative development projects at the same time as levels of opium poppy or coca cultivation fall are obvious, even if they might have been documented better or achieved more cost effectively (GTZ, 2006: 3).

Why alternative development has not failed

Despite the rather disappointing results detailed previously it must be said that alternative development cannot be dismissed as having failed altogether to address the illicit production of plant-based drugs. Indeed, dismissing alternative development completely would amount to throwing the baby out with the bath water. Alternative development as a strategy has not failed because it was the wrong approach to drug supply reduction but rather because it has barely been tried and because drug supply reduction has consistently been considered separate from poverty reduction. While the links between poverty and agricultural drug production have been widely and convincingly demonstrated worldwide, drug supply reduction has mainly focused on prohibition and repressive measures such as crop bans and forced eradication. The vast majority of the funds and of the material and human means that have been invested during almost forty years of a global war on certain drugs have been used to design, implement and reinforce repressive measures, which equates to increasing poverty (the main cause of illicit agricultural drug production) rather than to alleviating it.

This is the case in Afghanistan where peace-building, state-building, and nation-building are largely dependent on an economic reconstruction that is highly contingent upon international aid. Yet, despite the near general acceptance that 'high per capita aid in the early years of an intervention correlates with relative success', as demonstrated by a 2005 RAND study on the first two years of economic aid delivered in post-conflict situations, Afghanistan received far less aid per capita (US$ 57) than Bosnia (US$ 679), Iraq (US$ 206), or Kosovo (US$ 526) (Dobbins et al., 2005: xxviii). As stressed by Carl Robichaud, programme officer at the Century Foundation, from 2001 to 2005, according to the Congressional Research Service, the United States allocated $66.5 billion to the Department of Defense – almost two-and-a-half times Afghanistan's total reconstruction needs. The United States has spent 11 times as much on military operations as it has on reconstruction, humanitarian aid, economic assistance, and training for Afghan security forces combined. Robichaud then concludes: 'The plan has been more "martial" than "Marshall"' (Robichaud, 2006: 19).

While counter-narcotics is only a very small part of the overall United States financial contribution to Afghanistan's state-building and reconstruction (the United States has provided one-third of all development aid to Afghanistan between 2001 and 2007), it is also marked by a strong focus on repression. Out of the US$10.3 billion that the United States has pledged in assistance to Afghanistan between 2001 and 2006 (of these less than 5 billion were actually spent), approximately US$1.6 billion has been allocated to counter-narcotics efforts (OIG, 2007: 20). In one of the poorest countries of the world, where the opium economy amounts to more or less one-third of the overall economy, the United States allocated only US$420 million to counter-narcotics in fiscal year 2006: that is, less than the US$755 million value of Afghan opium at the farm gate and much less than the US$2.5 billion received by Afghan traffickers during the same year. In 2007, the Inspectors General of the US Department of State and of the US Department of Defense published an Interagency Assessment of the Counternarcotics Program in Afghanistan and noted that 'opium production increased dramatically in 2006 over 2005 while US Government funds allocated to CN [counter-narcotics] dropped from about $959 million in FY 2005 to about $480 million in FY 2006' (OIG, 2007: 10). Yet, the funds allocated to counter-narcotics were not only halved between 2005 and 2006 but the proportion of funds assigned to alternative development also decreased, from 37 per cent (US$344 million) to 28 per cent (US$120 million) of the annual counter-narcotics budget (OIG, 2007: 20). Therefore, in 2006, next to US$120 million allocated to alternative development, US$134 million went for eradication, US$109 million for interdiction, US$55 million for law enforcement and justice reform, and US$2 million for public information (OIG, 2007: 21). Another major problem is that most of the US funding of counter-narcotics programmes comes through Congressional supplemental appropriations that do not provide budget continuity, and therefore result in uneven programme implementation.

Of course, Afghanistan is far from being the only country where alternative development programmes are ill-funded. Considering the geopolitical and strategic importance of Afghanistan's economic reconstruction and state-building, and the considerable involvement of the United States in this process, other drug-producing countries can only be worse off. In fact, the US$120 million allocated in 2006 by the United States for alternative development in Afghanistan is ten times higher than the average made available on an annual basis for UNODC's alternative development programmes worldwide (Afghanistan, Burma, Laos, Vietnam, Bolivia, Colombia, Peru) (UNODC, 2005e: 18). Between 1998 and 2004, the budget of UNODC for alternative development activities worldwide averaged US$19 million only. Yet, UNODC is not to be blamed for not investing enough in alternative development as 'UNODC's low investment in AD is caused by the shortfall in donor pledges, not because UNODC has developed an especially cost effective way to do its work' (UNODC, 2005ee: 38). It is important to understand that the funding process of UNODC is unique in the United Nations, as 'ninety per cent of UNODC's budget comes from voluntary funding by a few countries' that 'determine on what project their funds are spent' (Jensema and Thoumi, 2003: 1). Among other consequences this funding process 'hampers UNODC's policy evaluation efforts because policy criticism can easily translate into a fund shortage' (Jensema and Thoumi, 2003: 1). The vast majority of UNODC's budget comes from the United States and Italy (respectively 23 and 20 per cent in 2002) who thereby largely influence the programmes undertaken by UNODC. Through its large funding, Italy also secures the post of Executive Director of UNODC for an Italian citizen. In the early 2000s, law enforcement projects received most of UNODC's funding, since most of the funds granted by the USA, Japan and the UK have been spent on law enforcement programmes. Italy and Sweden have mostly funded demand reduction projects and Germany alternative development projects. Ernestien Jensema and Francisco Thoumi explain that 'it is unclear whether this is due to earmarking or if UNODC directs the money this way' (Jensema and Thoumi, 2003: 1–2).

Of course, the low and unreliable budget of UNODC implies incongruous situations: Afghanistan programmes have long been hampered for many reasons, including funding shortages and, in Laos, where only '5 per cent of poppy-growing families [. . .] have received AD support', the North Phongsaly Alternative Development Project received only US$29,600 in 2005 (about 4 per cent of its estimated needs) to implement activities in 33 villages (CND, 2005: 5; UNODC, 2005e: 18). Therefore, 'in Asia, small budgets and restricted project areas mean that only a small proportion of poppy growers or potential poppy growers are assisted by AD projects' (UNODC, 2005e: 18). The 2005 global thematic evaluation on alternative development, conducted by the Commission on Narcotic Drugs, also stressed the extremely limited reach of alternative development in Asia and in the rest of the world:

'It is known that illicit-crop farmers receiving AD have been few: 23 percent in the Andes, 5 percent in Asia. But these few represent numerous successes. This suggests an unrealized potential' (CND, 2005: 2). Alternative development has obviously not been implemented widely enough for it to be considered a failure in addressing illicit drug crop cultivation. Until now, alternative development has mostly consisted of discreet area-based pilot projects that have often not only been ill-funded but also ill-designed and ill-implemented, whether by the United States or by UNODC.

But alternative development has also suffered from two things: from the fact that the traditional development community rarely invested in areas of illicit drug production; and from the fact that the UN agency with a drug mandate (UNODC) lacked the capacity and means to properly design and implement development projects. As David Mansfield explained in a 2006 report on alternative development or 'development in a drugs environment':

> UNODC, who has the mandate for providing technical support on alternative development projects, could have performed better.[54] There has been a lack of investment in building the necessary cadre of expertise that is required to support national governments and project managers in designing and implementing what should be catalytic projects aimed at establishing what works in moving farmers from illicit to licit livelihoods, and subsequently sharing this knowledge with those involved in larger scale rural development programmes. There has also been insufficient research into the drivers of opium poppy and coca cultivation and how these differ by locality, and socio-economic and gender groups, with which to inform project and programme design. Moreover, project managers, whilst rural development specialists, have typically been unfamiliar with illicit drug crop cultivation and how development and drug control impact might be maximised by better timing, targeting and sequencing interventions. Yet, due to the overall lack of capacity and limited knowledge base, these managers have generally been given insufficient technical support from their country office and headquarters (GTZ, 2006: 13–14).

Then the author concludes that UNODC should basically 'focus less on the implementation of alternative development projects as it did in the past, and more on developing partnerships with those development organisations, who typically have the comparative advantage in implementation, operating in source areas' (GTZ, 2006: 19).

So far alternative development has failed to achieve drug supply reduction, whether worldwide or in any given country. There are obviously many reasons for this, including: inadequate actors (lacking capacity and means); inappropriate funding; the focus on a 'detached string of "pilot projects"' rather than on holistic nationwide programmes; project design flaws; and wrong sequencing of counter-narcotics measures. Basically, alternative development has barely been tried as a measure to reduce the world's illicit drug crops and when it has been tried its programmes and projects have been mostly poorly designed and implemented. In addition to inappropriate funding and bad project design, alternative development has also suffered from the counterproductive effects of forced eradication or hastily implemented opium bans that were imposed too early (sometimes before development funds were even negotiated): 'As a systemic approach, AD should begin long before coercive measures are started so as to prevent and mitigate economic hardship during the process of economic realignment toward a stable licit economy' (UNODC, 2005e: 6). For too long, eradication, bans, and alternative development have tried to achieve supply reduction rather than demand reduction at the farm gate (reduction of drug crops rather than reduction of the drug trade). Also, the success of alternative development programmes has always been evaluated in terms of reduction of areas cultivated with illicit crops rather than in terms of poverty reduction and economic development indicators, while 'AD should continue, even after drug crops are gone, until the economy is robust enough to prevent reinvestment in drug crops' (UNODC, 2005e: 6). As Leik Boonwaat, then alternative development adviser for UNODC and the Lao National Commission for Drug Control and Supervision, declared: 'In the opium poppy growing regions of Laos, the same issues relate to opium and poverty. To eliminate both is a long-term process that cannot stop even after most farmers have stopped cultivation' (CND, 2005: 11).

Alternative livelihoods: no silver bullet but the most effective and least counterproductive solution

The report on alternative development issued in 2005 by the Commission on Narcotic Drugs began its executive summary as follows: 'A quarter-century on, Alternative Development donors and practitioners still underestimate the sociocultural, economic, political, and environmental milieu in which AD operates. This underestimation invites unrealistic expectations and projects set to fail' (CND, 2005: 1). Just as the importance of development has been underestimated in national and global counter-narcotics approaches, so the diversity and complexity of the factors that cause illicit opium production have been at best underestimated, at worse altogether ignored in the design and implementation of alternative development programmes and projects. For too long now, calls to address the issue of illicit agricultural production with measures that recognize the diversity of its causes have been left unanswered. In practice, simple – if not simplistic – solutions have mostly been favoured in answer to what have long been perceived as simple problems, whether it be calling for eradication to destroy the illicit crops of peasantries described as criminal, or advocating economic development to provide higher revenues to all opium producers without discriminating between the farmers economically dependent upon opium production and those who are acting opportunistically.

David Mansfield writes that 'research that actually documents the complexity of the factors that influence illicit drug crop cultivation is more often than not considered difficult to digest, or dismissed as too academic'. Instead, 'preference is given to quantitative data that gives a simple aggregate picture around which policy can be formed' (Mansfield, 2007b: 21). The problem is that there are obviously no simple ways to effectively address illicit drug cultivation: there are no shortcuts, quick fixes or other silver bullets, despite the many proposals made by well-meaning but misguided academics, politicians, journalists and activists of all persuasions. Among the most frequent alternative solutions proposed are buyout and licensing strategies that are not only not feasible but also share one of the main flaws of counter-narcotics strategies: they focus on the crops and their economic value rather than on the causes of their production. As will be shown below, the most widely advocated such solution – the licensing of Afghan opium for the pharmaceutical industry – is deeply flawed.

'Simple' solutions are still proposed (and implemented) to address issues that have been shown to be highly complex. Mansfield explains:

> given the diversity of assets and livelihood strategies of Afghan rural households, as well as the diversity in their dependency on opium poppy cultivation as a means of meeting basic needs, a corresponding diversity in policy and operational responses is required (Mansfield, 2007c: 67).

He also warns that 'designing policies that treat opium poppy farmers as homogenous will not only be ineffective, they will prove counter productive' (Mansfield, 2007b: 22). A drugs and development specialist himself, he argues that,

> policy makers and other commentators would do well to work with the diversity that exists amongst opium poppy cultivators and not resist it

simply due to complacency or because of the challenge it presents to the prevailing economic orthodoxy' (Mansfield, 2007b: 22).

He advocates an approach that would take the complexity and diversity of production contexts into consideration and especially one that would 'not focus on replacing the high level of income from opium as derived by the resource-rich, as the current economic model suggests', but one that would aim at 'improving the resource-poor's access to those assets that have hitherto been derived by a willingness to produce opium poppy' (Mansfield, 2007b: 22). In other words, development efforts should first and foremost focus on the conditions that make opium production imperative for the resource-poor farmers: access to credit, access to land, and development of off-farm and non-farm income opportunities. And although he, along with many others, warns against making development aid conditional upon crop reduction, he advises applying greater 'social and legal pressure' on opium farmers who are not economically reliant on opium poppy cultivation: 'whilst more complex, such a "targeted" approach is more likely to deliver on both drug control and development objectives' (Mansfield, 2007b: 22).

From simply trying to substitute one crop with another, to addressing the structural causes of illicit agricultural production, practice in drug-producing areas has evolved considerably – at least in theory. The emergence in the early 2000s of the 'alternative livelihoods' concept is the last step in a thirty-year trend that saw development programmes in drug contexts become increasingly complex. The alternative livelihoods approach has emerged in an attempt to overcome the limitations of previous development approaches that were 'designed as a specific response to reductions in opium production' but which did not address 'the underlying structural and institutional reasons that have led to the growth of opium poppy cultivation in the first place' (Mansfield, 2007c: 70). In order to promote alternative livelihoods, attempts to identify precisely the drivers and patterns of opium poppy cultivation at the district level have been successfully carried out by Adam Pain in Afghanistan's Balkh province, where cultivation has decreased in the mid-2000s. While the author argues that 'the recent decline in opium poppy area in Balkh is not likely to be durable', since 'evidence points to a consolidation of power with limited accountability and severe, negative welfare outcomes for particular social groups as a consequence of the decline in cultivation', he, again, warns that 'much greater attention needs to be paid to the diffusion and spread of opium poppy cultivation and what drives it, rather than simply focus on the aggregate statistics of area of production at the district or provincial levels' (Pain, 2007: 4, 6).

While real alternative livelihoods are still to be promoted, on paper they clearly differ from alternative development, as Mansfield and Pain detail. Unlike alternative development, alternative livelihoods should not be implemented through a discrete area-based approach but should be realized through mainstreaming counter-narcotics objectives into national development strategies and programming. Alternative livelihoods programmes should be designed to address the causes rather than the symptoms of cultivation and should 'address the factors that influence households' drug crop cultivation' rather than attempt 'to replace on-farm income generated by coca and opium poppy' (Mansfield and Pain, 2005: 4). By focusing on the causes of illicit agricultural drug production rather than on illicit cultivation itself, programmes to promote alternative livelihoods should also go 'beyond the metrics' of illicit crop cultivation, as progress should not be evaluated in terms of reduction of cultivated area but in terms of improved livelihoods (according to economic indicators but not these alone) and, also, of improved governance (Mansfield, 2007a; Mansfield and Pain, 2005: 4).

Obviously, in countries such as Afghanistan and Burma, poor governance at the national and provincial levels considerably hampers the development of the licit economy and therefore of the legal alternatives to opium poppy cultivation. Worse, existing power structures in Afghanistan and in Burma actually enable opium production because they maintain the inequalities that determine, perpetuate and reproduce poverty. While war and internecine conflict have stimulated opium production in the two countries, opium production not only encouraged the prolongation of such conflicts but also laid the foundation for the criminalization of these countries' peace economies. In both countries, opium production has long been a low-risk activity in a high-risk context where war and physical insecurity pushed many, if not most, farmers to favour short-term, risk-spreading economic strategies, notably by including opium production in their activities. While political developments and opium production trends in the mid-2000s are different in both countries, the overall context in each remains unfavourable to economic development, whether because physical insecurity prevents development programmes and projects to be carried out safely (as in Southern Afghanistan) or whether because national priorities and international sanctions and isolation prevent economic development from reaching opium-producing areas (as in Burma). Credible (if not durable) peace and an improved governance that addresses inequalities are prerequisites to any significant and sustainable decrease in illicit opium poppy cultivation and to economic development. In Afghanistan and Burma, where armed conflict considerably abated in the 1990s, sustainable drug supply reduction will necessarily take time, as the two countries have also, and firstly, to ensure their respective transitions from a war economy to a peace economy. Yet, if 'war is less about the breakdown of political and economic relations than about their reordering and transformation' (Goodhand, 2005: 209), peace and sustained economic development largely depend on addressing inequality and poverty and therefore on new political and economic relations. Since opium production is a consequence of both war and poverty, drug supply reduction can clearly only follow from peace and economic development. Addressing the causes of illicit opium production largely amounts to addressing the causes of poverty and the inequalities and grievances that contributed to war.

What both countries need more than anything is peace and economic development. Forced eradication (which has failed everywhere) entails exactly the opposite, since it relies on the use of force and destruction. With forced eradication parts of the economies of some of the world's poorest countries, and some of their poorest farmers, are ruined. It is more likely to give rise to social, political and economic conflict than to bring about peace in countries that have been at war for decades. The promotion of alternative livelihoods on the other hand, is more likely to bring, or reinforce, peace and economic development: what matters is to focus on reducing inequality, poverty, and food insecurity through economic and political measures. While both eradication and development have failed so far to reduce illicit drug production, development-based approaches are at least not counterproductive in the way that eradication has too often proven to be. Moreover, development-based approaches are much more likely to promote and enhance human rights than policies of forced eradication, which are mostly carried out by authoritarian or autocratic regimes. In fact, in 2007, the Amnesty International US Board of Directors eventually recognized that the 'War on Drugs has had a negative impact on human rights around the world'.[32]

LICENSING AFGHANISTAN'S OPIUM: SOLUTION OR FALLACY?

When interdiction, eradication and development failed to solve the 'opium problem' a new, but unrealistic, proposal has emerged in the mid-2000s. Described as 'a truly winning solution' by many – countless favourable editorials were published in the world's press – the proposal of the Senlis Council (now known as The International Council on Security and Development), a self-dubbed 'international drug policy think tank' based in Paris, entailed licensing Afghan opium so that it may be used for the production of legal medicines such as morphine and codeine. Such a solution would address the urgent need to reduce significantly Afghanistan's illegal opium trade but also provide a means of overcoming the 'significant global shortage of opium based medicines such as morphine and codeine', a problem 'felt most acutely in the developing world' (Senlis Council, 2005: 5). This proposal, however, is based on unsupportable premises: first regarding the world market for licit opiates and, secondly, regarding national and local opium farming communities (Chouvy, 2006a).

According to the International Narcotics Control Board (INCB), which is the body responsible for examining issues affecting the supply of and demand for opiates used for medical purposes, the supply of such opiates has, for years, been 'at levels well in excess of global demand' (INCB, 2004: 23). As yearly stocks continue to be more than sufficient to cover yearly global demand, INCB even recommends reducing the production of opiate raw materials. Nevertheless, INCB stresses that 'the low consumption of opioid analgesics for the treatment of moderate to severe pain, especially in developing countries, continues to be a matter of great concern', explaining that 'in 2003, six countries together accounted for 79 per cent of global consumption of morphine' while 'developing countries, which represent about 80 per cent of the world's population, accounted for only about 6 per cent' (INCB, 2004: 25). Thus, for INCB, the urgency is more 'to raise awareness of the necessity to assess the actual medical needs for opiates' in the world than to increase the production of medical morphine by authorizing more countries, including Afghanistan, to legally grow opium poppies.

Raising levels of morphine production, whether by licensing opium production in Afghanistan or by increasing the yields of current producers, is unlikely to increase the medical consumption of morphine and codeine in the world. The recommendations of the World Health Organization (WHO), that morphine and codeine be used as analgesics, are too often impeded by obstacles that are not, or not only, supply-related: e.g. concerns about drug addiction and drug diversion, restrictive national laws, insufficient importation or local production of opiates based medicine, but also deficiencies in national health-care delivery systems, insufficient training, etc. In addition, the demand for modern analgesics is also affected by local medical traditions and beliefs. In China, for example, according to WHO, traditional herbal preparations account for 30 to 50 per cent of total medicinal consumption, while in Africa as much as 80 per cent of the population uses traditional medicine for primary health care. In fact, a 2007 report prepared by Help the Hospices, a British charity that trains hospice workers and supports hospices in poor countries, 'has produced a disturbing portrait of the difficulties in offering pain relief to the dying in poor countries'.[33] Out of the 300 questionnaires that were sent to hospices and end-of-life specialists in poor countries only 69 were returned. The chief reasons cited by respondents for the shortages were 'restrictive national drug laws, fear of addiction, broken-down health care systems and lack of knowledge by doctors, patients and policy makers'.[34] According to David E. Joranson, director of the Pain Policy Study Group at the University of Wisconsin's medical school, the reason why morphine is not more readily available to patients in poor countries is 'the intense fear of addiction, which is often misunderstood'. Joranson, who aims at changing drug laws around the world, denounced the fact that 'pain relief hasn't been given as much attention as the war on drugs has'.[35] In a very significant way, morphine is almost impossible to get hold of for most of the population of India (with the exception of the state of Kerala), despite the fact that it is the only country in the world legally to produce opium gum for export for the pharmaceutical industry. In fact, 'legal morphine use in India plummeted 97 percent after 1985': i.e. after the Narcotic Drugs and Psychotropic Substances Act, designed to curb drug trafficking, was passed and corresponding state laws were enacted: 'the book outlining them is 1,642 pages, and even minor infractions can mean 10-year sentences'.[36]

Clearly, then, global medical consumption of opiates is far from directly dependent upon supply and demand, and price contingencies. This was actually hinted at by the Senlis Council itself when it stressed that, 'in 2002, 77 per cent of the world's morphine was consumed by seven rich countries: USA, the UK, Italy, Australia, France, Spain and Japan', but that, according to official figures, 'even in these countries only 24 per cent of moderate to severe pain relief needs were being met'. The fact that medical consumption of opiates is low even in rich morphine-producing countries clearly shows that the consumption of opiate-based pain-killers is determined by factors much more complex than the laws of the marketplace. A 2007 report produced by Macfarlan Smith, one of the world's oldest pharmaceutical companies and the world's largest morphine producer, severely criticizes the declarations and proposal of the Senlis Council, notably by stressing the fact that 'the actual consumption data of morphine is strongly influenced by cultural attitudes' and not only by price of availability: in 2005, while 2,559 kg of morphine were consumed in France, only 1,699 kg were consumed in the United Kingdom, 388 kg in Spain, and 184 kg in Italy. Therefore, the Macfarlan Smith report stated: 'We would strongly argue that morphine stocks are not a controlling factor for world demand.'[37]

Indian licit opium production vs. Afghan illicit opium production

Licensing the illicit opium supply is highly unlikely to bring economic development to Afghanistan and its opium farmers. First, it is important to understand that while licit opium poppy cultivation is undertaken for pharmaceutical use by nineteen countries around the world (Australia, Austria, China, the Czech Republic, Estonia, France, Germany, Hungary, Japan, India, the Netherlands, Poland, Romania, Slovakia, South Korea, Spain, Macedonia, Turkey and the United Kingdom) only four of them produce opium: China, India, Japan and South Korea. Among these, India is the only exporter of opium. The countries that do not produce opium actually grow opium poppies to harvest poppy straw and produce concentrate of poppy straw (CPS), using modern mechanised agriculture (for the most part combine harvesters on large tracts of cultivated land). Harvesting opium is, as we have seen, a long and arduous manual process that requires an abundant and above all cheap local workforce if the production process is to be economically viable. This, along with international agreements derived from the role of the opium economy in the country's colonial past, explains why India is the world's sole licit producer of opium for export.

But Indian opium production is also viable because it benefits from preferential access to the large US market in spite of very high opiates production costs: in 1999 the production costs for the equivalent of one kilogramme of morphine was said by INCB to be US$56 in Australia, under the CPS system, compared to US$159.77 in India (Mansfield, 2001: 7). According to the British Parliamentary Under-Secretary of State for Foreign and Commonwealth Affairs, Lord Triesman, in 2007 in Afghanistan the production of one kilogramme of morphine equivalent was thought to be approximately US$450. Yet, in 2008, a new British Parliamentary Under-Secretary, Meg Munn, explained that it cost less (US$300) to produce one kilogramme of morphine (end product, not morphine equivalent) in Australia in 2008 than in Afghanistan, where the farm-gate production cost of one kilogramme of morphine equivalent was US$385. The figure of US$385 is not the manufacturing cost of the final morphine product and therefore does not include the costs of 'regulation and security (policing of product, security of product transport from farm to factory); processing; equipment; chemicals; labour costs; and other business costs', all costs that are unknown for Afghanistan.[38] At such a price, legal Afghan opiates could hardly be marketed. Afghan CPS production is also very unlikely because shifting to the CPS method would increase national agricultural unemployment and poverty. And such a shift would be most difficult to implement as CPS production requires considerable quantities of water, which are not readily available in Afghanistan.

In India, legal opium production occurs in selected areas of the states of Madhya Pradesh, Uttar Pradesh and Rajasthan. The Indian Central Government sets an opium Minimum Qualifying Yield (MQY) according to the yields reported by farmers in previous years. During the 2004–5 crop year (8,770 licensed hectares) farmers were required to achieve an MQY of 58 kg/ha in Madhya Pradesh and Rajasthan, and 49 kg/ha in Uttar Pradesh to be eligible for the renewal of their license in 2005–6. Growers are issued a licence for growing poppies, and the entire opium crop produced by all farmers is purchased by – and only by – the Central Bureau of Narcotics (CBN) at a price fixed by Central Government. The price paid to the farmers depends on the yields achieved, with farmers producing more opium getting a higher price per kilogram. In 2004–5, the minimum price paid per kilogram was 750 rupees (US$17) for yields up to 44 kg/ha. The maximum price paid was 2,200 rupees (US$50/kg) for yields above 100 kg/ha. The average national yield was 56 kg/ha, attracting a price of 1,150 rupees/kg (US$26).[39] However, it is important to bear in mind that in an effort to better prevent diversion to the illicit market, in 2004–5 the maximum licensed area for the cultivation of opium poppies was 0.10 hectare per productive unit. The maximum income that Indian farmers can derive from legal opium production is therefore limited according to the price fixed by central government and by the area that each farmer is allowed to cultivate.

With such low prices paid to Indian opium farmers,[40] diversion to the illegal market, where opium can fetch prices as much as four to five times higher than the minimum government price, clearly takes place (there is no reliable estimate for such diversion). The 2005 International Control Strategy Report of the US Department of State stressed that 'in 2004, the Government of India discovered and shut down six morphine base laboratories in India's opium growing areas; four in Uttar Pradesh and two in Madhya Pradesh'. The fact that the Central Government raises the MQY and the official price paid to farmers is clearly not enough to prevent some farmers from diverting part of their harvest to the illegal market. It is worth noting that the CBN more recently tightened its controls on opium farming and diversion, drastically lowering both the number of hectares licensed (from 21,141 in 2003–4 to 8,771 in 2004–5) and the number of farmers licensed (from 105,697 in 2003–4 to 87,682 in 2004–5) (GOI, 2006: 113–16).

Large-scale diversion of licit opium to the illicit market is not the only problem in India, since illicit opium poppy cultivation is also prevalent: 6,200 hectares of illegally grown poppies were eradicated in West Bengal State alone in 2007. The same year, 800 hectares were eradicated in Arunachal Pradesh out of an estimated 2,000 hectares. In 2007 again, Maoist rebels allegedly resorted to illicit poppy cultivation on 8,000 hectares in Jarkhand state.[41] As illicit cultivation (which is unaccounted for by UNODC in its global estimates) is most likely larger[42] than licit cultivation in a country such as India, where the state is in a much stronger position than in

Afghanistan, it is difficult to see how licensing Afghanistan's opium production could prevent more poppies being grown for the illicit market.

The shortcomings of opium licensing in Afghanistan

The proposal to license opium production in Afghanistan thus raises an important question: would prices paid to opium farmers be high enough (1) to provide them with sufficient net returns, (2) to enable the development of Afghanistan's rural economy, and (3) to prevent the diversion of opium from the licit to the illicit market? In Afghanistan, opium prices have varied since the late 1990s, ranging from US$23 to US$350 per kilogram of fresh opium at harvest time. In 2005, the average farm-gate price of fresh opium at harvest time was US$102 per kilogram (average yield: 39 kg/ha) and 309,000 families, or about 2 million people (8.7 per cent of the population) were involved in opium poppy cultivation, itinerant workers not included. Such prices are far from enriching Afghan opium farmers. They merely allow them to cope with poverty. One need only compare such prices with Indian prices to realize that licit opium production in Afghanistan could not compete with illicit opium production, that most opium farmers would still have to give up opium production (considering the scope of opium production in Afghanistan) while the others would see their revenues plummet, and, considering the limited writ and power of the Afghan authorities, diversion from the licit to the illicit market would be unavoidable and would reach much higher proportions than in India.

In the Afghan sharecropping system, opium poppy growers keep only a small share of the revenue generated by opium cropping: 30 per cent of the crop goes to the landowner, 10 per cent goes to the Islamic tithe (*ushr*), and 15–25 per cent goes to the seasonal harvesters which labour intensive opium harvesting requires. Most of the poor growers sell the crop in advance at prices that are often around half the harvest price. In such a case, a sharecropper typically ends up receiving only half of the third that is left after the aforementioned deductions have been made. Considering the average licit Indian prices and opium yields, and the fact that Afghan growers produce opium on average on only one-fifth of a hectare, licit opium production is highly unlikely to provide a solution. It would basically require keeping opium farmers at poverty levels for it to be economically viable.

Licensing opium production in Afghanistan, therefore, would clearly be no better than eradication or alternative development at addressing the causes of illegal opium production and would thus fail to fulfil the international community's objective: the suppression of illegal opium production. If crop substitution has proved to be a failure in the past, why should the substitution of an illegal opium crop with a legal crop work any better, reducing, as it would, farmers' income and failing, as it would, to address the structural factors that cause illegal opium production?

It is crucial to understand that opium production is more a consequence of Afghanistan's lawlessness, instability and poverty than its cause. Opium production clearly proceeds from poverty and food insecurity, from Afghanistan to Burma and Laos, where it is a coping mechanism and a livelihood strategy. Opium production is a vital element in the livelihood strategies of sector of the Afghan rural population, providing peasants not only with a source of income but also with access to land and credit. It is poverty and the shortcomings of the Afghan agrarian system that need to be tackled if illicit opium production is to be curtailed.

9. Forced eradication of an opium poppy field, Thailand.

Conclusion

The rich and complex history of illicit opium production in Asia clearly shows that prohibition and drug supply reduction have largely failed to attain their goal. Many explanations have been put forward for this failure; in the end it would appear that ill-conceived policies and programmes are largely responsible. Yet, despite its oft denounced failure, the war on drugs has been regularly re-launched and augmented rather than scaled down, partly because of the long and heated debate between the proponents of forced eradication and the advocates of development in a drugs environment, with the deadlock between the two leading to the repetition of past mistakes.

Drug supply reduction has long been a highly controversial issue, not only because of the enduring opposition between ideology and rationality but also because of ignorance, misunderstanding and disagreement about the causes of illicit opium production and the motivations of opium farmers. As a consequence, the failure of both forced eradication and alternative development has not been properly analysed and understood. Yet, it now appears that the main reason why anti-drug policies have failed lies largely in the fact that both eradication and alternative development have focused on illicit drug *production* and not on its *causes*. Alternative development has proved no more successful than forced eradication in suppressing or reducing illicit opium production, notably because it has never been properly implemented (either in scope or means). Forced eradication not only fails to achieve its goal, it often proves counterproductive because it ends up exacerbating poverty rather than reducing it. Economic development – whether it is called 'alternative development' or not – has produced mixed results, mostly because of design and implementation flaws, not necessarily because it is the wrong approach.

As we have seen by comparing the diverse yet similar contexts of illicit opium production in Southwest and Southeast Asia, poverty and food insecurity are the main drivers of illicit opium production. Yet they cannot be eradicated in the same way that opium poppies can: it is necessary to identify and address the causes of poverty and food insecurity, no matter how diverse and complex they may be, if illegal poppy cultivation is to be reduced or suppressed. Ultimately, since illicit opium production stems from the need of farmers to cope with poverty and food insecurity, what is required in order to achieve drug supply reduction is broad and equitable economic development, especially in rural areas. Since illicit agricultural production tends to take place in remote and inaccessible areas where the writ of the state barely extends, economic development must find a way of reaching even the most far-flung areas and populations. Yet, history shows us that just as alternative development has never been properly funded, so on a global basis rural development and agriculture have also been long neglected.

Significantly, the 2008 World Development Report of the World Bank was the first report since 1982 to focus on agriculture. Titled *Agriculture for Development*, the report stresses that 'three of every four poor people in developing countries live in rural areas', that 'most depend on agriculture for their livelihoods', and that it is 'time to place agriculture at the center of the development agenda' (World Bank, 2007: 1). The report insists on the fact that agriculture contributes to development in many ways, as a source of livelihoods and as a source of economic growth. Of course, placing agriculture at the centre of the development agenda is important, as staple and cash crop productions can significantly reduce not only food insecurity but also poverty, i.e. a large part of what opium farmers need to achieve before they can safely renounce illicit opium production (World Bank, 2007: 2–3). Yet, 'agriculture has been vastly underused for development' the report declares, and advises both an increase in access to assets such as land and water, and also increasing the productivity and sustainability of smallholder farming: 'improving the productivity, profitability, and sustainability of smallholder farming is the main pathway out of poverty in using agriculture for development' (World Bank, 2007: 8–10). Of course, 'because of demographic pressures and land constraints, the agenda for transforming countries must jointly mobilize all pathways out of poverty: farming, employment in agriculture and the rural non-farm economy, and migration' (World Bank, 2007: 21). However, while the World Bank report rightly addresses many of the challenges faced by the world's illicit cannabis, coca and opium poppy growers (lack of or inadequate access to land, water, credit, off-farm employment, etc.) and puts forward proposals that fit many of their needs, curiously it does not once refer to illicit agricultural drug production. Basically, while the advice of the World Bank report on *Agriculture for*

Development is to put agriculture at the centre of anti-poverty efforts, it fails to mention some of the world's poorest and most vulnerable farmers who, despite the risk of forceful eradication, grow illicit crops in order to combat poverty and food insecurity.

However, from a more political point of view, it is obvious that no development agenda can be reasonably set without first strengthening the institutions of state, civil society and democracy. Economic development, whether in rural or in urban areas, can only occur in countries and regions where peace prevails and is sustainable. The problem is that this is hardly the case in either Afghanistan or Burma, the world's premier illicit opium producing countries. In late 2008, seven years after the Taliban regime was toppled, Afghanistan was still a long way from peace, notably because the Taliban-led insurgency has considerably eroded the overall security necessary to reconstruction and economic development. Of course, the drug trade is often denounced for allegedly widely funding – if not driving – insurgency and for fuelling the wide-scale corruption of Afghan authorities. Yet, while it is true that the large cash inflows generated by the opium economy do fund insurgency and fuel corruption (at least to some extent), it is wrong to assume that the suppression of opium production would end insurgency and corruption (after all, corruption is also funded by diverted economic aid). In the same way that failure to address the causes of opium production will compromise any anti-drug policy, so neglecting the causes and mechanisms of conflict and corruption will prevent (or largely postpone) their solution. The causes of conflict and corruption and the drivers of opium production must be addressed if peace-building, state-building, reconstruction and the development of a licit economy are to take place in Afghanistan – or anywhere else. In a similar way, the prolonged political and territorial crisis of Burma – where many rebel ethnic groups and private armies have signed ceasefire agreements but have not brokered official peace agreements with the military junta – needs a long-lasting solution if a sustainable decrease in illicit opium production is to be achieved. In fact, until the conflicts and political crises of Afghanistan and Burma have been solved all anti-drug efforts will most likely be vain.

Ultimately, it appears that proper sequencing is the key to successful anti-drug policies. No matter how adequately designed and funded counter-narcotics policies may be, if forced eradication is undertaken before or during economic development programmes (whatever their scope and however they are labelled), or if economic development is undertaken before peace-building and state-building are well under way, no decrease in illicit opium production will be possible. In 2007 Tiri, an NGO, warned that when post-war reconstruction aid is spent without transparency and accountability, war-torn countries risked being propelled back into open conflict. Its report is especially critical of the sequencing of reforms in post-war countries: Jeremy Carver, one of Tiri's founders, explains how,

> too often the actions of the international community in post-war societies directly lead to new conflict. It is driven by the insistence of countries and international organisations that reconstruction follows their agendas and tight timetables.[1]

This is clearly the case with the prioritising of anti-drug goals in the complex and brittle scenarios of Afghanistan and Burma, where fragile transitions from war economies to peace economies are underway but constantly at risk of being jeopardized, notably by hasty eradication campaigns. In Burma and Laos, tens of thousands of poor hill tribe farmers bear the brunt of forced eradication programmes, being left to cope with both the loss of their only cash crop and the lack of economic aid. In Afghanistan, also – reportedly the fifth least developed country in the world[2] – it is frequently and oddly advised that one-third of an otherwise shattered economy be wiped out in order for peace, national reconciliation, reconstruction and state building to be possible. Despite the obvious risks of political destabilization that such programmes present, and in spite of the inevitable human costs that would entail for the affected populations, measures that are ultimately repressive and destructive continue to be proposed as the only realistic solutions – when exactly the opposite is needed: (re)construction and economic development. Illicit opium production will not abate until its root causes are addressed. In the meantime, despite their repeated failure, counter-narcotics policies continue to be proposed in the name of security and legality but at the expense of food security, fairness and human rights.

Postscript

September 2009

With the election of Barack Obama, a new US strategy for Afghanistan was quickly called for, both in terms of counter-insurgency and counter-narcotics. For a start, the new president appointed Richard Holbrooke, a former US ambassador to the United Nations, as his Special Representative for both Afghanistan and Pakistan, or what is now widely referred to as 'AfPak'.

The need for a new strategy for Afghanistan called for new military leadership. Obama prematurely replaced General David McKiernan, the top commander of US and NATO troops in Afghanistan, with Lieutenant General Stanley McChrystal, a former commander of the Joint Special Operations Command and until recently in command of US special forces in Iraq. Meanwhile, Obama ordered 21,000 additional troops into Afghanistan, so that the American force level could reach about 68,000 by the end of 2009. He also replaced the US ambassador to Afghanistan, William Wood, a.k.a. 'Chemical Bill', with now-retired Lieutenant General Karl Eikenberry, who had served two tours in post-2001 Afghanistan. Eikenberry had also served as the Deputy Chairman of the NATO Military Committee and had long put a strong emphasis on enhancing Afghan governance, in particular the Afghan army.

The appointment of Richard Holbrooke and the replacement of William Wood signify a change in US counter-narcotics strategy in Afghanistan. Indeed, in a 2008 newspaper article,[1] Holbrooke reminded his readers that President Bush, during his 2006 trip to Afghanistan, had declared himself a 'spray man', thereby paving the way for his next ambassador to Afghanistan, William Wood (2007–2009). Holbrooke referred to Wood as 'an enthusiastic proponent of aerial spraying in his previous assignment, in Colombia'. Holbrooke also staunchly denounced the US counter-narcotics strategy in Afghanistan, declaring:

But even without aerial eradication, the program, which costs around $1 billion a year, may be the single most ineffective program in the history of American foreign policy. It's not just a waste of money. It actually strengthens the Taliban and al-Qaeda, as well as criminal elements within Afghanistan.[2]

Yet, while Holbrooke dismissed crop eradication as costly, ineffective, and counterproductive, he also pointed out that talk 'about "alternative livelihoods" and alternative crops as the solution to the drug problem' was 'true in theory', but not in practice: 'this theory has been tried elsewhere with almost no success'.[3]

As we have seen, this holds true mainly because the vast majority of alternative development programs and projects have long been ill-designed and ill-funded. Since September 2001, the US Congress has passed 17 separate emergency funding bills totalling $822.1 billion for the wars in Iraq and Afghanistan. Yet, out of the $75.5 billion asked for in the Supplemental Appropriations Request for 2009 for Afghanistan and Iraq, 'only $170 million [was] earmarked to support economic growth in Afghanistan, including agriculture sector development'.[4] Congress eventually agreed to add $100 million for agricultural reconstruction, and the administration has asked lawmakers for an additional $235 million for fiscal year 2010, a more than fourfold increase from 2008.[5]

Holbrooke said that the new administration needed 'to fix' what it had 'inherited': not just 'the single most wasteful, most ineffective program' that he had ever seen, but actually what constituted 'a benefit to the enemy' (the fact that forced eradication drives farmers into the hands of the Taliban). Of course, opium does not only benefit the Taliban and the other various jihadist insurgent groups. As journalist Gretchen Peters writes in a recent book:

> The Taliban and their allies may be earning hundreds of millions from the drug trade, but one thing almost everyone interviewed for this project agreed on was that crooked members of Hamid Karzai's administration are earning even more.[6]

In late 2008, UNODC Executive Director Antonio Maria Costa declared that the Taliban and other anti-government forces were able to make huge profits from the drugs business, netting up to $400 or $500 million.[7] Yet, in September 2009, a US congressional report mentioned that UNODC had miscalculated the amount of drug payments in taxes and protection money paid to the Taliban and that it now estimated it to be around $125 million in 2009. According to the report, 'U.S. officials in Afghanistan said the CIA and the

Pentagon's Defense Intelligence Agency estimate annual Taliban revenue from drugs at about $70 million a year'. The report goes even further by denying that Al Qaeda is benefiting from the opium industry in Afghanistan:

> Surprisingly, there is no evidence that any significant amount of the drug proceeds go to Al Qaeda. Contrary to conventional wisdom, numerous money laundering and counter-narcotics experts with the United States Government in Afghanistan and Washington said flatly that they have seen no indication of the Taliban or traffickers paying off Al Qaeda forces left inside the country.[8]

Still, the report makes it clear that 'Fighting the drug traffickers who help finance the Taliban and similar groups is one of the priorities of the new strategy in Afghanistan', and that 'Military officers now regard it as part of the mission'.[9] As a matter of fact, the Pentagon has drawn up 'a list of 367 "kill or capture" targets, including 50 nexus targets who link drugs and insurgency'. According to a US general quoted in the congressional report, the 'long-term approach is to identify the regional drug figures and corrupt government officials and persuade them to choose legitimacy or remove them from the battlefield'.[10] Of course, targeting individuals in a deliberate assassination policy 'was a hard sell in NATO', said General John Craddock, NATO's supreme allied commander until he retired in July.[11]

Apart from what can be likened to the 'extrajudicial, arbitrary and unlawful killings' that took place during Thailand's war on drugs in 2003, members of Obama's 'national security team have concluded that the country requires not just more money and personnel for reconstruction but also a fundamental overhaul of the U.S. approach to development'.[12] On 27 June 2009, at a G8 meeting on Afghanistan, Holbrooke announced the new US counter-narcotics policy and declared that the new US administration 'was phasing out funding for eradication efforts and using it for drug interdiction and alternate crop programs instead'.[13] At the time I am writing this, it is unclear, though, if the funds previously allocated to eradication will be reinvested into alternative livelihoods or into interdiction. In any case, we have seen that broad economic development, not interdiction (for it is only slightly less counterproductive than eradication), is key to successful counter-narcotics policies.

What is undeniably an important shift in US counter-narcotics policy in Afghanistan occurred amidst worldwide denunciations of either prohibition or the war on drugs. In March 2009, on the eve of the meeting of the High Level Segment of the Commission on Narcotic Drugs (follow-up of the 1998 UNGASS),[14] a European Commission report claimed that the UN strategy on drugs over the past decade had failed. The authors of the report declared that they had found 'no evidence that the global drug problem was reduced'. They wrote: 'For some nations the problem declined but for others it worsened and for some of those it worsened sharply and substantially. The drug problem generally lessened in rich countries and worsened in a few large developing or transitional countries'.[15] Then, in May 2009, twenty years after it first argued for legalisation of drugs, the British weekly *The Economist* stressed again that 'prohibition itself vitiates the efforts of the drug warriors', that 'far from reducing crime, prohibition has fostered gangsterism on a scale that the world has never seen before', and that 'prohibition seems even more harmful [than the health risks implied by legalisation], especially for the poor and weak of the world'.[16] Later, in September 2009, Fernando Henrique Cardoso, the former president of Brazil (1995–2003), argued the case for a new global policy in an article in *The Observer*. He wrote: 'It is time to admit the obvious. The "war on drugs" has failed, at least in the way it has been waged so far'. He then explained: 'Continuing the drugs war with more of the same is ludicrous. What is needed is a serious debate that will lead to the adoption of more humane and more effective strategies to deal with the global drug problem'.[17] Latin America is now searching for an alternative to the US-led war on drugs, with Mexico and Argentina taking significant steps towards decriminalisation, something that Brazil and Ecuador are also considering.[18]

On 15 September 2009, in the Presidential Determination for Major Drug-Transit and Major Illicit Drug-Producing Countries, the US president 'has determined that three countries, Bolivia, Burma, and Venezuela, "failed demonstrably" during the last 12 months to adhere to international counter-narcotic agreements and take counter-narcotic measures set forth in U.S. law'.[19] Nonetheless Bolivia and Venezuela were issued national interest waivers, but the United States withheld funding from Burma because of its poor human rights records, including human trafficking.[20]

Burma has largely reduced its illicit opium production in the recent years, but it has not convinced past and present US administrations of its dedication to adhere to international drug treaties. Burma's military junta also sparked international uproar in August 2009 when it prolonged Aung San Suu Kyi's house arrest for an additional 18 months in citing a 'violation' after a US citizen trespassed on her property in Rangoon. The year 2009 actually bodes ill for the future of Burma: some cease-fire groups have rejected an order to transform their armed militias into Burmese-controlled border guard forces, and this has led the junta to attack and defeat Pheung Kyashin's Myanmar National Democratic Alliance Army in the Kokang region. The junta's move has raised concerns in China, whose border trade has been disrupted and where more than 30,000 people from Kokang have fled. The risks are high now that the military junta may enter into open conflict with the Kachin, the Shan, and the Wa along the Chinese, Laotian and Thai borders.

For decades now, the United States and other Western governments have utterly failed to address the ongoing crises of Afghanistan and Burma. The past decade (2000s) has seen opium production explode in Afghanistan and production decrease in Burma (and Laos). While counter-narcotics policies may be changing for the better in Afghanistan, the ongoing Afghan conflict (July 2009 was the deadliest month since 2001 for both coalition troops and civilians) and the current tensions in Burma raise serious doubts about the prospects for peace and economic development in these two nations. This is something I will keep following, along with opium production trends and counter-narcotics policies in Asia, in the years to come. And I will keep updating my website, www.geopium.org, as I have been doing since 1998.

Drug Trafficking Routes

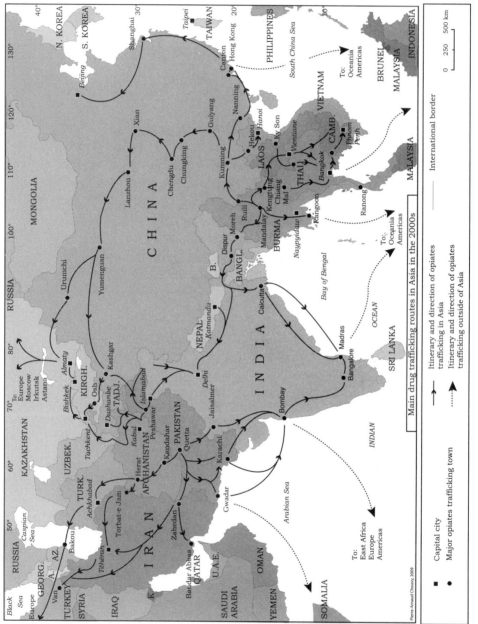

Map 1: Main drug trafficking routes in Asia in the 2000s.

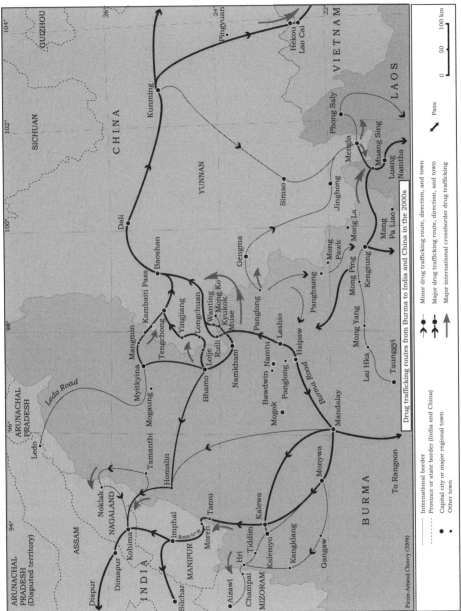

Map 2: Golden Triangle: drug trafficking routes from Burma to India and China in the 2000s.

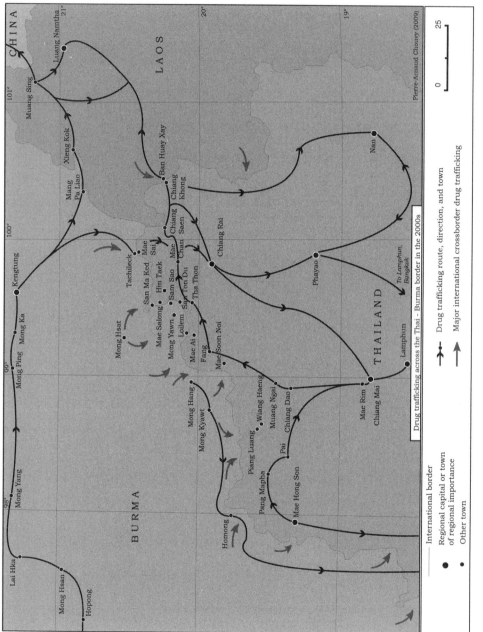

Map 3: Golden Triangle: drug trafficking across the Thai–Burma border in the 2000s.

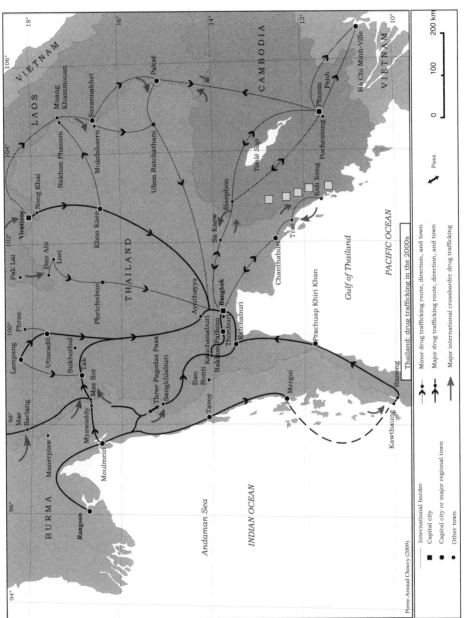

Map 4: Golden Triangle: Thailand: drug trafficking in the 2000s.

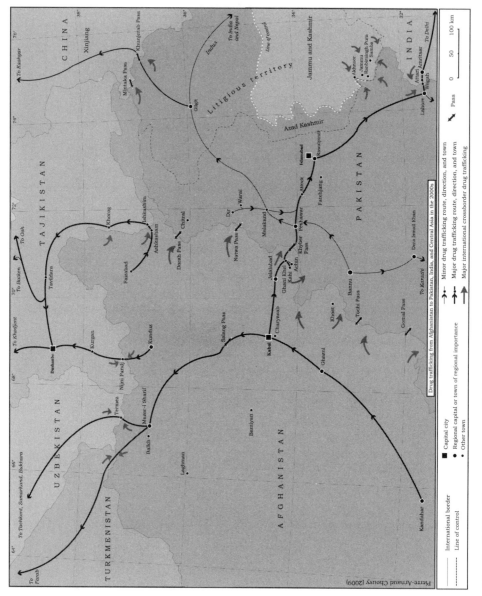

Map 5: Golden Crescent: drug trafficking from Afghanistan to Pakistan, India and Central Asia in the 2000s.

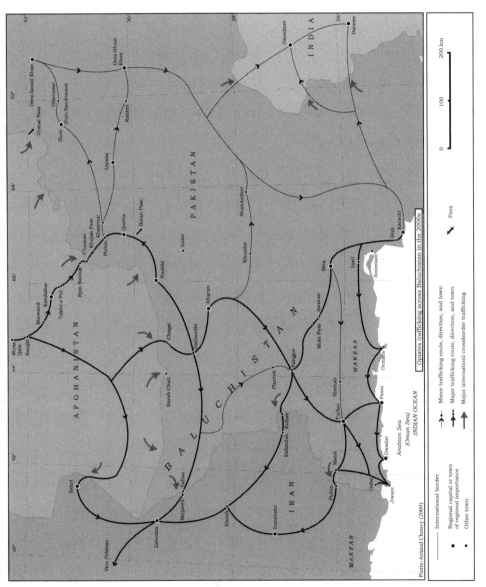

Pierre-Arnaud Chouvy (2009)

Map 6: Golden Crescent: opiates trafficking across Baluchistan in the 2000s.

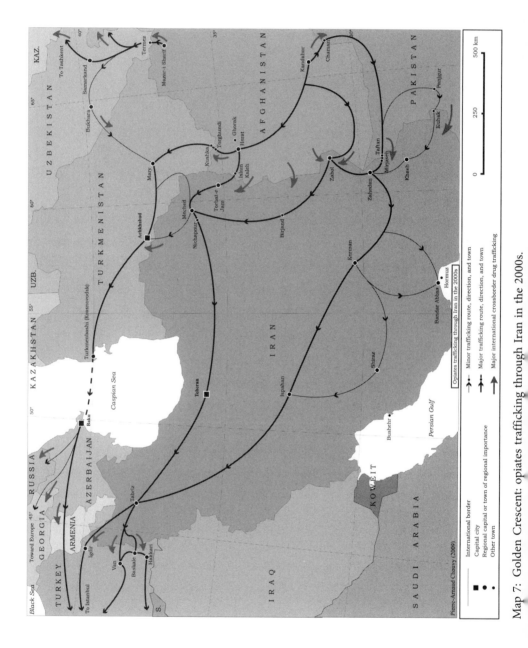

Pierre-Arnaud Chouvy (2009)

Map 7: Golden Crescent: opiates trafficking through Iran in the 2000s.

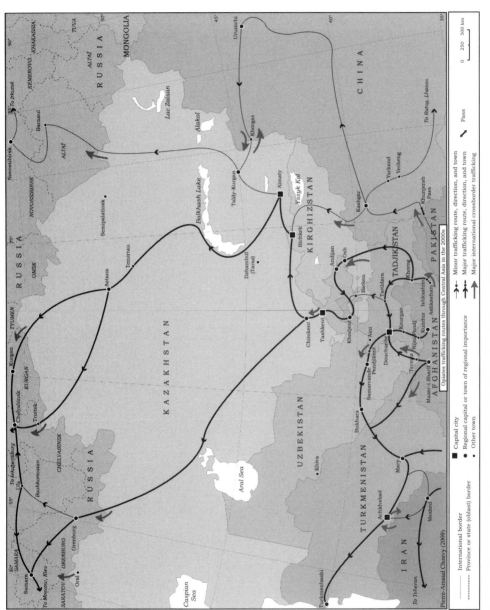

Map 8: Opiates trafficking routes through Central Asia in the 2000s.

Notes

INTRODUCTION

1   The Union of Burma was renamed 'Myanmar' on 25 June 1989 by the military dictatorship then known by the acronym 'SLORC' (State Law and Order Restoration Council). Rangoon, the capital, was renamed Yangon. In 1997 the SLORC became the SPDC (State Peace and Development Council). In March 2006, the SPDC made the newly built city of Naypyidaw the capital of 'Myanmar'. The change from 'Burma' to 'Myanmar' was recognized by the United Nations and by a number of countries, including France, but not by others such as the United Kingdom and the United States. A statement by the UK Foreign Office says: 'Burma's democracy movement prefers the form "Burma" because they do not accept the legitimacy of the unelected military regime to change the official name of the country. Internationally, both names are recognised'. BBC, 'Should it be Burma or Myanmar?', 26 September 2007: http://news.bbc.co.uk/2/hi/uk_news/magazine/7013943.stm (visited on 12 November 2007). Hereafter the country will be mentioned as 'Burma' and not as 'Myanmar'.

Chapter 1

1   Opiates can also be extracted directly from opium poppies (pharmaceutical morphine is produced from concentrate of poppy straw, which is extracted from so-called poppy straw).
2   The three major international drug control treaties are the Single Convention on Narcotic Drugs (1961), the Convention on Psychotropic Substances (1971), and the Convention against the Illicit Traffic in Narcotic Drugs and Psychotropic Substances (1988). See www.unodc.org
3   Diamorphine, or diacetylmorphine, is a semi-synthetic derivative of morphine most commonly know as heroin. With similar pharmacological properties but with greater potency than morphine, diamorphine is used medically almost only in the United Kingdom: it is unavailable for medical use in most countries of the world and is strictly prohibited in the United States (since

1924). 'By the early 1980's British doctors were writing just under 99% of the world's prescriptions for medicinal diamorphine and consuming 95% of the worldwide legally produced annual quantity of about 300 kg of diamorphine' (Gossop *and* Keaney, 2004). Because there has been a shortage of diamorphine in the United Kingdom since December 2004, in 2007, some, including members of the parliament, were reported in the British press as supporting the idea that opium production be licensed in Afghanistan. Yet, despite the many shortcomings of such a proposition (see last chapter), the British diamorphine shortage is 'caused by a lack of capacity of producing the sterile injection and not due to a shortage of the active ingredient itself' (Letter – in author's possession – from David Mercer, managing director of Macfarlan Smith, the world's largest producer and user of morphine, to Isabelle Izzard, UK Department of Health, 11 October 2007).

4 F. Dikötter, L. Laamann, and Zhou Xun underline: 'As John Quincy Adams commented in a lecture before the Massachusetts Historical Society in December 1841, opium was a "mere incident to the dispute but no more the cause of war [between Great Britain and China] than the throwing overboard of the tea in Boston harbour was the cause of the North American revolution"'. As the authors argue, 'free trade and the "opening" of China prompted the first Sino-British War in 1839' (Dikötter *et al.*, 2004: 45).

5 www.incb.org

6 Transnational Institue (TNI): http://www.tni.org/drugsungass-docs/ungass1998.htm and http://www.tni.org/drugsungass-docs/ungass.htm (visited on 7 February 2007).

7 http://www.un.org/ga/20special/poldecla.htm (visited on 7 February 2007).

Chapter 2

1 The People's Republic of China, the Democratic Republic of Korea, and Japan also produce opium legally but it is for their *domestic* markets and in much lesser quantities than India (Mansfield, 2001: 1). India and Turkey benefit from the 80:20 rule imposed by the US Drug Enforcement Administration, which states that 80 per cent of all Narcotic Raw Material imported in the US for pharmaceutical use must come from India and Turkey. Only 20 per cent of the US pharmaceutical requirement can come from other countries.

2 Sanjay Dutta, Pradeep Thakur, '6,000 hectares of opium crop destroyed in WB', *Times of India*, 5 May 2007.

3 For the sake of comparison, British India exported about 960 tonnes of opium to China in 1824, 1,600 in 1832, 2,400 in 1835, 3,200 just before the first Opium War (1838–9), and an average of 5,440 tonnes during the 1850s (Butel, 1995: 73, 129).

Chapter 3

1 The Karen National Union (KNU) has fought Burma's central government since the country's independence in 1948.

Chapter 4

1 UNODC Web site: http://www.unodc.org/myanmar/projects_icmp.html (visited on 29 May 2007).
2 UNODC Web site: http://www.unodc.org/myanmar/en/supply_reduction.html (visited on 29 May 2007).
3 Press Release, US Department of State, 'Justice Department Charges Eight in Burma with Drug Trafficking', 25 January 2005, http://usinfo.state.gov/eap/Archive/2005/Jan/25–265264.html (visited on 29 May 2007).
4 Steve Hirsch, 'Interview with UNODC Myanmar Representative Jean-Luc Lemahieu', *Asian Tribune*, 19 December 2003.
5 Bertil Lintner, 'UN fiddles while Myanmar burns', *Asia Times*, 23 October 2007.
6 Larry Jagan, 'Mixed Progress for Yangon's Drug War', *Asia Times*, 9 May 2003.
7 'The Legacy of the Taliban is a Sad and Broken Land', *New York Times*, 31 December 2001.
8 Florence Chipaux, 'Des mines d'émeraude pour financer la résistance du commandant Massoud', *Le Monde*, 18 July 1999.
9 Frontier Post, 'Afghan Opposition Involved in Drug-trafficking', 3 March 1999.
10 UN Press Release GA/SHC/3636, 10 October 2001.
11 Secretary Colin L. Powell, 'Statement at Press Briefing on New US Humanitarian Assistance for Afghans', 17 May 2001.
12 Press Release (07/75), International Committee of the Red Cross, 'Afghanistan: Insecurity Spreads Amid Escalating Conflict', 12 June 2007.
13 Afghan Ministry of Counter-Narcotics, 'Progress Report on Implementation of National Drug Control Strategy', January 2007.

Chapter 5

1 Cantonese pronunciation of *Teochiu*, largely used by the police and press of Hong Kong, where many Teochiu are strategically settled.
2 The Hokkien are mainly based in Taiwan, Singapore, Malaysia, the Philippines, and in Indonesia.
3 Father of Chatichai Choonhavan, Foreign Minister between 1975 and 1976, and democratically elected Prime Minister of Thailand between 1988 and 1991.
4 'Meth Still Pouring in to Thailand', *Bangkok Post*, 26 September 2004.

5 'Thaksin Declares New Drug War', *Bangkok Post*, 4 October 2004.

6 'Thaksin to Revitalise War on Drugs', *Bangkok Post*, 19 May 2006.

7 United Nations Information Service, 'Iraq Emerging as a Transit Country for Drugs, INCB President Says', 12 May 2007; IRIN, 'Iraq: Officials Complain of Rising Drug Use, Trafficking', 31 March 2006; *Los Angeles Times*, 'Iraq and Afghanistan: Post-invasion Chaos Blamed for Drug Surge', 4 October 2004; *The Independent*, 'Opium: Iraq's Deadly New Export', 23 May 2007; *The Independent*, 'Opium Fields Spread across Iraq as Farmers Try to Make Ends Meet', 17 January 2008.

8 Text of the 1907 Romanes Lecture on the subject of 'Frontiers' by Lord Curzon of Kedleston, Viceroy of India (1898–1905) and British Foreign Secretary (1919–24): Website of The International Boundaries Research Unit: http://www-ibru.dur.ac.uk/docs/curzon1.html (visited on 8 June 2007).

Chapter 6

1 Based on the entry, 'Drug trafficking', by Pierre-Arnaud Chouvy, in the *Encyclopaedia of the Cold War* (2007, ABC-CLIO).

2 Gaston Bouthol (1896–1980) founded the discipline of polemology (from the Greek *polemos* for war) after the Second World War in order to study the causes and drivers of wars and conflict

3 Transnational Institute, 'UNODC World Drug Report 2006 Full of Scientific Insults', TNI Press Release, 26 June 2006.

4 Transnational Institute, 'Wishful thinking clouds independent assessment in World Drug Report', TNI Press Release, 26 June 2007.

5 Drug Enforcement Administration, 'DEA Staffing and Budget', http://www.usdoj.gov/dea/agency/staffing.htm (visited on 18 July 2007).

6 Office of National Drug Control Policy, *Certification for Major Illicit Drug Producing and Transit Countries*, http://www.whitehousedrugpolicy.gov/publications/international/factsht/cert_major_illct.html (visited on 18 July 2007).

7 White House Press Release, 'Memorandum for the Secretary of State: Presidential Determination on Major Drug Transit or Major Illicit Drug Producing Countries for Fiscal Year 2007', 15 September 2006.

8 *Join Together*, 'US Mayors Declare Drug War a Failure', 18 July 2007.

9 In Thailand, opium poppy eradication is still carried out every year. In 2006, out of 157 cultivated hectares, 153 were eradicated (97 per cent). The Thai case illustrates how the war on drugs translates into the militarization of counter-narcotics operations as the Third Army and the Border Patrol Police respectively carried out 77 per cent and 10 per cent of the total eradication in the country (UNODC, 2006d: 127).

10 After the 2006 military coup d'Etat established the Council for National Security (CNS) to rule over the country, ISOC was turned into something akin to the US Department of Homeland Security.

11 Coca cultivation has increased according to US statistics but has decreased

according to UN statistics. In 2006, despite the largest use of fumigation in the country's history, 157,200 hectares of coca were reported by the United States, that is, 13,200 hectares more than in 2005. To the great dismay of Colombian President, Álvaro Uribe, the difference between the US and the UN statistics amounted to 80,000 hectares in 2006. The US and the UN explain such a huge gap by different methodologies.

12   Embassy of the United States in Afghanistan, Statement by Ambassador William B. Wood on Drug Day, 26 June 2007, http://kabul.usembassy.gov/speech_amb_062607.html (visited on 19 July 2007).

13   DeGrasse B., Bajraktari Y., 2005, 'Dealing With the Illicit Drug Trade: The Afghan Quandary', USIPeace Briefing, April 2005, http://www.usip.org/pubs/usipeace_briefings/2005/0407_dealing.html (visited on 20 July 2007).

14   Tiron R., 2006, 'Key House GOP Members Support Dem Anti-Narcotic Measure', The Hill, 19 September 2006 http://thehill.com/business—lobby/key-house-gop-members-support-dem-anti- narcotic-measure-2006-09-19.html (visited on 20 July 2007).

15   Ibid.

16   Bigwood J., 2001, 'DynCorp in Colombia: Outsourcing the Drug War', CorpWatch, 23 May 2001, http://www.corpwatch.org/article.php?id=672 (visited on 20 July 2007).

17   Ibid.

18   *Eurasianet*, 'Afghanistan Stands on Brink of Becoming "Narco-State"', 10 February 2004; *BBC*, 'UN Calls for War on Afghan Drugs', 10 February 2004.

19   'Narco-Terrorism: International Drug-Trafficking and Terrorism – A Dangerous Mix', Testimony of Steven W. Casteel, Assistant Administrator for Intelligence, Drug Enforcement Administration, Hearing of the United States Senate Judiciary Committee, 13 May 2003.

20   Warner D., 'For the West, a War on Terrorism Makes No Sense', *International Herald Tribune*, 21 September 2001.

21   Council on Foreign Relations, *Terrorism: Questions & Answers. Narcoterrorism*, http://cfrterrorism.org/terrorism/narcoterrorism.html (visited on 15 May 2004).

22   Hearing before the Subcommittee on Asia and the Pacific of the Committee on International Relations, House of Representatives, One Hundred Eighth Congress, First Session, March 20, 2003, Serial No. 108–15, p. 24.

23   National Commission on Terrorist Attacks Upon the United States, http://www.9-11commission.gov/staff_statements/911_TerrFin_Ch1.pdf

24   9-11 Commission, Staff Monograph, Monograph on Terrorist Financing: 2, http://www.9-11commission.gov/staff_statements/911_TerrFin_Ch2.pdf (visited on 23 September 2004).

25   9-11 Commission, Staff Monograph, Monograph on Terrorist Financing: 2, http://www.9- 11commission.gov/staff_statements/911_TerrFin_Ch2.pdf (visited on 23 September 2004

26   Tom Barry, 'The Neo-Con Philosophy of Intelligence', *Asia Times*, 19 February 2004.

27   Eleanor Thomas and Lindsay Thomas, 'US Southern Command (SouthCom)

Struggles to Justify its Role in the War on Terror', Council on Hemispheric Affairs, 2 September 2004, http://www.coha.org

28 Ibid.

29 Tom Barry, 'The Neo-Con Philosophy of Intelligence', *Asia Times*, 19 February 2004.

Chapter 7

1 While UNODC reported that multiple cropping, including off-season monsoon cropping, occurred in Burma, Laos and Thailand, it did not report on the yields achieved during what are likely to be much less favourable cultivation seasons.

2 In 2003, only 32 per cent of Afghan agriculture was mechanized. 42 per cent of the farm work was done with animals and 26 per cent was manual: http://www.fao.org/inpho/content/documents/vlibrary/ac311f/ac311f04.htm (visited on 31 July 2007).

3 A household may correspond to one family – extended or not – or include a few families. In Afghanistan, the National Surveillance System defines a household as 'a group of individuals sharing income and expenditure and that are living within the same compound'. For example, during a survey conducted in eastern Afghanistan in 2004, it was found that while there were on average 15 persons per household (46 per cent of adults and 54 per cent of children, equal distribution of males and females), the total number of persons varied between 2 and 52 (Mansfield, 2004: 5).

4 For opium production, the slash-and burn process is not accounted for, as poppy cultivation directly follows maize cultivation: 30 more days would be needed if opium production was not following maize production. Yet, 55 person-days of work (roughly 20 per cent of the work needed for opium production) are needed to clear the harvested maize fields from weeds, possibly maize stubble, and for ploughing.

5 In 2006, in Afghanistan, UNODC documented the use of 16 varieties of opium poppy (UNODC, 2006b: 50).

6 The Lahu people are an ethnic group of Southern China and Mainland Southeast Asia that belongs to the Tibeto-Burman family. They are, or were until recently, predominantly swiddeners, like the Hmong.

7 United Nations Office for the Coordination of Humanitarian Affairs, Afghanistan Drought Joint Appeal (July 2006): http://ochaonline.un.org/cap/webpage.asp?Page=1396 (visited on 5 June 2007).

8 Khueunsai Jaiyen, 'Opium-free Wa: A Costly Sacrifice', *The Nation* (Bangkok), 4 July 2007.

9 Obviously, the extent of illicit drug crops in a given country tells a lot about the power and authority of the state, or at least about its priorities: Afghan opium production benefits both from a nation-wide favourable climate and from a weak state with more urgent priorities than counter-narcotics.

10 Press Release, 'Promoting Alternatives to Poppy Cultivation in Afghanistan', *Food and Agricultural Organization*, 15 November 2004.

11 'The Rich Potential of Horticulture in Afghanistan', *International Center for Agricultural Research in the Dry Areas (ICARDA)*: http://www.icarda.org/Afghanistan/Rich.htm (visited on 13 August 2007).

12 Since the 1990s, with the price increase in opium, landowners have increasingly calculated the rent of their land to tenants on the basis of the potential yield of opium, rather than wheat, that it could produce.

13 'Burma's Unemployed Turn to Drug Producers for Survival', *Bangkok Post*, 16 January 2003.

14 Agarwood is cut for oil and wood but is only worth harvesting if infected with a fungi: a tree not infected by the fungi will not have the sought-after fragrance: http://www.enfleurage.com/aa- agarwood.html

Chapter 8

1 Mathea Falco, 'Drug Prevention Makes a Difference', *USIA Electronic Journal*, Vol. 2, No. 3, June 1997: http://usinfo.state.gov/journals/itgic/0697/ijge/gj-5.htm (visited on 21 August 2007).

2 Misha Glenny, 'The Lost War', *Washington Post*, 19 August 2007.

3 Lee Hudson Teslik, 'The Forgotten Drug War', *Council on Foreign Relations*, 6 April 2006: http://www.cfr.org/publication/10373/#Online_Library_The_Forgotten (visited on 21 August 2007).

4 Office of National Drug Control Policy, Historical Drug Control Funding by Function FY2002 – FY 2009, http://www.whitehousedrugpolicy.gov/publications/policy/09budget/tbl_3.pdf (visited on 2 October 2008).

5 *Ibid.*

6 United Nations Economic and Social Council, CND resolution n° 45/14, 'The role of alternative development in drug control and development cooperation', 1223rd meeting, 15 March 2002: http://www.unodc.org/documents/commissions/CND-Res-2000-until-present/CND-2002- Session45/CND-resolution-45.14.pdf (visited on 11 June 2008).

7 'The EU Drugs Strategy (2005–2012)': http://europa.eu/scadplus/leg/en/cha/c22569.htm (visited on 6 November 2007).

8 In fact, as stressed by Frank Dikötter, Lars Laamann and Zhou Xun, from the late nineteenth century to the mid-twentieth century, Chinese nationalism also rested upon 'narcophobia' and the successful anti-drug campaigns it generated: 'Opium represented both the enemy within – the morally depraved and physically weak addict – and the enemy outside – conniving foreign powers bent on enslaving the country. Opium became the rallying point around which social unity could be asserted, as both addicts and imperialists could be defined' (Dikötter *et al.*, 2004: 93 and 93–117).

9 Data regarding Pakistan's opium production in UNODC's World Drug Report

2006 is erroneous but has not been the subject of any erratum: it was just modified in the 2007 report.

10 Tom Fawthrop, 'Lao Tribes Suffer from Drug Crackdown', *BBC*, 15 July 2005.

11 UNDCP, 'Alternative Development at its Best: A Success Story From Laos', *Eastern Horizon*, n° 1 March 2000: 5.

12 Letter available on the Website of Maurizio Turco, former Italian deputy to the European Parliament: www.maurizioturco.it/arlacchi/arlacchi.htm (Page visited on 13 August 2007). Formerly available from the Website of the Transnational Radical Party: http://coranet.radicalparty.org/pressreview/arlacchi1.php

13 Tow Fawthrop, 'Kill or Cure: Bio-weapons in the War on Drugs', *Asia Times*, 26 June 2002.

14 UNHCHR, 2001, 'What is Poverty?', http://www.unhchr.ch/development/poverty-02.html (visited on 19 September 2007).

15 Ahto Lobjakas, 'Afghanistan: Multipronged Drug Eradication Effort Set for Helmand', *RFERL*, 30 January 2007.

16 UN, 'Towards an Opium-free Lao (PDR)', *Perspectives*, n° 2, 2006, United Nations: http://www.unodc.org/newsletter/en/200602/page005.html (visited on 19 September 2007).

17 Regarding how a 'narcophobic discourse gradually established itself' during the first decades of the twentieth century and how 'the image of China as an opium slave became the *locus classicus* of the modern drug debate, the cornerstone of the anti-opium movement and the founding case of concerted international efforts to enforce increasingly draconian measures not only against opium but against all illicit drug use in America, Europe and Asia', read: Dikötter *et al.*, 2004: 68-70, 74-88, and 2007. From nineteenth-century China to twenty-first century Laos, opium has been 'portrayed in narcophobic discourse as a drug which produced an irresistible compulsion to increase both the amount and frequency of the dosage, although the historical evidence shows that very few users were "compulsive addicts" who "lost control" or suffered from a "failure of will"' (Dikötter *et al.*, 2007: 20–1). As R. Newman underlines: 'Careful accounts of Muslim societies, such as Russel's much-quoted *History of Aleppo*, made it clear that opium was not taken as often as was commonly supposed. Dallaway agreed, and made the point that the addict was considered "with as much pity and disgust" as the inveterate drunkard in the West' (Newman, 2007: 59).

18 Vanda Felbab-Brown quoted in Drug War Chronicle, 'As Afghan Opium Production Goes Through the Roof, Pressure for Aerial Eradication, Increased Western Military Involvement Mounts', Issue n° 500, 7 September 2007, http://stopthedrugwar.org/chronicle/500/afghanistan_opium_production_record_eradication_military (visited on 19 September 2007)

19 IRIN, 'Afghanistan: Interview with UN drug agency on Opium Proliferation', *IRIN News*, 30 November 2004.

20 Sayed Yaqub Ibrahimi, 'Poppy Eradication on the Cheap', *IWPR*, 1 June 2006

21 Barnett Rubin, 'Counter-Narcotics in Afghanistan III: The False Promise of Crop Eradication', *Informed Comment: Global Affairs*, Blogspot Blog, 31 August

2007: http://icga.blogspot.com/2007/08/counter-narcotics-in-afghanistan-iii_31.html (visited on 1 October 2007).

22 Kirk Semple, Tim Golden, 'US Renews Bid to Destroy Opium Poppies in Afghanistan', *New York Times*, 8 October 2007.

23 Kim Sengupta, 'US Wants to Bring Colombia Tactics to Afghan Drugs War', *Independent*, 4 October 2007.

24 Sue Branford, 'Lesson from Colombia', *New Statesman*, 9 August 2007.

25 Chiade O'Shea, 'Kabul Rejects US Pleas to Spray Opium Poppies', *Guardian*, 9 October 2007.

26 'Remarks About an Intensified Program for Drug Abuse Prevention and Control', Richard Nixon, 17 June 1971: http://www.presidency.ucsb.edu/ws/index.php?pid=3047&st=&st1=

27 USAID started the first development project in South America's coca growing areas in 1981, in Peru's Alto Huallaga Valley.

28 Commission on Narcotic Drugs, *Draft Action Plan on International Cooperation on Eradication of Illicit Drug Crops and Promotion of Alternative Development Programmes and Projects*, United Nations General Assembly, E/CN.7/1998/PC/7, 14 January 1998: http://www.unodc.org/unodc/document_1998-01-14_1.html

29 Xaisomboun Special region was created in 1994 and dissolved in 2006 with districts reassigned either to the province of Vientiane (including the Hom district) or to the province of Xiang Khouang.

30 Clifford McCoy, 'Seedlings of Evil Growing in Myanmar', *Asia Times*, 23 August 2007.

31 *Ibid.*

32 Amnesty International, Resolution n° 5 (2007), 'The War on Drugs and Human Rights', http://www.amnestyusa.org/members/agmdecisions/detail.do?personid=149

33 Donald G. McNeil, 'Painkillers in Short Supply in Poor Countries', *New York Times*, 9 October 2007.

34 Ibid.

35 Donald G. McNeil, 'Drugs Banned, Many of the World's Poor Suffer in Pain', *New York Times*, 10 October 2007.

36 Donald G. McNeil, 'In India, a Quest to Ease the Pain of the Dying', *New York Times*, 11 October 2007.

37 'Afghanistan Poppies': unpublished Macfarlan Smith report, September 2007.

38 http://www.publications.parliament.uk/pa/ld200607/ldhansrd/text/70208w0001.htm and http://www.parliament.the-stationery-office.co.uk/pa/cm200708/cmhansrd/cm080715/text/80715w0002.htm (visited on 2 October 2008).

39 Ministry of Finance, Government of India: http://finmin.nic.in/the_ministry/dept_revenue/revenue_headquarters/nc-I/index.html (visited on 7 January 2006).

40 In late December 2007, the Indian press reported that poppy growers from Uttar Pradesh were increasingly switching from opium to vegetable production, not only because of advantageous returns but also because of

lesser constraints and pressure from the narcotics department and from smugglers and traffickers: Indo-Asian News Service, 'Farmers abandoning opium cultivation in Uttar Pradesh', 30 December 2007.

41   Sanjay Dutta, Pradeep Thakur, '6,000 Hectares of Opium Crop Destroyed in WB', *Times of India*, 5 may 2007; Surajit Khaund, '800 Hectares of Opium Cultivation Destroyed in Arunachal', *The Assam Tribune*, 16 July 2007; Amarnath Tewary, 'India Rebels Turn to Poppy for Funds', *BBC News*, 29 May 2007.

42   The Indian Central Bureau of Narcotics revealed in 2008 that, in 2007, the country's illicit opium poppy cultivation was more important than licit cultivation, indicating that 7,753 hectares of illicit poppy cultivation had been eradicated in 2007 when only 6,300 hectares had been licensed for legal cultivation: Pradeep Thakur, 'Illicit Opium Trade Thriving in India: Narcotics Bureau', *The Times of India*, 7 March 2008.

CONCLUSION

1   Tiri Media Release, 'Post-War Reconstruction Aid Risks Fuelling More Conflict', 16 January 2007, http://www.tiri.org/dmdocuments/NIR%20Press%20release%201801.pdf (visited on 14 November 2007).

2   According to the UN global human development index: IRIN, 'Afghanistan: Fifth Least Developed Country in the World', 18 November 2007.

POSTSCRIPT

1   R. Holbrooke, 'Still Wrong in Afghanistan', *Washington Post,* 23 January 2008.

2   Ibid.

3   Ibid.

4   A. Mojumdar, 'Old military hardware in a new bottle', *Asia Times,* 23 April 2009. See also the amendment to the Supplemental Appropriations Request for 2009: http://www.whitehouse.gov/omb/assets/budget_amendments/supplemental_04 _09_09.pdf. Accessed on 14 September 2009.

5   R. Chandrasekaran, 'U.S. Pursues a New Way To Rebuild in Afghanistan', *Washington Post,* 19 June 2009.

6   G. Peters, *Seeds of Terror. How Heroin Is Bankrolling the Taliban and Al Qaeda* (New York: Thomas Dunne Books, 2009), pp. 133–34.

7   UN News Centre, 'Opium trade finances Taliban war machine, says UN drug tsar', 27 November 2008.

8   United States Congress, *Afghanistan's Narco War: Breaking the Link Between Drug Traffickers and Insurgents.* A Report to the Committee on Foreign Relations, United States Senate, 11th Session, 2009, p. 10.

9   Ibid., p. 13.

10 Ibid., pp. 15–16.

11 R. Norton-Taylor, 'Pentagon puts Afghan drug-traffickers on hitlist', *The Guardian,* 10 August 2009.

12 R. Chandrasekaran, 'U.S. Pursues a New Way To Rebuild in Afghanistan', *Washington Post,* 19 June 2009.

13 'Holbrooke: US changing Afghan drug policy', *Associated Press,* 27 June 2009.

14 For more on the 2009 CND meeting, see the Transnational Institute's dedicated Website: http://www.ungassondrugs.org.

15 European Commission, *A Report on Global Illicit Drug Markets 1998–2007,* 10 March 2009.

16 'How to Stop the Drug Wars', *The Economist,* 5 May 2009.

17 F. Cardoso, 'The war on drugs has failed. Now we need a more humane strategy', *The Observer,* 6 September 2009.

18 R. Carroll, J. Tuckman, T. Phillips, 'Mexico and Argentina move towards decriminalising drugs', *The Guardian,* 31 August 2009.

19 US Department of State, Press Release, 15 September 2009, http://www.state.gov /r/pa/prs/ps/2009/sept/129236.htm. Accessed on 15 September 2009.

20 L. Jha, 'Burma Fails to Meet Global Counter-narcotics Measures', *Irrawaddy,* 16 September 2009.

Bibliography

ADDENS, T.J., 1939, *The Distribution of Opium Cultivation and the Trade in Opium*, Haarlem: J. Enschedé en Zonen.

ALAGAPPA, M. (ed.), 1995, *Political Legitimacy in Southeast Asia. The Quest for Moral Authority*, Stanford: Stanford University Press.

ANDERSON, E.F., 1993, *Plants and People of The Golden Triangle. Ethnobotany of the Hill Tribes of Northern Thailand*, Chiang Mai: Silkworm Books.

ANDERSON, J.L., 2006, 'The Man in the Palace. Hamid Karzai and the Dilemma of Being Afghanistan's President', *The New Yorker*, 6 June 2006.

ANDERSON, J.L., 2007, 'The Taliban's Opium War. The Difficulties and Dangers of the Eradication Program', *The New Yorker*, 9 July 2007.

ANF (ANTI NARCOTIC FORCE), 2006, *Analysis of Domestic Seizures 2005–2006*, Pakistan Ministry of Narcotics Control, Islamabad.

BANUAZIZI, A. and WEINER, M. (eds), 1986, *The State, Religion, and Ethnic Politics. Afghanistan, Iran, Pakistan*, New York: Syracuse University Press.

BARKER, R., 1990, *Political Legitimacy and the State*, Oxford: Clarendon Press.

BAUDRAN, E., 2000, *Derrière la savane, la forêt. Etude du système agraire du nord du district de Phongsaly (Laos)*, Paris: Comité de coopération avec le Laos (CCL).

BERTRAM, E., BLACMAN, M., SHARPE, K. and ANDREAS, P., 1996, *Drug War Politics. The Price of Denial*, Berkeley – Los Angeles: University of California Press.

BEWLEY-TAYLOR, D.R., 2001, *The United States and International Drug Control, 1909– 1997*, London – New York: Continuum.

BEYRER, C. et al., 2000, 'Overland heroin trafficking routes and HIV-1 spread in South and South-East Asia', *AIDS*, 2000, Vol. 14 N° 1: 75–83.

BLICKMAN, T. and BEWLEY-TAYLOR, D., 2006, 'The UNGASS Evaluation Process Evaluated', Briefing Paper, International Drug Policy Consortium, June 2006. http://www.idpc.info/docs/Ungass_evaluation.pdf

BLUMENSON, E. and NILSEN, E., 1998, 'Policing for Profit: The Drug War's Hidden Economic Agenda', *University of Chicago Law Review*, Winter 1998, n° 65, pp. 35–114.

BOONWAAT, L., 2004, 'The Balanced Approach to Opium Elimination in the Lao PDR'. Proceedings from NAFRI Uplands Workshop on Shifting Cultivation Stabilization and Poverty Eradication, Luang Prabang: 95–100.

BOOTH, M., 1998, *Opium. A History*, New York: St Martin's Press.

232   PIERRE-ARNAUD CHOUVY

BOUTHOUL, G., 1991 (1951), *Traité de polémologie. Sociologie des guerres*, Paris : Payot.

BROOK, T. and WAKABAYASHI, B.T. (eds), 2000, *Opium Regimes. China, Britain, and Japan, 1839–1952*, Berkeley: University of California Press.

BUDDENBERG, D. and BYRD, W., 2006, *Afghanistan's Drug Industry. Structure, Functioning, Dynamics, and Implications for Counter-Narcotics Policy*, Vienna – Washington, D.C: UNODC – World Bank.

BURKE, J., 2004, *Al-Qaeda: Casting a Shadow of Terror*, London: I.B. Tauris.

BUTEL, P., 1995, *L' opium. Histoire d'une fascination*, Paris: Perrin.

CANFIELD, R.L., 1986, 'Ethnic, Regional, and Sectarian Alignments in Afghanistan', in Banuazizi and Weiner M., 1986, *The State, Religion, and Ethnic Politics*: 75–103.

CARE, 2006, *No Quick Fix. Curbing Opium Poppy Cultivation in Afghanistan*, CARE, December 2006.

CARE-CIC, 2005, *Too Early to Declare Success: Counter-Narcotics Policy in Afghanistan*, Afghanistan Policy Brief, CARE-CIC (Center on International Cooperation), March 2005.

CARPENTER, T.G., 2000, 'Collateral Damage : The Wild-Ranging Consequences of America's Drug War', in T. Lynch (ed.), 2000, *After Prohibition: An Adult Approach to Drug Policies in the 21st Century*, Washington, Cato Institute (Online document).

CHOISEUL PRASLIN, C.-H. de, 1991, *La drogue, une économie dynamisée par la répression*, Paris : Presses du CNRS.

CHOUKOUROV, C. and CHOUKOUROV, R., 1994, *Peuples d'Asie centrale*, Paris: Syros.

CHOUVY, P.-A., 1999a, 'Taliban's Drug Dilemma: Opium Production vs. International Recognition', *Central Asia – Caucasus Analyst*, 8 December 1999.

CHOUVY, P.-A., 1999b, 'Drug Diversity in the Golden Triangle', *Crime and Justice International*, Vol. 15, N° 33, October 1999: 5,6,18.

CHOUVY, P.-A., 2001, 'Le pavot à opium et l'homme. Origines géographiques et premières diffusions d'un cultivar'. *Annales de géographie*. 618 : 182–194.

CHOUVY, P.-A., 2002a, *Les territoires de l'opium. Conflits et trafics du Triangle d'Or et du Croissant d'Or*, Geneva: Olizane.

CHOUVY, P.-A., 2002b, *Drug trade in Asia ; Golden Triangle ; Golden Crescent. In* Levinson, D. and Christensen, K. (eds), *Encyclopedia of Modern Asia*, Chicago: Scribners.

CHOUVY, P.-A., 2002c, 'New drug trafficking routes in Southeast Asia'. *Jane's Intelligence Review*, July 2002, Vol. 14, n° 7: 32–34.

CHOUVY, P.-A., 2002d, 'Drug and war destabilize Thai-Myanmar border'. *Jane's Intelligence Review*, April 2002, Vol. 14, n° 4: 33–35.

CHOUVY, P.-A., 2002e, 'Afghanistan-s opium production rises post-Taliban'. *Jane's Intelligence Review*, December 2002, Vol. 14, n° 12: 28–29.

CHOUVY, P.-A., 2003a, 'Opiate smuggling routes from Afghanistan to Europe and Asia'. *Jane's Intelligence Review*, March 2003, Vol. 15, n° 03: 32–35.

CHOUVY, P.-A., 2003b, 'La production illicite d'opium en Afghanistan, dans le contexte de l'enclavement, de l'isolement et de l'isolationnisme', *CEMOTI*, n° 35: 71–82.

CHOUVY, P.-A., 2003c, 'The ironies of Afghan opium production', *Asia Times*, 17 September 2003.

CHOUVY, P.-A., 2004a, 'Drogues illicites, territoire et conflits en Afghanistan et en

Birmanie', *Hérodote* n° 112 : *Géopolitique des drogues illicites* (P.-A. Chouvy and L. Laniel) : 84–104.

CHOUVY, P.-A., 2004b, 'Myanmar's Wa: Likely losers in opium war', *Asia Times*, 24 January 2004.

CHOUVY, P.-A., 2004c, 'Opium ban risks greater insecurity for Wa in Myanmar', *Jane's Intelligence Review*, Vol. 16 n° 2, February 2004: 39–41.

CHOUVY, P.-A., 2004d, 'Narco-Terrorism in Afghanistan', *Terrorism Monitor*, Vol. 2, Issue 6, 25, March 2004: 7–9.

CHOUVY, P.-A., 2004e, 'Drugs and the Financing of Terrorism', *Terrorism Monitor*, Vol. 2, Issue 20, 21 October 2004: 3–5.

CHOUVY, P.-A., 2005a, 'The dangers of opium eradication in Asia', *Jane's Intelligence Review*, Vol. 17 n° 1, January 2005: 26–27.

CHOUVY, P.-A., 2005b, 'Opium et danger de crise humanitaire dans le Triangle d'Or', *Questions internationales*, n° 11, January-February 2005: 100–107.

CHOUVY, P.-A., 2005c, 'Morocco said to produce nearly half of the world's hashish supply', *Jane's Intelligence Review*, Vol. 17, Issue 11, November 2005: 32–35.

CHOUVY, P.-A., 2006a, 'Afghan Opium: License to Kill'. *Asia Times Online*, 1 February 2006.

CHOUVY, P.-A., 2006b, 'Afghanistan's Opium Production in Perspective', *The China and Eurasia Forum Quarterly*, Central Asia – Caucasus Institute, Silk Road Studies Program, Vol. 4, n° 1, February 2006: 21–24.

CHOUVY. P.-A., 2006c, 'Le défi afghan de l'opium', *Etvdes*, December 2006, tome 405/6: 597–607.

CHOUVY. P.-A., LABROUSSE, A. and KOUTOUZIS, M., 2003, *Background to the drug routes*, International ministerial conference: *The drug routes from Central Asia to Europe*, 21–22 May 2003, G8 Meeting, Ministry of Foreign Affairs, Paris, France.

CHOUVY, P.-A. and LANIEL, L., 2004, 'De la géopolitique des drogues illicites', *Hérodote*, n° 112 : *Géopolitique des drogues illicites* (P.-A. Chouvy and L. Laniel) : 7–26.

CHOUVY, P.-A. and LANIEL, L., 2006, *Drug Production and State Stability*, Policy Brief, Secrétariat général de la Défense nationale (SGDN), Centre d'études et de recherches internationales (CERI), May 2006.

CHOUVY, P.-A. and MEISSONNIER, J., 2004, *Yaa Baa : Production, Traffic, and Consumption of Methamphetamine in Mainland Southeast Asia*, Singapore: Singapore University Press.

CND (COMMISSION ON NARCOTIC DRUGS), 2005, *Alternative Development: A Global Thematic Evaluation*, Final synthesis report to the forty-eighth session of the CND, Vienna (7–14 March 2005), 28 February 2005.

COLLIER, P. and HOEFFLER, A., 2001, *Greed and Grievance in Civil War*, Economics of Civil War, Crime, and Violence Research Project, Policy Research on the Causes and Consequences of Conflict in Developing Countries, Washington: World Bank.

COMMISSION ON NARCOTIC DRUGS (CND), 2005, *Alternative Development: A Global Thematic Evaluation*, Final Synthesis Report, Commission on Narcotic Drugs, Forty-eighth Session, Vienna, 7–14 march 2005, E/CN.7/2005/CRP.3, 28 February 2005.

COUNCIL OF THE EUROPEAN UNION, 2006, *The EU Approach on Alternative Development*, Brussels: European Union, 18 May 2006.

COURTWRIGHT, D.T., 2001, *Forces of Habit. Drugs and the Making of the Modern World*, Cambridge: Harvard University Press.

CRESSEY, G.B., 1960, *Crossroads : Land and Life in Southwest Asia*, Chicago/New York/Philadelphia: J.B. Lippincott Company.

DAVENPORT-HINES, R., 2001, *The Pursuit of Oblivion. A Social History of Drugs*, London: Phoenix Press.

DAVIDSON, G., 1991, 'Terrorism and the Rule of Law: Dangerous compromise in Colombia', *Commentary*, N° 13, Canadian Security Intelligence Service.

DICHTER, D., 1967, *The North-West Frontier of West Pakistan : A Study in Regional Geography*, Oxford: Clarendon Press.

DI COSMO, N., 1999, 'State formation and periodization in inner Asian history', *Journal of World History*, January 1999, Vol. 10 No. 1.

DIKOTTER, F., LAAMAN L. and ZHOU XUN, 2004, *Narcotic Culture. A History of Drugs in China*, Chicago: University of Chicago Press.

DIKOTTER, F., LAAMAN, L. and ZHOU XUN, 2007, *China, British Imperialism and the Myth of the 'Opium Plague'*, in J.H Mills and P. Barton (eds), 2007, *Drugs and Empires*: 19–38.

DOBBINS, J. *et al.*, 2005, *The UN's Role in Nation-Building. From the Congo to Iraq*, RAND Corporation: Santa Monica.

DRUG ENFORCEMENT ADMINISTRATION (DEA), 1993, *Opium poppy cultivation and heroin processing in Southeast Asia*, Washington: U.S. Department of Justice, Drug Enforcement Administration, Intelligence Division, Strategic Intelligence Section, 31 p.

DRUG ENFORCEMENT ADMINISTRATION (DEA), 2001, *The Price Dynamics of Southeast Asia Heroin*, Intelligence Brief, February 2001, Washington: U.S. Department of Justice, Drug Enforcement Administration, Intelligence Division, Strategic Intelligence Section.

DUCOURTIEUX, O., 2004, 'Shifting Cultivation and Poverty Reduction in the Uplands of Lao PDR: A Complex Issue'. Proceedings from NAFRI Uplands Workshop on Shifting Cultivation Stabilization and Poverty Eradication, Luang Prabang: 71–94.

DUCOURTIEUX, O., 2005, 'L'abattis-brûlis: éradication ou stabilization ?', in D. Gentil and P. Boumard (eds), 2005, *Le Laos doux et amer. Vingt-cinq ans de pratiques d'une ONG*, Paris : Comité de coopération avec le Laos (CCL) – Karthala : 193–209.

DUDOUET, F.-X., 2002, *Le contrôle international des drogues, 1921–1999*, Thèse de doctorat de science politique, Université Paris X – Nanterre, U.F.R. des sciences juridiques et politiques, Nanterre.

EDWARDS, M.W. and BAUMANN, J.B., 1977, 'An Eye for an eye: Pakistan's Wild Frontier', *National Geographic*, January 1977: 111–139.

ELLIOT, J..-G. (Major-General), 1968, *The Frontier: 1839–1947, The Story of the North-West Frontier of India*, London: Cassell.

FELBAB-BROWN, V., 2005, '*Afghanistan: When Counternarcotics Undermines Counterterrorism*', *The Washington Quarterly*, Volume 28, Number 4, Autumn 2005, pp. 55–72.

FELDAFING DECLARATION (THE), 2002, *The Feldafing Declaration*, 'International Conference on the Role of Alternative Development in Drug Control and Development Cooperation', Feldafing, Germany, 8–12 January 2002.

FISKESJO, M., 2000, 'The Fate of Sacrifice and the Making of Wa History', Dissertation submitted to the Faculty of the Division of the Social Sciences Department of Anthropology and the Faculty of the Division of the Humanities Department of East Asian Languages and Civilizations in Candidacy for the Degree of Doctor of Philosophy, Chigaco, Illinois.

FORBES, A.D.W., 1986, 'The 'Cin-Ho' (Yunnan Chinese) Muslims of North Thailand'. *Journal Institute of Muslim Minority Affairs*, Vol. 7, n° 2: 173–186.

FORBES, A.D.W. and HENLEY, D., 1997, *The Haw: Traders of the Golden Triangle*, People and Cultures of Southeast Asia, Bangkok: Teak House Publications.

FREY, R. and LINTNER, B., 1995, 'Jade in Burma: The Major Jadeite Source. The Jade Trade in Burma', *in* Keverne R., *Jade*: 266–271.

FRIEDMAN, M., 2000, 'Foreword', in T. Lynch (ed.), 2000, *After Prohibition: An Adult Approach to Drug Policies in the 21st Century*, Washington, Cato Institute (Online document).

GETTMAN, J., 2006, 'Marijuana Production in the United States (2006)', *Bulletin of Cannabis Reform*, Issue n° 2, December 2006.

GOI (GOVERNMENT OF INDIA), 2005, *Annual Report 2004–2005*, Ministry of Finance, New Delhi.

GOI (GOVERNMENT OF INDIA), 2006, *Annual Report 2005–2006*, Ministry of Finance, New Delhi.

GOODHAND, J., 2005, 'Frontiers and Wars: the Opium Economy in Afghanistan', *Journal of Agrarian Change*, Vol. 5 n° 2, April 2005: 191–216.

GOSSOP, M. and KEANEY, F., 2004, 'Prescribing diamorphine for medical conditions: a very British practice'. *Journal of Drug Issues*, Spring 2004, Volume 34, n° 2.

GOUDINEAU, Y. and EVRARD, O., 2004, 'Planned Resettlement, Unexpected Migrations and Cultural Trauma in Laos', *Development and Change*, Vol. 35, n° 5: 937–962.

GOVERNMENT OF INDIA (GOI), 2006, *Annual Report 2005–2006*, Ministry of Finance, New Delhi.

GRARE F., 2008, *Anatomy of a Fallacy: The Senlis Council and Narcotics in Afghanistan*, The Centre for International Governance Innovation, Working Paper n° 34, February 2008.

GTZ (DEUTSCHE GESELLSCHAFT FÜR TECHNISCHE ZUSAMMENARBEIT), 1998, *Drugs and Development in Asia. A background and discussion paper*, Drugs and Development Programme, Eschborn: GTZ.

GTZ (DEUTSCHE GESELLSCHAFT FÜR TECHNISCHE ZUSAMMENARBEIT), 2006, *Drugs and Development in a Drugs Environment: A Strategic Approach to 'Alternative Development'*, Discussion Paper, Drug-oriented Drug Control Programme, Eschborn: GTZ.

HARRISON, L.D., BACKENHEIMER, M. and INCIARDI, J.A., 1995, *Cannabis Use in the United States: Implications for Policy*, 1995, http://www.cedro-uva.org/lib/harrison.cannabis.05.html (Page consulted on July 24, 2003).

HAUDRICOURT, A.-G. and HEDIN, L., 1943, *L'homme et les plantes cultivées*, Paris: Métaillé.

HODGSON, B., 1999, *Opium, histoire d'un paradis infernal*, Paris: Seuil.

HUMAN RIGHTS WATCH, 2004, *Not Enough Graves. The War on Drugs, HIV/AIDS, and Violations of Human Rights*, Human Rights Watch Report, Vol. 18, n° 8, June 2004.

HUSAIN A. and SHARMA, J.R., 1983, *The Opium Poppy*, Lucknow: Central Institute of Medicinal & Aromatic Plants.

HRW (HUMAN RIGHTS WATCH), 2007, *The Human Cost. The Consequences of Insurgent Attacks in Afghanistan*, Vol. 19 n° 6, April 2007.

INTERNATIONAL DRUG POLICY CONSORTIUM (IDPC), 2007, *The World Drug Report 2007: Still Winning the War on Drugs?*, Briefing Paper, n° 6, August 2007.

INTERNATIONAL NARCOTICS CONTROL BOARD (INCB), 2004, *Report 2004*, Vienna: International Narcotics Control Board.

ISACSON, A., 2005, 'Le Plan Colombie : bilan négatif', *Cahiers de la sécurité*, 'Drogues et antidrogue en Colombie', n° 59, Quatrième trimestre 2005, pp. 169–192.

ISPAHANI, M.Z., 1989, *Roads and Rivals : the Politics of Access in the Borderlands of Asia*, London: I.B. Tauris.

JELSMA, M., 2002, 'Alternative Development And Drug Control: A Critical Assessment', Keynote speech, International Conference on The Role of Alternative Development in Drug Control and Development Cooperation, Feldafing, Germany, 8 January 2002.

JELSMA M., KRAMER T. and VERVEST, P. (eds), 2005, *Trouble in the Triangle. Opium and Conflict in Burma*, Chiang Mai: Silkworm Books.

JENSEMA, E.H. and THOUMI, F.E., 2003, 'Drug Policies and the Funding of the United Nations Office on Drugs and Crime', Senlis Council, Paris, October 23.

JONNES, J., 1996, *Hep-cats, Narcs, and Pipe Dreams. A History of America's Romance with Illegal Drugs*, Baltimore – London: Johns Hopkins University Press.

KAPOOR, L.D., 1995, *Opium Poppy. Botany, Chemistry, and Pharmacology*, New York: Food Products Press, Haworth Press.

KEVERNE, R. (Consultant Editor), 1995, *Jade*, London: Lorenz Books.

KHAN I. and WADUD K, A., 1977, 'Drug abuse policy in Pakistan'. *Bulletin on Narcotics*, United Nations, Issue 4: 21–40.

KOBAYASHI, M., 2000, *Drug Operations by Resident Japanese in Tianjin*, in T. Brook and T.B. Wakabayashi, 2000, *Opium Regimes, China, Britain, and Japan, 1839–1952*: 152–166.

KO LIN CHIN and ZHANG, S.X., 2007, 'The Chinese Connection: Cross-border Drug Trafficking Between Myanmar and China', Final report to the United States Department of Justice (unpublished), National Criminal Justice Reference Service, April 2007.

KRAMER, T., 2005, *Ethnic Conflict and Dilemmas for International Engagement*, in M. Jelsma, T. Kramer and P. Vervest (eds), *Trouble in the Triangle. Opium and Conflict in Burma*, Chiang Mai: Silkworm Books, pp. 33–59.

KRAMER, T., 2007, *The United Wa State Party: Narco-Army or Ethnic Nationalist Party?*, East-West Center, Policy Studies n° 38, Singapore: Institute of Southeast Asian Studies / Washington: East-West Center.

LABROUSSE, A., 2002, 'Drogue et terrorisme : les liens du sang', *Politique internationale*, n° 98, hiver 2002–2003, pp. 379–392.

LABROUSSE, A., 1992, 'La culture du pavot dans le district de Dir', in P. Salama and M. Schiray (eds), 1992, 'Drogues et développement', *Revue Tiers-Monde*, XXXIII – 131, juillet –septembre: 623–644.

LABROUSSE, A., 2005, *Afghanistan. Opium de guerre, opium de paix*, Paris: Mille et une nuits.

LAMB, A., 1968, *Asian Frontiers. Studies in a Continuing Problem*, London: Pall Mall Press.

LAMOUR, C. and LAMBERTI M, R., 1972, *Les grandes manœuvres de l'opium*, Paris: Editions du Seuil.

LANIEL, L., 2003, 'La 'guerre à la drogue' aux États-Unis après le 11 septembre 2001', *Diplomatie Magazine*, n° 1, janvier-février: 27–34.

LANIEL, L., 2007, 'Colombie, la guerre perdue contre la drogue', in B. Badie, S. Tolotti (eds.), *L' état du monde 2008*, Paris: La Découverte: 132–135.

LATIMER, D. and GOLDBERG, J., 1981, *Flowers in the Blood: The Story of Opium*, New York – London: Franklin Watts.

LEBAR, F.M., HICKEY, G.C. and MUSGRAVE, J.K., 1964, *Ethnic Groups of Mainland Southeast Asia*, New Haven: Human Relations Area Files Press.

LEVY, A. and SCOTT-CLARCK, C., 2002, *The Stone of Heaven. The Secret History of Imperial Green Jade*, Londres: Phoenix.

LIFSCHULTZ, L., 1992, *Pakistan: The Empire of Heroin*, in A. McCoy and A. Block (eds), 1992, *War on Drugs: Studies in the Failure of U.S. Narcotics Policy*, Boulder: Westview Press, pp. 319–357.

LINTNER, B., 1994, *Burma in Revolt: Opium and Insurgency since 1948*, Boulder: Westview Press.

LINTNER, B., 1998, 'Drugs and Economic Growth, Ethnicity and Exports', in R.I. Rotberg (ed), 1998, *Burma, Prospects for a Democratic Future*, Cambridge / Washington: The World Peace Foundation / Harvard Institute for International Development / Brookings Institution Press, pp. 165– 183.

LISTER, S., 2007, *Understanding State-Making and Local Government in Afghanistan*, Crisis Research Centre, Working Paper n° 14, May 2007, LSE, London.

LUDDEN, D., 1994, 'History Outside Civilization and the Mobility of South Asia', *South Asia* 17, n° 1, June 1994, pp. 1–23.

LYTTLETON, C., 2004, 'Relative Pleasures: Drugs, Development and Modern Dependencies in Asia's Golden Triangle', *Development and Change*, Vol. 35, n° 5: 909–935.

MACCOUN, R.J. and REUTER, P., 2001, *Drug War Heresies: Learning from Other Vices, Times, and Places*, Cambridge: Cambridge University Press.

MACDONALD, D., 2007, *Drugs in Afghanistan. Opium, Outlaws and Scorpion Tales*, London – Ann Arbor: Pluto Press.

MALEY, W. (ed.), 1998, *Fundamentalism Reborn? Afghanistan and the Taliban*, Lahore: Vanguard Books.

MALIK, J.M., 1995, 'China-India relations in the post-Soviet era : the continuing rivalry', *The China Quarterly*, June 1995, n° 142, pp. 317–355.

MANSFIELD, D., 2001, 'An analysis of licit opium poppy cultivation: India and Turkey'. Unpublished document available on http://www.geopium.org.

MANSFIELD, D., 2002, *Economic Superiority of Illicit Drug Production: Myth and Reality. Opium Poppy Cultivation in Afghanistan*, Paper (unpublished) prepared for the International Conference on The Role of Alternative Development in Drug Control and Development Cooperation, Feldafing/Munich, Germany, January 2002.

MANSFIELD, D., 2004a, *Diversity and Dilemma: Understanding Rural Livelihoods and Addressing the Causes of Opium Poppy Cultivation in Nangarhar and Laghman*,

Eastern Afghanistan, A Report for the Project for Alternative Livelihoods (PAL) in Eastern Afghanistan, Internal Document n° 2, GTZ.

MANSFIELD, D., 2004b, *What is Driving Opium Poppy Cultivation? Decision Making Amongst Opium Poppy Cultivators in Afghanistan in the 2003/4 Growing Season*, Paper for the UNODC/ONDCP Second Technical Conference on Drug Control Research, 19–21 July 2004.

MANSFIELD, D., 2004c, *The Role of Opium as a Source of Informal Credit in Rural Afghanistan*, in *Rural Finance in Afghanistan and the Challenge of the Opium Economy*, Report on a two-day workshop, Kabul, Afghanistan, 13–14 December 2004: 75–88.

MANSFIELD, D., 2006, *Exploring the 'Shades of Grey': An Assessment of the Factors Influencing Decisions to Cultivate Opium Poppy in 2005-2006*, A Report for the Afghan Drugs Inter Departmental Unit of the UK Government, London.

MANSFIELD, D., 2007a, *Beyond the Metrics: Understanding the Nature of Change in the Rural Livelihoods of Opium Poppy Growing Households in the 2006/07 Growing Season*, A Report for the Afghan Drugs Inter Departmental Unit of the UK Government, London.

MANSFIELD, D., 2007b, '"Economical with the truth": The limits of price and profitability in both explaining opium poppy cultivation in Afghanistan and in designing effective responses', in A. Pain and J. Sutton (eds), *Reconstruction Agriculture in Afghanistan*, Colchester: Practical Action Publishing: draft version.

MANSFIELD D., 2007c, 'Responding to the challenge of diversity in opium poppy cultivation in Afghanistan', in D. Buddenberg and W. Byrd (eds), *Afghanistan's Drugs Industry: Structure, functioning, dynamics and implications for counter narcotics policy*, Kabul: UNODC/World Bank. November 2007: 47–76 (draft version).

MANSFIELD, D. and PAIN, A., 2005, *Alternative Livelihoods: Substance or Slogan?*, AREU Briefing Paper, October 2005, Kabul.

MANSFIELD, D. and PAIN, A., 2006, *Opium poppy eradication: How to raise risk when there is nothing to lose?*, AREU Briefing Paper, August 2006, Kabul.

MANSFIELD, D. and PAIN, A., 2007, *Evidence from the Field: Understanding Changing Levels of Opium Poppy Cultivation*, AREU Briefing Paper, November 2007, Kabul.

MAREZ, C., 2004, *Drug Wars. The Political Economy of Narcotics*, Minneapolis, University of Minnesota Press.

MAULE, R., 1991, 'Tea Production on the Periphery of the British Empire'. *Thai-Yunnan Project Newsletter*, n° 14, September 1991.

McCOY, A.W., 1972, *The Politics of Heroin in Southeast Asia*, New York: Harper & Row.

McCOY, A.W., 1991, *The Politics of Heroin. CIA Complicity in the Global Drug Trade*, New York: Lawrence Hill Books.

McCOY, A.W., 2003, *The Politics of Heroin. CIA Complicity in the Global Drug Trade (Afghanistan, Southeast Asia, Central America, Colombia)*, New York: Lawrence Hill Books.

McCOY, A.W., 2004, 'The Stimulus of Prohibition. A Critical History of the Global Narcotics Trade', in M.K. Steinberg, J.J Hobbs and K. Mathewson (eds), 2004, *Dangerous Harvest. Drug Plants and the Transformation of Indigenous Landscapes*, Oxford – New-York: Oxford University Press, pp. 24–111.

McGIRK, T., 2004, 'Terrorism Harvest', *Time Asia Magazine*, Volume 164, n° 6, 9 August 2004.

McLAUGHLIN, G.T., 1976, 'The Poppy is not an Ordinary Flower: A Survey of Drug Policy in Iran', *Fordham Law Review*, pp. 702–766.

McLAUGHLIN, M., 2007, 'Opium Production and Consumption in Afghanistan and Iran'. *Iranian.com*, 23 February 2007.

McNICOLL, A., 1983, *Drug Trafficking: A North-South Perspective*, Ottawa: The North-South Institute.

MERLIN, M.D., 1984, *On the Trail of the Ancient Opium Poppy*, Rutherfold: Fairleigh Dickinson University Press.

MEYER, K. and PARSSINEN, T., 1998, *Webs of Smoke. Smugglers, Warlords, Spies, and the History of the International Drug Trade*, Lanham: Rowman & Littlefield.

MILLS, J.H. and BARTON, P. (eds), 2007, *Drugs and Empires. Essays in Modern Imperialism and Intoxication, c. 1500-c. 1930*, Basingstoke / New York: Palgrave Macmillan.

MILSOM, J., 2005, *The Long Hard Road Out of Drugs: The Case of the Wa*, in M. Jelsma, T. Kramer and P. Vervest (eds), *Trouble in the Triangle. Opium and Conflict in Burma*, Chiang Mai: Silkworm Books, pp. 61–93.

MINTZ, S.W., 1985, *Sweetness and Power. The Place of Sugar in Modern History*, New York: Penguin.

MYA MAUNG, 1991, *The Burma Road to Poverty*, New York: Praeger Publishers.

NADELMANN, E., 1993, *Cops Across Borders: The Internationalization of U.S. Criminal Law Enforcement*. University Park: Pennsylvania State University Press.

NAIM, M., 2005, *Illicit*, New York: Anchor Books.

NATIONAL COMMISSION ON TERRORIST ATTACKS UPON THE UNITED STATES, 2004, *Monograph on Terrorist Financing*, Staff Report to the Commission, Washington, http://www.9-11commission.gov.

NAWA, F., 2006, *Afghanistan, Inc.*, A Corpwatch Investigative Report, Oakland: Corpwatch, April 2006.

NEPOTE, J., 1977, 'In the Golden Triangle With a Handful of Dollars', *Bulletin on Narcotics*, 1976, Issue 1: http://www.unodc.org/unodc/en/bulletin/bulletin_1976-01-01_1_page002.html.

NEWMAN, R., 2007, *Early British Encounters with the Indian Opium Eater*, in J.H Mills and P. Barton (eds), 2007, *Drugs and Empires*: 57–69.

OFFICE OF INSPECTOR GENERAL (OIG), 2007, *Interagency Assessment of the Counternarcotics Program in Afghanistan*, Offices of Inspectors General of the Department of State and of the Department of Defense, Washington, July 2007.

PAIN, A., 2007, *Water Management, Livestock and the Opium Economy. The Spread of Opium Poppy Cultivation in Balkh*, Afghanistan Research and Evaluation Unit (AREU), Case Study Series, June 2007, Kabul.

PASUK PHONGPAICHIT, 2003, 'Drug policy in Thailand', First International Symposium on Global Drug Policy, Senlis Council, Lisbon, 23–25 October 2003.

PELT, J.-M., 1983, *Drogues et plantes magiques*, Paris: Fayard.

PLANHOL, X. de, 1993, *Les Nations du Prophète. Manuel géographique de politique musulmane*, Paris: Arthème Fayard.

RASHID, A., 1998, *Pakistan and the Taliban*, in W.Maley (ed.), 1998, *Fundamentalism Reborn? Afghanistan and the Taliban*, pp. 72–89.

RASHID, A., 2000, *Taliban. Islam, Oil and the New Great Game in Central Asia*, London – New York: I.B. Tauris.

RENARD, R. D., 1996, *The Burmese Connection. Illegal drugs and the making of the Golden Triangle*, Studies on the Impact of the Illegal Drug Trade, Volume 6, Boulder-London: Lynne Rienner Publishers.

RENARD, R.D., 2001, *Opium Reduction in Thailand 1970-2000. A Thirty-Year Journey*, Bangkok: UNDCP – Silkworm Books.

REUTER, P., 1983, *Disorganized Crime: The Economics of the Invisible Hand*, Cambridge: MIT Press.

ROBERTS, M., TRACE, M. and KLEIN, A., 2004, 'Thailand's "War on Drugs"', Drugscope Briefing Paper, n° 5, Drug Policy Programme, Beckley Foundation.

ROBICHAUD, C., 2006, 'Remember Afghanistan? A Glass Half Full, On the Titanic', *World Policy Journal*, Spring 2006: 17-24.

ROMAGNY, L., 2004, 'Resettlement: An Alternative for Upland Development?', Proceedings from NAFRI Uplands Workshop on Shifting Cultivation Stabilization and Poverty Eradication, Luang Prabang: 117-128.

ROTBERG, R.I. (ed.), 1998, *Burma, Prospects for a Democratic Future*, Cambridge / Washington: The World Peace Foundation / Harvard Institute for International Development / Brookings Institution Press.

RUBIN, B.R., 1995, *The Fragmentation of Afghanistan: State Formation and Collapse in the International System*, New Haven / London: Yale University Press.

RUBIN, B.R., 1999, "The Political Economy of War and Peace in Afghanistan', Paper presented at the meeting of the Afghanistan Support Group, Stockholm, Sweden, 21 June 1999.

RUBIN, B.R., 2004, *Road to Ruin: Afghanistan's Booming Opium Industry*, Center for American Progress & Center on International Cooperation, 7 October 2004, New York.

RYDELL, C.P. and EVERINGHAM, S.S., 1994, *Controlling Cocaine*, Prepared for the Office of National Drug Control Policy and the United States Army, Santa Monica, CA: Drug Policy Research Center, RAND Corporation.

SAIN (SOUTHEAST ASIAN INFORMATION NETWORK), 1998, *Out of Control. The HIV/AIDS Epidemic in Burma. A Report on the Current State of the HIV/AIDS and Heroin Epidemics, Policy Options, and Policy Implications*, Chiang Mai.

SCHENDEL, W. and van ABRAHAM, L., 2000, 'Beyond Borders : (II)licit Flows of Objects, People, and Ideas', Discussion Paper, New York: Social Science Research Council.

SCHULTES, R.E., KLEIN, W.M., PLOWMAN, T. and LOCKWOOD, T.E., 1975, *Cannabis: An Example of Taxonomic Neglect,* in V. Rubin (ed.), *Cannabis and Culture*, Paris: Mouton.

SCOTT, J.G. and HARDIMAN, J.P., 1900-1901, *Gazetteer of Upper Burma and the Shan States, Compiled from Official Papers by J.G Scoot, assisted by J.P. Hardiman*, Rangoon: Printed by the Superintendent, Government Printing, Burma, 5 volumes.

SEAGRAVE, S., 1995, *Lords of the Rim, The Invisible Empire of the Overseas Chinese*, London: Corgi Books.

SEDRA, M., 2003, *Security sector transformation in Afghanistan*, Working Paper, n° 143, Geneva Centre for the Democratic Control of Armed Forces.

SENLIS COUNCIL, 2005, *Feasibility Study on Opium Licensing in Afghanistan for the Production of Morphine and Other Essential Medicines*, Initial Findings, September 2005, Paris: Senlis Council.

SHAN (SHAN HERALD AGENCY FOR NEWS), 2003, *Show Business. Rangoon's 'War on Drugs' in Shan State*, Chiang Mai, December 2003.

SHAN (SHAN HERALD AGENCY FOR NEWS), 2005, *Show Business II*. Rangoon's 'War on Drugs' in Shan State, Chiang Mai, April 2005.

SHAN (SHAN HERALD AGENCY FOR NEWS), 2006, *Hand in Glove. The Burma Army and the Drug Trade in Shan State*, Chiang Mai, August 2006.

SHAW, M., 2006, 'Drug Trafficking and the Development of Organized Crime in Post-Taliban Afghanistan', in D. Buddenberg and W. Byrd (eds), *Afghanistan's Drug Industry*: 189–214.

SMITH, M., 1991, *Burma: Insurgency and the Politics of Ethnicity*, London: Zed Books.

SPENCER, B. and AMATANGELO, G., 2001, 'Drug Certification', *Foreign Policy in Focus*, Vol. 6 N° 5, March 2001.

STEINBERG, D., 2006, 'The U.S.-Burmese Relationship and its Vicissitudes', in N. Birdsall, M. Vaishnav, and R. Ayres (eds), *Short of the Goal: U.S. Policy and Poorly Performing States*, Washington: Center for Global Development, pp. 209–244.

STEINBERG, M.K., HOBBS, J.J. and MATHEWSON, K. (eds), 2004, *Dangerous Harvests. Drugs Plants and the Transformation of Indigenous Landscapes*, Oxford: Oxford University Press.

TARAPOT, P., 1997, *Drug Abuse and Illicit Trafficking in North Eastern India*, New Delhi: Vikas Publishing House.

TNI (TRANSNATIONAL INSTITUTE), 2002, *A Failed Balance. Alternative Development and Eradication*, Drugs and Conflicts, Debate Papers n° 4, March 2002, Amsterdam: TNI.

TNI (TRANSNATIONAL INSTITUTE), 2003, *Drugs and Conflict in Burma (Myanmar). Dilemmas for Policy Responses*, Drugs and Conflicts, Debate Papers n° 9, December 2003, Amsterdam: TNI.

TNI (TRANSNATIONAL INSTITUTE), 2005, *Downward Spiral. Banning Opium in Afghanistan and Burma*, Drugs and Conflicts, Debate Papers n° 12, June 2005, Amsterdam: TNI.

TNI (TRANSNATIONAL INSTITUTE), 2006, *Losing Ground. Drug Control and War in Afghanistan*, Drugs and Conflicts, Debate Papers n° 15, December 2006, Amsterdam: TNI.

TNI (TRANSNATIONAL INSTITUTE), 2007, *Missing Targets. Counterproductive Drug Control Efforts in Afghanistan*, Drug Policy Briefing n° 24, September 2007, Amsterdam: TNI.

TNI (TRANSNATIONAL INSTITUTE), 2008, *Withdrawal Symptoms. Changes in the Southeast Asian Drugs Market*, Debate Papers n° 16, August 2008, Amsterdam: TNI.

TONGCHAI WINICHAKUL, 1994, *Siam Mapped, A History of the Geo-body of a nation*, Chiang Mai: Silkworm Books.

TROCKI, C.A., 1999, *Opium, Empire and the Global Political Economy. A Study of the Asian Opium Trade 1750–1950*, London: Routledge.

TULLIS, L., 1996, *Unintended Consequences. Illegal Drugs and Drug Policies in Nine Countries*, Boulder: Lynne Rienner Publishers.

UNAIDS (JOINT UNITED NATIONS PROGRAMME ON HIV/AIDS), 2000, *Report on the Global HIV/AIDS Epidemic*, Geneva, UNAIDS, June 2000.

UNITED SATES DEPARTMENT OF STATE, 2000, *International Narcotics Control Strategy Report 1999*, Bureau of International Narcotics and Law Enforcement Affairs, US State Department, March 2000.

UNITED STATES DEPARTMENT OF STATE, 2004, *2003 Country Reports on Human Rights Practices*, Bureau of Democracy, Human Rights, and Labor, US State Department.

UNITED SATES DEPARTMENT OF STATE, 2004, *International Narcotics Control Strategy Report 2003*, Bureau of International Narcotics and Law Enforcement Affairs, US State Department, March 2004.

UNITED SATES DEPARTMENT OF STATE, 2005, *2005 International Narcotics Control Strategy Report*, Bureau of International Narcotics and Law Enforcement Affairs, US State Department, March 2005.

UNDCP (UNITED NATIONS INTERNATIONAL DRUG CONTROL PROGRAMME), 1998, *Afghanistan Strategic Study #2. The Dynamics of the Farmgate Opium Trade and the Coping Strategies of Opium Traders*, October 1998, Islamabad: UNDCP.

UNDCP, 1999, *Afghanistan Strategic Study #4, Access to Labour: The Role of Opium in the Livelihood Strategies of Itinerant Harvesters Working in Helmand Province*, June 1999, Islamabad: UNDCP.

UNDCP, 2000, *Afghanistan Annual Opium Poppy Survey 2000*, United Nations.

UNDCP, 2001a, *Afghanistan Annual Opium Poppy Survey 2001*, United Nations.

UNDCP, 2001b, *Global Impact of the Ban on Opium Production in Afghanistan*, United Nations, July 2001.

UNDCP, 2001c, *Laos Annual Opium Poppy Survey 2001*, United Nations, October 2001.

UNDCP, 2002a, *Myanmar Opium Survey 2002*, United Nations, August 2002.

UNDCP, 2002b, *Afghanistan Annual Opium Poppy Survey 2002*, United Nations.

UN GASC (UNIED NATIONS GENERAL ASSEMBLY SECURITY COUNCIL), 2008, *The situation in Afghanistan and its implications for international peace and security*, General Assembly sixty-second session, Agenda item 19, 6 march 2008, New York: United Nations.

UNODC (UNITED NATIONS OFFICE ON DRUGS AND CRIME), 2003a, *Global Illicit Drugs Trends 2003*, United Nations.

UNODC, 2003b, *Afghanistan Opium Survey 2003*, United Nations, October 2003.

UNODC, 2003c, *The Opium Economy in Afghanistan. An International Problem*, New York, United Nations.

UNODC, 2003d, *Maroc. Enquête sur le cannabis 2003*, United Nations, December 2003.

UNODC, 2003e, *Myanmar Opium Survey 2003*, United Nations, June 2003.

UNODC, 2004a, *Afghanistan Opium Survey 2004*, United Nations, November 2004.

UNODC, 2004b, *Myanmar Opium Survey 2004*, United Nations, October 2004.

UNODC, 2004c, *Afghanistan. Farmer's Intentions Survey 2003/2004*, United Nations, February 2004.

UNODC, 2004d, *Laos Opium Survey 2004*, United Nations, July 2004.

UNODC, 2005a, *Afghanistan Opium Survey 2005*, United Nations, November 2005.

UNODC, 2005b, *Myanmar Opium Survey 2005*, United Nations, November 2005.

UNODC, 2005c, *Thematic Evaluation of UNODC Alternative Development Initiatives*, Independent Evaluation Unit, Vienna, United Nations.

UNODC, 2005d, *Laos Opium Survey 2005*, United Nations, June 2005.

UNODC, 2005e, *Thematic Evaluation of UNODC Alternative Development Initiatives*, Independent Evaluation Unit (Dir. Allison Brown), Vienna, United Nations, November 2005.

UNODC, 2005ee, *Thematic Evaluation of UNODC Alternative Development Initiatives*, Independent Evaluation Unit (Dir. Allison Brown), Draft version, 4 September 2005.

UNODC, 2006a, *Afghan opium cultivation soars 59 percent in 2006, UNODC survey shows*, Kabul, United Nations, Press Release, September 2, 2006.

UNODC, 2006b, *Afghanistan Opium Survey 2006*, United Nations, October 2006.

UNODC, 2006c, *2006 World Drug Report*, Volume 1, Vienna, United Nations.

UNODC, 2006d, *Opium Poppy Cultivation in the Golden Triangle. Lao PDR, Myanmar, Thailand*, United Nations, October 2006.

UNODC, 2007a, *2007 World Drug Report*, Vienna, United Nations.

UNODC, 2007b, *Afghanistan Opium Survey 2007. Executive Summary*, United Nations, August 2007.

UNODC, 2007bb, *Afghanistan Opium Survey 2007*, United Nations, October 2007.

UNODC, 2007c, *Opium Poppy Cultivation in South East Asia. Lao PRD, Myanmar*, United Nations, October 2007.

UNODCCP (UNITED NATIONS OFFICE FOR DRUG CONTROL AND CRIME PREVENTION), 2001, *Global Illicit Drug Trends 2001*, United Nations.

UNODCCP, 2002, *Afghanistan Opium Survey 2002*, United Nations, October 2002.

VEEN, H.T. van der, 1999, 'The International Drug Complex', Centre for Drug Research, Universiteit van Amsterdam.

WALDMANN, P., 2002, '*Existe una politica europea de lucha contra el terrorismo y el crimen organizado?*', Colloque du Comité universitaire européen pour la Colombie, Institut des Hautes études d'Amérique latine, Paris, 20 mars 2002.

WALKER, A.R., 1980, 'The Production and Use of Opium in the Northern Thai Uplands: An Introduction'. *Contemporary Southeast Asia*, September 1980, Vol. 2, N° 2: 135–154.

WET, J.M. de and HARLAN, J.R., 1975, 'Weeds and Domesticates: Evolution in the Man-Made Habitat'. *Economic Botany*. April-June 1975, Vol. 29, N° 2: 99–107.

WALKER, J.,1995, 'Jade: A Special Gemstone', in R. Keverne, 1995, *Jade*: 20–41.

WILD, O., 1992, *The Silk Road*, University of California, Irvine, http://www.ess.uci.edu/~oliver/silk.html (page visited on April 16, 2007).

WORLD BANK, 2004, *Afghanistan. State Building, Sustaining Growth, and Reducing Poverty*, Washington, D.C.: The World Bank.

WORLD BANK, 2007, *World Development Report 2008*, Washington D.C.: The World Bank.

YEGAR, M., 1966, 'The Panthay (Chinese Muslims) of Burma and Yunnan'. *Journal of Southeast Asia History,* Vol. 7, N° 1: 73–85.

ZHOU YONGMING, 1999, *Anti-Drug Crusades in Twentieth-Century China. Nationalism, History, and State Building*, Lanham: Rowman & Littlefield.

Index